LIVING RESPONSIBLY IN COMMUNITY

*Essays in Honor of
E. Clinton Gardner*

Edited by

**Frederick E. Glennon
Gary S. Hauk
Darryl M. Trimiew**

University Press of America, Inc.
Lanham • New York • London

Copyright © 1997 by
University Press of America,® Inc.
4720 Boston Way
Lanham, Maryland 20706

12 Hid's Copse Rd.
Cummor Hill, Oxford OX2 9JJ

Library of Congress Cataloging-in-Publication Data

Living responsibly in community : essays in honor of E. Clinton
Gardner / edited by Frederick E. Glennon, Gary S. Hauk, Darryl M.
Trimiew.
p. cm.
Includes bibliographical references and index.
l. Social ethics. 2. Christian ethics. 3. Responsibility. I. Gardner,
E. Clinton (Edward Clinton). II. Glennon, Frederick E. III. Hauk,
Gary S. IV. Trimiew, Darryl M.
HM216.L57 1997 303.3'72--dc21 96-39550 CIP

ISBN 0-7618-0638-5 (cloth: alk. ppr.)

Contents

Foreword

Professor E. Clinton Gardner was a founder—along with the late Professor Earl D. C. Brewer—of the Department of Ethics and Society in the Graduate Division of Religion of Emory University. Across the years of his long tenure, Clinton Gardner chaired the Department for several terms and helped shape its character and policies, develop its faculty, and attract, admit, advise, educate, and place its students. He was the Department's principal teacher in the field of Christian Ethics. He was *Doktorvater* to numerous Ph.D. candidates and continued the supervision of several doctoral dissertations even after his retirement in 1990. He established important and productive links between the faculties of the Graduate Division of Religion and the Candler School of Theology and those of the schools of medicine, law, nursing, business, and public health. He is what is known in the trade as a "productive scholar," i.e., the author of several books and many articles. He was a founding member (1959), president, and executive secretary of what became the Society of Christian Ethics in the United States and Canada. It is a splendid testimony to his service and influence that graduates of the Department of Ethics and Society should honor him with this collection of their essays.

Also, it is appropriate that the editors should select the theme of "responsibility" as the rubric for these essays, for that was the theoretical framework and much of the substance of Professor Gardner's own constructive work in ethics. As a scholar in the field of Christian Ethics, he taught his students the history of Christian moral teaching, the critical approach to texts, and the types of methods of moral analysis. As a normative ethicist, he drew upon all this learning to develop a responsiblist approach to Christian moral identity and to proposals for public policy. By adopting "responsibility" as the defining term for his normative theological and social ethics, Gardner placed himself deliberately and with acknowledgment in the following of our great and honored teacher in Yale University, Professor H. Richard Niebuhr. In developing the concept, however, Professor Gardner contributed his own distinctive methodological refinements, especially with regards to medical ethics, health policy, and issues of racial justice. These methodological developments are extended in the essays contributed by his former students.

There is another reason—ultimately of greater importance—why the theme is the appropriate choice. Clinton Gardner is himself the embodiment of responsibility. I shall not belabor the point, because he would find it embarrassing. But to say at least a little more would be "fitting"—to use Professor Niebuhr's ethical criterion. In Clinton Gardner's case, responsibility embodies a noble deontological element: a strong sense of duty, of loyalty, of commitment, of propriety, of distinction between right and wrong—but prompted by love and administered with pragmatic discernment of context. He held his students and holds himself to high standards. Yet they found him to be concerned, available, and pastoral. He held his colleagues also to high standards, and reminded them on occasion that expectations should be met and rules in place should be enforced. Yet he was himself the most reliable—as well as the most considerate—of colleagues, and he understood fully that enforcement of rules was a dimension of contextual responsibility and not a mandate of rigid legalism.

One aspect of personal responsibility deserves special mention: Dr. Gardner's passionate and profound commitment to racial justice. Clinton Gardner is a white southern male whose speech betrays unmistakably (and marvelously) the accents of middle Tennessee. He is also an educated agrarian, a United Methodist clergyman, and a racial liberal who challenged prophetically the unjust and repressive racial practices of his native southland long before it was popular and easy to do so—and from within the segregated South, not from outside. He made his witness in various ways, but most constantly and effectively in his course on Christianity and Race Relations, which he taught for a number of years in the Candler School of Theology of Emory University, and in the large, required course on Christian Ethics. In those courses Gardner destroyed the myths of racism and segregation, delineated the injustice of contemporary practices, identified the proper roles for the church as that of prophetic community, and invited the members of his classes—most of them preparing for pastoral ministry—to lead their congregations to a new day of liberation and reconciliation. This emphasis was somewhat less in evidence in graduate seminars, but it was present there nonetheless, and it always is manifest in his personal stance and in his comportment towards persons of other races. If it does not emerge explicitly in the essays, it must be lifted up here as testimony to Clinton Gardner's personal embodiment of the ethics of responsibility.

It is a great privilege for me to share with our former students, now our colleagues, in acknowledging and honoring Professor E. Clinton Gardner's career and ministry with this volume of essays.

Theodore R. Weber
Professor of Social Ethics
Emory University

Preface

Three and a half decades have passed since H. Richard Niebuhr last proposed, in the posthumous publication of a slender book called *The Responsible Self*, that "responsibility" can serve as a touchstone in ethics. In the years since, Niebuhr's proposition has become so familiar as to be almost taken for granted; the notion of "response" itself has become important—and, by a perverse irony, often trivialized—in many other disciplines besides ethics, from psychotherapy to literary criticism. Perhaps for this reason alone, the current volume will prove worthwhile: it takes a fresh look at what might otherwise appear, at best, commonplace or, at worst, hackneyed. More than this, however, the essays presented in this volume seek to carry forward the project of bringing Niebuhr's "Essay in Christian Moral Philosophy" into a place where, as Marx would have it, philosophy might change the world.

But if these essays seek to lay the groundwork for a deeper understanding of Niebuhr's concept of responsibility, they also seek to make that concept aptly useful in framing some of the more pressing social questions of our day. In this, the essays carry forward the work of one of Niebuhr's responsible and exemplary students, E. Clinton Gardner. To the extent that they succeed in their aim, the essays—and their authors—honor a scholar and teacher who, himself, has sought to engage responsibly in ethical inquiry. E. Clinton Gardner's work, studied under the rubrics of "responsibility" and "covenant" in Chapter 1, has been a lifelong response not only to the formative questions posed by

Niebuhr but also to the faithful impulse that has carried Professor Gardner, as a Christian believer, toward concern for racial equity, fair access to health care, compassionate treatment of the unfortunate, and keeping human life humane in an increasingly dehumanizing world.

Each essay in this volume is itself a kind of response—to the mind of the teacher and the spirit of the pastor who is Clinton Gardner. All are also responses to the particular—one might say peculiar—callings of their authors, friends, and colleagues in the past decade and a half of the Ethics and Society Program in Emory University's Graduate Division of Religion.

Two of the essays, by Janet Jakobsen and Rosetta Ross, are wonderfully nuanced explorations of the ethical experience of women in American society, the one more general in scope and the other precisely attuned to the experience of an individual African-American woman. Two other essays, by William Thurston and Darryl Trimiew, call for attention to the ethical heritage of the American schizophrenia caused by our history of racial consciousness: on the one hand, Thurston's constructive proposal for furthering the work of three great African-American activist/theorists; on the other hand, Trimiew's urgent plea for reasoned yet compassionate response to the racial imbalances in capital punishment.

Sharing Clinton Gardner's long and deep interest in the understanding of the Word, the life of the church, and the ministry of the faithful, three essays—those of Louis Ruprecht, Christine Pohl, and James Thobaben—extend in important ways our understanding of, respectively, the nature of the Gospels as they call forth a faithful response; the character of betrayal of moral response, including response to the demands of the church and other institutions; and the changing identity and self-understanding of the church as it responds to contemporary life.

The largest single "cluster" of essays, six in number, bring Niebuhr's and Gardner's constructive concepts to bear on social and institutional policies. In doing this, they share an emphasis that Professor Gardner brought to and infused into the Ethics and Society Program that he helped to shape. This is an emphasis lies in making ethical inquiry important to a community's collective determination: of what it values, where it will use its energy and resources for good, and how it will perpetuate its mode of ethical being and doing. In addition to Trimiew's cogent analysis of capital punishment, there are essays by Frederick Glennon on the ethics of welfare economics; by Adele Resmer on the need for covenantal relationships in health care; by Peter Gathje on the nature of responsible political communities; by Leslie Weber on the role of schools in educating "responsible selves"; and by Russell Willis on policy responses to the growing "technopolis."

It is especially fitting—to use a Niebuhrian term—that this volume should be brought into being by ethicists who gathered as a small community of scholars at Emory University in the 1980s. This was a time when Emory as an institution was striving to claim more vigorously and forthrightly its heritage of "education of the heart," to quote a phrase often used by its then-president, James T. Laney. If the University has in any measure grown in its capacity to respond to the moral demands of our time, it is in no small measure owing to the writers of these essays and to their teachers. In honoring E. Clinton Gardner, these ethicists also honor this much larger purpose to which he, himself, has contributed so much.

Gary S. Hauk
Secretary of the University
Emory University

Section I

The Promise and Limits of Responsibility and Covenant for Christian Social Ethics

Chapter 1

Responsibility and Covenant in the Work of E. Clinton Gardner

Frederick E. Glennon and Russell E. Willis

In this book, *Living Responsibly in Community*, the editors and contributors have two basic purposes. First, we seek to contribute to the field of Christian social ethics by exploring two central concepts, responsibility and covenant. To that end, these essays critically appropriate and reconceptualize responsibility and covenant within diverse Christian ethical traditions and explore the concepts' significance for critical social issues. Second, we hope to pay honor to E. Clinton Gardner. Not only is Professor Gardner one of the finest teachers and mentors in contemporary Christian ethics, he is also one of the premier contemporary theological ethicists and has explored the meanings of responsibility and covenant for Christian ethics for the past forty years. It is fitting, therefore, to begin this book by reviewing Professor Gardner's own use of these concepts in his writings.

Responsibility

"Responsibility defines the basic structure of human morality generally, including that of Christian ethics."[1] In these words, E. Clinton Gardner suggests the pivotal role of responsibility in his theological ethics. This particular quotation is an appropriate opening for this essay for two reasons. First, it indicates the centrality of responsibility to

Gardner's understanding of human moral existence, and particularly of Christian vocation. According to Gardner, responsibility not only must lie at the heart of an adequate theory of moral agency but also suggests a theoretical paradigm for theological ethics and serves as the basic ingredient of a pragmatic moral vision for contemporary Christians. Guided by this paradigm and moral vision, Gardner constructs a theological ethics that is best characterized as "responsiblist."

Second, when placed in context, this statement also points to the source of Gardner's responsiblist approach to ethics, namely the work of his teacher and intellectual mentor, H. Richard Niebuhr. From the beginning of Gardner's scholarly career, he has insightfully, appreciatively, and critically appropriated Niebuhr's notion of the "responsible self." Indeed, Gardner used the quotation above to invoke Niebuhr's ethics as the basis for construing justice in terms of covenantal responsibility. This is just one of many ways in which Gardner critically analyzes Niebuhr's use of the concept of responsibility or uses Niebuhr's responsiblist approach as a foundation for his own normative ethics.

This is not to say that Gardner's responsiblist ethics is influenced only by H. Richard Niebuhr. One of Gardner's earliest essays, for example, focused on the metaphor of "response" in Horace Bushnell's theology.[2] In Gardner's second book, *The Church as a Prophetic Community*, he used Bonhoeffer's metaphor of "deputyship" to describe the nature of responsibility in the context of the covenant community of faith.[3] As his career developed, Gardner sharpened his conceptualization of responsibility in a host of critical analyses focusing on both methodological and substantive uses of the concept of responsibility.[4] This body of work (which culminates in *Christocentrism and Christian Social Ethics*) is part of Gardner's broader project, to provide an extensive and in-depth comparative study of twentieth-century Christian ethics, especially of his Protestant contemporaries.[5] In much of this work Gardner appreciatively acknowledged the influence of such colleagues as James Gustafson.[6] He was also positively influenced by several contemporary Catholic moral theologians, such as Karl Rahner. Nevertheless, it was Niebuhr who laid the groundwork that Gardner found most conducive to the construction of a Christian ethics of responsibility.

Gardner's critical analysis of Niebuhr is spread throughout his oeuvre. In-depth consideration of Niebuhr's use of the concept of responsibility can be found in such works as "Responsibility and Moral Direction in the Ethics of H. Richard Niebuhr," "Character, Virtue, and Responsibility in Theological Ethics," and *Christocentrism in Christian Social Ethics*.[7] In several other works—including his recent book, *Justice and Christian Ethics*—Gardner invokes Niebuhr's responsiblist approach to flesh out issues from justice and law, to abortion, to medicine and health care.[8]

In these works, Gardner focuses on three main themes suggested by Niebuhr's approach: the idea that the lineaments of responsibility provide the basic structure of ethics; the view that the responsiblist approach copes with moral ambiguity and particularity in moral decision making more adequately than either deontological (rules-oriented) or teleological (ends-oriented) systems (including so-called "virtue ethics"); and the conviction that theocentrism (God-centeredness) is the appropriate moral stance of the responsible self. For each of these themes, Niebuhr provides a foundation that Gardner discerns, qualifies, fills in, and transcends.[9]

In the first place, Gardner takes Niebuhr's lead in construing responsibility as the basis of the moral life, and ethics as reflection on the moral life. In fact, Gardner agrees with Niebuhr that the "responsiblist" approach represents a fundamental shift in ethics, away from perspectives based on duty or rights as well as approaches grounded on good or value. What is proposed with such a shift, Gardner argues,

> is not so much a new conceptual norm which would provide a substitute for rights and/or values as it is a shift in the perspective of the moral agent. Such a shift in perspective does, however, entail a redefinition of the notion of responsibility itself.[10]

The redefinition of responsibility Gardner suggests is based on the definition of responsibility first proposed by Niebuhr.[11]

Responsibility, in this perspective, entails four major features: response to prior actions, interpretation of those prior actions, a willingness to be held accountable for one's action, and participation within an ongoing moral community. Generally Gardner treats the first three of these features of responsibility as rather obvious, and therefore unremarkable; however, he focuses significant attention on the fourth. In fact, it is this fourth feature that Gardner views as revolutionary for ethics.

The responsiblist position, he argues, should not ignore concepts of duty/rights or good/value. Rather, "considerations of both right and values . . . would be transformed by being placed in the context of a community of claims."[12] That is to say, this paradigm shift defines "the fundamental structure of moral relationships in terms of the responses of the self in an ongoing moral community rather than in terms of aspiration after an ideal good (teleology) or obedience to abstract duties or absolute laws (deontology)."[13] The ethics of responsibility seeks the "fitting" or "appropriate" response. In so doing,

[t]he notion of Responsibility does not make the language of duty and the good unnecessary. Rather, it qualifies the latter and places these concepts in a relational, interactive context so that their meaning becomes concrete rather than abstract.[14]

Ultimately Gardner describes the moral basis of community in terms of *covenant*, the other major theme explored in this volume.

In *The Church as a Prophetic Community*, Gardner uses Bonhoeffer's metaphor of "deputyship" to locate responsibility (and freedom) within the covenant community.[15] The covenant community is "the concrete place where freedom and responsibility meet and where it is possible for the Christian to love the neighbor in a concrete, other-centered, human way." In this early work, Gardner focuses on the church itself as a basic covenant community, within which Christian responsibility takes a concrete form.[16] In his later works, especially *Justice and Christian Ethics*, he expands the view of covenant community to include all humanity, but he remains steadfast in suggesting that Christian moral responsibility is concretely expressed within the covenant community. More will be said about his use of covenant shortly.

Another of Gardner's main themes vis-à-vis the ethics of responsibility is that such an approach addresses moral ambiguity and particularity in moral decision-making more adequately than other approaches. This is vividly demonstrated in a personal account related in a recent article on medical and health-care ethics.

Some months ago I was invited to participate in Grand Rounds in the Department of Urology in the Medical School. The case under discussion was that of a patient with end-stage kidney disease who had been placed on dialysis. Over time the dialysis treatment had become increasingly burdensome. Eventually, the patient requested to be taken off dialysis and allowed to die. As a competent adult, he had a legal right to discontinue treatment; nevertheless, the physician felt morally obligated to try to persuade him to remain on dialysis. In the end the physician was unsuccessful, and he eventually supported the patient's decision. In summarizing the case the physician said that the health care team and the patient had reached "an appropriate" decision. The terms "right" and "good" seem strangely inadequate to capture the moral ambiguity and particularity of that decision, including the patient's own sense of moral integrity which was at stake in it.[17]

In the context of the abortion debate, Gardner again claims that the responsiblist approach provides the most adequate moral perspective for such a complex, ambiguous situation. Gardner states that, viewed from the perspective of responsibility, values and rights are perceived as concrete and relational rather than as abstract and absolute. [The] concept of responsibility takes seriously the freedom of the moral agent as a participation in the decision-making process, i.e., in the process of deciding *what* present acts would be responsible in a particular set of moral relationships. . . . [The] concept of responsibility offers promise as a mediating symbol between the religious traditions of Judaism and Christianity, on the one hand, and our contemporary moral experience on the other. More particularly, the responsiblist method of structuring moral questions seems to provide a more adequate and authentic bridge between these religious traditions and the contemporary experience of freedom, complexity, moral ambiguity, and guilt than do appeals finally to rights or to values. Moreover, while it does not resolve the difficult issue of the humanity of the fetus, the responsiblist approach to normative ethics does suggest a less dogmatic and possibly less arbitrary way of dealing with this problem—a method suggested in fact, by the general recognition in theological ethics as well as in civil and common law that abortion is not murder.[18]

These examples illustrate Gardner's contention that responsibility is more in touch with our common moral experience than either deontological or teleological ethics. Human life lived in relationship in a community with a past, present, and future is full of moral complexity and ambiguity. What is good or right is not always clear in particular historical circumstances. Moral action requires the ability to discern which actions are most fitting or most appropriate in a given context, and the capacity to discriminate among competing goods and duties. Moreover, from the perspective of faith, the moral agent needs to perceive what God is doing in the context as well.

This emphasis on discerning what God is doing illustrates the final theme in Gardner's ethics: theocentrism. As did Niebuhr, Gardner contends that all moral action is ultimately a response to God's creating, ordering, and redeeming activity in the world. Human moral responsibility is ultimately "*to* God and *for* the neighbor in an inclusive moral community."[19] Human beings are relational beings; we become human only in relationship with others. This is also true for our moral selves. By advocating a theocentric ethic, Gardner, with Niebuhr, contends that relationality is not simply endemic to human life; relationality is central to all life, that is, it is universal. Through God's creating, ordering, and reconciling activity all life is brought together in ways that lead to its fulfillment and completion. In addition, a theocentric ethic provides a transcendent, universal perspective from which to evaluate and transform all moral relationships. Those actions are fitting and responsible that enhance God's purposes in creation and redemption. The term Gardner uses to understand this universal community is covenant, of course, the second major theme in Gardner's work.

Covenant

Like his treatment of responsibility, Gardner's reflections on covenant as the basis for human community probe and expand the use of the concept by his mentor, H. Richard Niebuhr. Gardner agrees with Niebuhr that covenant best describes human moral experience. As social beings, we ground our relationships with others on the promises we make and the promises we keep. Moreover, Gardner suggests that covenant is the fundamental way in which God relates to the created order. Thus, at one level in Gardner's ethics, covenant serves a descriptive function.

As a social ethicist, however, Gardner is concerned with relevance to the society in which he lives. He wants to make moral claims about how we ought to live our lives in community with one another. In other words, he wants to be prescriptive as well as descriptive, and the notion of covenant provides the communal basis for his prescriptions. In particular, his understanding of covenant enables him to engage in discussions about justice and public policy. Gardner acknowledged Niebuhr's critics, who charged that Niebuhr's work lacked norms for moral action. At the communal level, Gardner contends, covenant provides such norms, especially a norm of justice, which not only becomes foundational for a variety of public policies but also provides insight into the debate in Christian ethics regarding the relationship between love and justice. Finally, covenant is the basis upon which Gardner can advocate for a theocentric social ethic over the christocentric ethics championed by many prominent Protestant ethicists.

The Nature of Covenant Community

Following Niebuhr, Gardner contends that "the fundamental form of human society is covenant, i.e., the making and keeping of promises."[20] Covenant structures all of our communal lives; all our relationships rely on trust and the mutual promise of fidelity. All people participate in covenants, by birth and by choice. Families, voluntary associations, and political communities, are all covenantal in structure. For example, while the family has a natural basis in sex and parental love, its essence is found in the promise-making and promise-keeping between husbands and wives, parents and children. When members of the family fail to keep their promises or fulfill their obligations to one another, the experience of community disintegrates, in spite of the bonds of nature and affection.

Underlying this conception of community is a relational ontology of human life and moral agency. Human beings are fundamentally social; that is, we exist and are sustained through our relationships with others. We find meaning, become selves, by expressing and fulfilling ourselves in these acts of mutual promise and trust. There is, thus, a strong connection between an ethics of responsibility and a covenantal conception of community.

Like responsibility, covenant community is always triadic, involving the parties in faithfulness both to one another and to a common cause that they attempt to realize. In a political context, this cause is generally understood as the "public good" or "commonweal." The unity of the people is based upon mutual commitment to each other for a common purpose or end, a commitment based on promise to and trust in one another. According to Gardner, John Winthrop's sermon "A Model of Christian Charity," is the quintessential expression of this concept in the American context.

> Thus stands the cause between God and us. We are entered into covenant with him for this work. . . . For this end, we must be knit together in this work as one man. . . . We must delight in each other, make others' conditions our own, rejoice together, mourn together, labor and suffer together, always having before our eyes our commission and community in the work, our community as members of the same body.[21]

This sermon illustrates the deep bonds between and the level of commitment expected from members of a covenantal community. The sermon also suggests that membership in a political covenant includes commitment to a common cause, a cause to which members will sacrifice private interests if necessary.

Another dimension of Winthrop's sermon that is important to Gardner is its theocentric focus. No less than the theocentric notion of responsibility, which claims that we respond to others as if to God, the concept of covenant claims that promises and commitments are made in the presence of God. Human action in relationship to the covenant community is always done in response to the God of all. Our moral agency is best understood "as the response of the self to the action of other selves (individuals and groups) in the context of ultimate dependence upon the moral ordering of history."[22] The author of that moral ordering is God; thus our response is always response to divine action.

While Gardner affirms certain aspects of christocentrism in Christian social ethics, he is ultimately critical of christocentrism, because it inadequately understands God as Creator. Christocentric social ethics tend to focus on the work of God as Redeemer. But there is an ordering process that God initiates in the world from creation. The Puritans spoke of this as the "covenant of works."[23] The order is understood as a law of nature, knowable through human reason. Although sin required that this law be supplemented by divine law revealed in Scripture, the implant of the law of nature still remains in the hearts of all people. This is important, because the law of nature provides a transcendent moral order against which all institutions and positive law are measured. Through both the law of nature and divine law God orders human history.

Based upon this descriptive account of covenant community, Gardner contends that this understanding of community provides a more solid foundation for social ethics than either contract views of community or more recent communitarian and sectarian views. Gardner's use of covenant thus becomes prescriptive: covenant not only *is* the basis for most forms of human community; covenant *ought* to be the basis for human community. Covenant community offers the best possibility that a human community will provide fulfillment for all members, and it most connects us with our God.

Covenant contrasts sharply with notions of contract. Some would contend that conceptions of contract and covenant are identical. They do have common roots. They are both agreements based on the mutual consent of the parties involved. They both emphasize individual freedom and mutual responsibility. Some Puritan covenantal theologians even used the terms interchangeably, leading some to argue that the notion of covenant is inherently individualistic.[24] While covenant makes use of contract, however, the terms are not equivalent.

Contract views of community are inherently individualistic. Although the blame for this individualism is often laid at the feet of John Locke, Gardner suggests that Locke's social compact has deeply communal dimensions.[25] Gardner admits, however, that because of Locke's underlying concept of human nature, Locke believes human beings exist as individuals prior to membership in society, and Locke's conception of natural rights is essentially individualistic. It is this emphasis on individual rights, Gardner claims, that dominates later American thinking regarding Locke's social contract, and that is why contract has become perceived in largely individualistic terms. The self implicit in contract thought makes of society a collection of autonomous agents who relate to one another to promote their mutual values, interests, or advantages.

Covenant, on the other hand, is fundamentally communal. Covenant recognizes the patterns of interdependence in which people are enmeshed with one another. Moreover, covenant affirms that the well-being of one is intricately connected to the well-being of others. One cannot pursue one's own good without concern for the well-being of others. Freedom is important in a covenantal framework, but freedom is conceived relationally rather than individualistically. Instead of meaning the capacity to choose among goods, true freedom means the ability to commit oneself to a cause.[26]

Gardner argues that covenant is a stronger foundation for community than the communitarian and sectarian views that underlie advocates of virtue ethics, such as Alasdair MacIntyre and Stanley Hauerwas. Their conception of community is narrow and includes only those who share a moral narrative. As a result, they appear exclusive and elitist, failing to appreciate human diversity, and lacking sufficient foundation for political responsibility.[27] Covenant, on the other hand, is inclusive and pluralistic. Conceived theocentrically, the covenant with God includes all of creation; all life has a relationship to that transcendent power.[28] Covenant also affirms the diversity in the created order. Gardner argues, "pluralism is part of God's design for the enrichment and ordering of human history."[29] The mutual promise and entrustment that we do is not limited to those who share the same moral tradition, as MacIntyre supposes.

> In a covenantal understanding of public life, accountability is the willingness to give an account to the community *as a whole*. Pluralism, because it widens the scope of the community, provides the broadest possible resources not only for a fuller insight into the meaning of justice but also for the practical implementation of justice within the limits of history.[30]

Clearly, sectarian views of community fail to achieve this end, and thus, as we shall see, limit their ability to generate justice in the community.

Gardner's prescriptive use of the concept of covenant community is not without its critics. Many feminist ethicists and others claim rightly that the concept of covenant community has been used to exclude large groups of people, especially women and persons of color. Historically, the Puritans, advocates of covenant community, did not tolerate diversity within their midst. Covenantal or federal symbols and language, which were foundational for the United States. Constitution, did not prohibit the United States from excluding women, slaves, and the poor from full membership in the body politic. Even recently, "protective covenants" were used in real estate to restrict minorities and others from moving into communities. Gardner recognizes these problem as well. He insists, however, that those who use the concept of covenant to exclude others from community have lost sight of the inclusive nature of covenant, especially as it has been intended from a theocentric framework. Covenant can provide a basis for a broader conception of human community, a greater affirmation of pluralism, and a more dynamic concept of justice than it sometimes has been used to do. Let us turn to this broader conception of justice that Gardner suggests is implicit in covenantal notions of justice.[31]

Covenant and Justice

Covenantal justice, according to Gardner, is fundamentally creative, "reconciling justice," which "seeks the transformation of all forms of human society and culture."[32] This form of justice differs from "preserving justice," those forms of justice that seek to sustain the existing social order, which is what the Aristotelian view of justice intends. Preserving justice is about social order, even if that order includes systemic injustice. Reconciling justice, on the other hand, affirms the fundamental freedom and equality of all persons before God and seeks to change structures toward the greater realization of freedom and equality for all groups, especially those who are marginalized and oppressed. Covenantal justice is also positive in that it seeks to build new forms of inclusive community.

A covenantal view of justice includes both rights and duties. From a theocentric perspective, all rights claims are based on the notions of the "image of God" and covenant. Being created in the "image of God" means that all persons are created free and equal, entitled to certain human rights that provide the fundamental conditions for human flourishing. These rights include negative rights—protections against unjustified interference, such as rights to life, freedom of speech, and freedom of religion. They also include positive rights—claims for assistance from others, including rights to shelter, work, and education. Any just community must respect the freedom and equality of all members of the community; however, we are also created for covenant relationship with God and one another. This means that our freedom and equality are relational rather than absolute, always finding their fulfillment in community. Thus our rights are set within a framework of obligation and duty: our rights to participate freely and equally in the civil and economic benefits of society entail a corresponding duty to exercise those rights responsibly, with an eye toward the common good as well as our individual goods.[33]

That people can act irresponsibly points to the negative function of justice. Both the biblical and Puritan discussions of covenant recognized clearly the pervasiveness of human sin. Power can corrupt, and people can use their power to violate the rights and usurp the goods of others. Such violations were the fundamental basis for the prophetic judgment of Israel (Amos). That is why Protestant ethics traditionally has associated justice with God's restraining or ordering activity. Justice requires structures that limit the harm that people can do to one another. Yet a covenantal conception of community also recognizes a positive role for justice, relating it to God's creative activity to bring about human fulfillment. With regard to distributive justice, the proper allocation of society's benefits and burdens, this means not only that all persons share meaningfully in the distribution of society's goods but also that all members of the community share in the determination of what the good entails.[34]

In light of this positive function, a covenantal view of justice entails some conception of the "common good," a phrase that has meant many things. The Puritans understood the public good to be a part of the calling and vocation of every member of the community. Using one's vocation purely for private interests was an abuse of one's calling. This idea is also embedded in the Puritan concept of the "holy common-wealth." The proper purpose of government and ruling authorities is to promote the well-being of all.[35] The other notions of political community noted above do not share this perspective. Contract views of community lack a strong commitment to the common good but, rather, affirm the rights of individuals to pursue individual goods. We hear much today about trust as the basis of government. But what is clear is that, in contract views, the trustworthiness expected of government is limited to the faithfulness of protecting the lives, liberties, and possessions of individuals. In covenantal thought, Gardner contends, the public trust "means faithfulness to the promise to promote the good of the whole even at the expense of private interest."[36] Similarly, in sectarian and communitarian views, the common good is limited to those who share the same religious or moral traditions. On the other hand, covenant's affirmation of pluralism and inclusiveness means that justice extends to all. The demand for justice "is a demand for public account-ability both in those individuals and in those collective relationships in which we meet the neighbor."[37]

In addition to affirming the common good, covenant allows us to unify conceptions of justice as both virtue and law in a concept of polit-ical community based upon mutual trust and fidelity to a common cause. In some ways, this unifying function of covenant resembles the unifying nature of responsibility as a paradigm for moral relationships. Responsibility brings together teleological and deontological forms of ethics; it takes abstract principles of the good and the right and makes them concrete in human relationships. Covenant does the same with justice. Neither justice as virtue nor justice as law is complete by itself. A covenantal view of justice stresses the internal disposition to act justly ("virtue") and the faithfulness to obey the moral law ("rules of

justice"). It also provides the transcendent norm by which all systems
of human justice are measured: the cause of true human fulfillment for
all intended in God's creating and covenanting activity.[38]

Gardner demonstrates that covenant provides the basis upon which to
resolve the tension between love and justice discussed so much in
Christian ethics. Reinhold Niebuhr, among many, has contended that
love is the highest ideal for Christian ethics, but that it is an eschatological hope. The most we can expect in this world is some form of
justice, some balance of the liberty and equality of all persons in the
community. Admittedly, Reinhold Niebuhr recognized that the ideals
of love and justice were in dialectical tension, with love pushing justice
to become more just. Gardner suggests, however, that the notion of
covenant brings the ideals of love and justice into closer relationship,
because "in its covenantal form justice provides a basis for the transformation of law and justice itself by self-giving love." In covenant, the
aim of justice is more than preserving the existing forms of community.
It also includes a reconciling dimension. "Love makes use of secular
forms of reciprocal, distributive, and juridical justice in the earthly city,
but love transforms them by directing them beyond justice proper to
the restoration of broken relationships and to the creation of new and
fuller forms of community."[39]

Implication of Covenant for Social Policy

Gardner's use of covenant and its conception of justice also has implications for public policy, implications that Gardner intends.[40] He
suggests, however, that because we live in a pluralistic society, the
language of moral discourse will remain primarily secular. How, then,
can his view of covenant be relevant to policy debate? Why should
American public policy be influenced by the language of covenant,
which for Gardner is clearly theological? The answer he provides is that
the notion of covenant is foundational to American society. The symbol of covenant is a part of the American heritage. As such, it provides
"an indispensable metaphor for our self-understanding as a people under
the sovereignty and providence of God."[41] The language of covenant
resonates deeply with our collective soul, and it has been given count-
less public expressions, most recently by President Clinton. Thus,
Gardner is quite comfortable with exploring its relevance for public policy, particularly for health care policy.

Gardner agrees with those ethicists who contend that covenant ought
to form the foundation for the doctor-patient relationship; however, he
goes further in his application of covenant to health-care policy.[42]
Gardner suggests that health-care policy involves three issues: the accessibility of health care, the level of care provided, and the allocation

of scarce medical resources. He explores each issue from the perspective of distributive justice, which as we noted above, includes not only the distribution of the goods but also voice in the determination of what goods are distributed.

With regard to the issue of accessibility, Gardner notes that America has a two-tiered system of health-care delivery. Those with resources, money, and insurance get more health care than those without. For Gardner this state of affairs is problematic:

> From a covenantal perspective the moral right to a basic level of care is grounded in the equality of human worth and in the recognition that health care is not only a fundamental good but also a public good. Such a right, however, is neither absolute nor unconditional. Health care is both a mutual responsibility and a mutually shared good.[43]

Clearly, stressing a moral right to a basic level of health care places the covenantal view at odds with those who suggest that health care is a commodity, subject to the forces of the free market and its fee-for-service calculations. What they do not see, Gardner argues, is that health care is not simply a commodity but a public good, which means that together we have determined that society should distribute it to all regardless of ability to pay. Moreover, denying millions of people access to certain kinds of health care because of their inability to pay is wasteful. As a result, we spend billions of dollars on curative care that we might avoid if we spent more on preventive care.

What level of health care we should provide to one another is a second policy issue Gardner addresses. The idea of a "basic" level is obviously open to interpretation. When we say that people ought to have an "adequate" level of care, we recognize that equality is a relational rather than a fixed idea. At the least, equality is qualified by need; not every person needs a heart transplant. Moreover, what we can provide to one another is limited by scarcity and cost. The right to health care is contingent upon the resources of the community. People should also use the resources available to them responsibly and not frivolously. Finally, Gardner contends that the idea of a basic level of care "implies an emphasis upon prevention rather than treatment."[44] On the one hand, this means that people have a responsibility to take care of their health, to limit behaviors they know are detrimental. On the other hand, any health-care policy must include education about the genetic, nutritional, and environmental factors that support good health and those that promote disease.

Finally, the question emerges regarding the allocation of medical resources. The availability of medical resources is greater than at any previous time in America; yet some resources remain scarce. How much should America invest in health care, and how should those funds be distributed? In part the answer to this question is determined by where the medical needs are. As our population ages, more resources will go into taking care of the aging. AIDS and breast cancer continue at epidemic levels. Covenant, with its emphasis on mutual responsibility and commitment, affirms that we need to devote more resources to these needs. But covenant also demands that we become more efficient in the utilization of resources. Finally, covenant also means that we must place more emphasis on prevention. People can and should do more to keep themselves healthy, so that scarce medical resources will be available for those who truly need them.

To bring the issue of the allocation of resources into perspective, Gardner suggests: "from a covenantal perspective, greater attention should be given to human finitude, quality of life, and proportionality in decisions concerning termination of treatment of terminally ill patients."[45] Although he does not spell out the implications of this idea, his suggestion points to the need for members in a covenantal community to consider the well-being of others as well as of themselves, even promoting the good of the whole at the expense of private interest. Should we allocate tremendous medical resources to extend the lives of terminally ill patients whose chances for enhanced quality of life are slim, if doing so means that we cannot provide basic health care for poor children? A covenantal perspective would lead us to think not. Instead, we should accept our finitude and be willing to live a few days or weeks, less so that others can live life more fully.

Conclusion

For over thirty years, in his teaching and his writing, Clinton Gardner has explored and developed the themes of responsibility and covenant and their implications for Christian ethics. In so doing, he has enabled others, colleagues and students alike, to do the same.

A good example of this work is his book *Christocentrism in Christian Social Ethics.* Here Gardner's purpose is not merely to discuss various perspectives in recent Christian ethics. Rather, it is to create a dialogue among the six ethicists, and even to enter the conversation himself. The positions are not simply presented to the reader; they engage each other and the reader. The positions are not merely investigated, they interact. The result is not just an accurate portrait of various views in juxtaposition (though it is certainly that). It is a snapshot of the evolution of a community whose membership includes Gardner, the ethicists discussed in the book, and the readers who engage the text. In many ways it is the dialogue, and the chance that the dialogue will continue and grow beyond the text, that counts most.

Yet Professor Gardner's work on responsibility and covenant does not stop with his writings. Instead, he embodies these themes in all of his relationships, as teacher, mentor, and colleague. For Gardner, acting responsibly is a vocation that is fundamentally relational, dialogical, other-centered, covenantal, and ultimately, we believe, a faithful response to God. In both his teaching and writing, Gardner does not give the final answer. Rather, he offers all with whom he relates an invitation to engage in meaningful conversation. His quiet, welcoming demeanor is a significant part of his vocation. Through it, other voices are heard without having to shout. These other voices include not only his mentors and his colleagues but also his students, whom he welcomed into his pedagogical and moral community. In these and many other ways, Clinton Gardner exemplifies what living responsibly in community is all about.

Notes

[1] E. Clinton Gardner, "Justice, Virtue, and Law," Journal of Law and Religion II/2 (November 2, 1984): 409.

[2] E. Clinton Gardner, "Horace Bushnell's Concept of Response," *Religion in Life* 17/1 (Winter, 1957-58): 212-222.

[3] E. Clinton Gardner, *The Church as a Prophetic Community* (Philadelphia: Westminster Press, 1967), 226ff.

[4] See, for example, E. Clinton Gardner, "Responsibility in Freedom," in *Storm Over Ethics*, ed. John C. Bennett (Minneapolis: United Church Press, 1967), 38-66, a sustained analysis of Joseph Fletcher's ethics; "Abortion from the Perspective of Responsibility," *Perkins Journal* 30/3 (Spring 1977): 10-28; "Responsibility and Moral Direction in the Ethics of H. Richard Niebuhr," *Encounter* 40/2 (spring 1979): 143-168; "Character, Virtue, and Responsibility in Theological Ethics," *Encounter* 44/4 (Autumn 1983): 315-339; and *Christocentrism in Christian Social Ethics* (Washington, D.C.: University Press of America, 1983), chapter 5, 7.

[5] In addition to *Christocentrism in Christian Social Ethics*, see, for example, "Justice and Love," in *Social Ethics: Issues in Ethics and Society*, ed. Gibson Winter (New York: Harper Forum Books, 1968), 66-77; "Christian Ethics: Contemporary Developments," in *Contemporary Christian Trends*, ed. William M. Pinson, Jr., and Clyde E. Fant, Jr. (Waco: Word Books, 1972); "Ethical Traditions in American Methodism," in *Encyclopedia of World Methodism*, ed. Nolan B. Harmon (Nashville: Abingdon Press, 1974); "Phenomenological Analysis and Normative Ethics in Selected Theological Ethicists," in The American Society of Christian Ethics, *Selected Papers, Sixteenth Annual Meeting* (Missoula, Mont.: Scholars Press, 1975), 29-47; and "Ethics in the South," in

Encyclopedia of Religion in the South, ed. Samuel S. Hill (Macon, Georgia: Mercer University Press, 1984).

[6]See, for example, *Christocentrism in Christian Social Ethics*, chapter 7; and "Abortion From the Perspective of Responsibility."

[7]E. Clinton Gardner, "Responsibility and Moral Direction in the Ethics of H. Richard Niebuhr," 143-168; "Character, Virtue, and Responsibility in Theological Ethics," 315-339; and *Christocentrism in Christian Social Ethics*.

[8]E. Clinton Gardner, *Justice and Christian Ethics* (Cambridge: Cambridge University Press, 1995), 120-123. See also, for instance, "Justice, Virtue, and Law," *Journal of Law and Religion* 2/2 (1984), 393-412; "Abortion: From the Perspective of Responsibility," 10-28; and "Theology, Medicine and Health," *Quarterly Review* 12/3 (Fall 1992): 71-82.

[9]In fact, much of Gardner's work, including the focus on these three themes, is related to his attempt to overcome several problems associated with Niebuhr's position. Gardner directly addressed these three issues in "Responsibility and Moral Direction in the Ethics of H. Richard Niebuhr."

[10]E. Clinton Gardner, "Abortion: From the Perspective of Responsibility," 10.

[11]Several essays in this volume expand on Niebuhr's concept of responsibility. They include Janet Jakobsen, "The Gendered Division of Moral Labor"; Christine Pohl, "Responsibility and Moral Betrayal"; Adele Resmer, "The Ethics of Leaving Ms. Smith Alone"; William Thurston, "Transformationist Responsiblist Ethic of Justice"; and Russell Willis, "Technology and Complex Responsibility."

[12]"Abortion: From the Perspective of Responsibility," 10.

[13]*Justice and Christian Ethics*, 120.

[14]"Theology, Medicine, and Health," 78.

[15]*The Church as a Prophetic Community*, 236ff.

[16]Ibid, 239-240

[17]"Theology, Medicine and Health," 78

[18]"Abortion: From the Perspective of Responsibility," 11.

[19]"Theology, Medicine, and Health," 78.

[20]*Christocentrism in Christian Social Ethics*, 213.

[21]John Winthrop, "A Model of Christian Charity," in *The Puritans in America: A Narrative Anthology*, ed. Alan Heimert and Andrew Delbanco (Cambridge: Harvard University Press, 1985), 82.

[22]*Justice and Christian Ethics*, 121.

[23]See E. Clinton Gardner, "Justice in the Puritan Covenantal Tradition," *Journal of Law and Religion* 6/1 (1988): 39-60. For an essay in this volume that advocates christocentrism over theocentrism in Christian social ethics, see James Thobaben's essay, "Ecclesiology and Covenant: Christian Social Institutions in a Pluralistic Society."

[24]"Justice in the Puritan Covenantal Tradition."

[25]E. Clinton Gardner, "John Locke: Justice and the Social Compact," *Journal of Law and Religion* 9/2 (1992): 347-371.

[26]*Christocentrism in Christian Social Ethics*, 201

[27]Peter Gathje's essay in this volume, "Virtue Ethics and Political Responsibility," provides a possible corrective to this concern.

[28]"Justice, Virtue, and Law," 410.

[29]*Justice and Christian Ethics*, 124.

[30]"Justice, Virtue, and Law," 410.

[31]In light of recent reappropriation of the concept of covenant among some feminist ethicists, Gardner may indeed be right. See, for example, Rosemary Radford Ruether, *Gaia and God* (San Francisco: Harper & Row, 1995). There she argues that the notion of covenant may be redeemable for environmental ethics. See also Margaret Farley, *Personal Commitments* (New York: Harper and Row, 1986), chapter 8.

[32]*Justice and Christian Ethics*, 52.

[33]Ibid., 130-133.

[34]Gardner writes: "In a democratic form of government justice requires the participation of all the citizens in the determination of the public good, and also in its distribution." Ibid., 138.

[35]"Justice in the Puritan Covenantal Tradition," 50.

[36]*Justice and Christian Ethics*, 140.

[37]"Justice, Virtue, and Law," 410.

[38]Ibid., 410-411.

[39]*Justice and Christian Ethics*, 142.

[40]Several of the essays in this volume spell out the implications of covenant for public policy. They include Fred Glennon, "Renewing the Covenant"; Darryl Trimiew, "Casting One Stone After Another"; and Leslie Weber, "The Covenant with Distant Neighbors."

[41]*Justice and Christian Ethics*, 141.

[42]See William F. May, *The Physician's Covenant* (Philadelphia: Westminster Press, 1983).

[43]*Justice and Christian Ethics*, 136.

[44]"Theology, Medicine, and Health," 81.

[45]*Justice and Christian Ethics*, 137.

Chapter 2

The Gendered Division of Moral Labor: Radical Relationalism and Feminist Ethics

Janet R. Jakobsen

The task of feminist ethics, in both its critical and its constructive aspects, is to contribute to the historical project of liberation by taking seriously women's moral agency. In order for feminist ethics to fulfill its commitments, it is necessary to question whether women's ethical articulations and actions are themselves implicated in structures of domination. Thus, the relationship between women's moral voices and feminist ethics is complicated, in that the ratification of women's norms alone is not necessarily resistant to domination. Chandra Mohanty points out that to have the identity woman/women is not necessarily to be a feminist—to adopt a particular politics. But Mohanty's distinction does not necessarily valorize feminist over "woman/women," in that feminist politics can misrepresent women; to enact feminist politics is not necessarily to represent women.ᵛ As a result of these complexities, there has been much debate within feminist theory as to whether and how feminism can represent the diverse and complex group of persons articulated by the category "women." Rather than configuring feminism as a movement that represents "women," I argue that feminist movements and ethics represent a political commitment to resist the domination of all women. This commitment is based on knowledge developed through processes of building relationships among women.[1] Moreover, while feminist ethics highlights political commitment, it must recognize its limitations as a "partial vision."[2] Feminism is not coextensive with either representations of "women" or "women's" movements (as clearly indicated by lesbian and womanist movements). Thus, I will develop a model of feminist ethics that draws on the experiential knowledge of women without uncritically accepting women's moral labor as resistant.

The Gendered Division of Moral Labor

Charlotte Perkins Gilman, socialist and feminist writer in the late nineteenth and early twentieth centuries, titled her critique of patriarchal religion *His Religion and Hers: A Study of the Faith of Our Fathers and the Work of Our Mothers*.[3] She argues that while men pursue ideological interests related to their own experience, women work to build and maintain the communities that sustain and reproduce those men and their ideals. Thus, the structure of gender complementarity dividing labor into male and female roles that are supposed to be complementary halves actually produces a hierarchy. While the construction of Gilman's argument in terms of a simple male/female dichotomy is problematic from the perspective of contemporary feminist theory, her central point—that labor can be structured to support the ideological interests of a privileged few—remains salient.

The premise of my argument is that morality, like faith, requires work, and that moral labor can also be divided so that the labor of many persons is in service of norms produced by a privileged few. By moral labor I mean all those undertakings that contribute to the development and maintenance of moral relationships and moral communities. My use of the term "moral" to describe a relationship or community is not to pass a particular value judgment, but to imply that the parties to a relationship or members of a community have normative expectations of themselves, of others, and of the relationship or community itself. These expectations may vary, or be in conflict, but as long as there are such expectations, moral labor will be necessary to the existence of that relationship or community. Thus, all the work that goes into establishing a community and developing an understanding of that community as a moral community, with a set of normative expectations of community members and of the community as a whole, is moral labor. I have chosen to emphasize the labor necessary to morality because much of the work that women do is moral work and, like most women's work, is often devalued. To name women's labor as labor and as moral is to cut to the heart of such denials and trivializations.

Moreover, if we analyze the structure of moral labor, then the issue raised by Gilman comes to the fore: specifically, if morality is constructed through social labor, what are the implications for a society where this labor is not commonly shared? As with divisions in material labor, divisions in moral labor tend to enact and reinforce unequal power relations along lines of social differentiation. In particular, the social differentiation of gender is one of the axes that structure moral labor so as to narrow public discourse and reinforce a complex set of dominations.[4] The normative nature of gender in conjunction with gendered understandings of divided moral labor creates a set of mutually reinforcing exclusions by narrowing the meaning of gender to a division between two (and only two) separate and complementary categories of persons and roles. Moreover, the division of society into two separate and complementary genders is interstructured with divisions along lines of race, class, and sexuality so as to further marginalize persons and groups who might otherwise make claims in the public sphere.

Historically, in relation to the United States public sphere the division of moral labor through gendered complementarity has worked to structure hierarchy and exclusion in two ways—by separating "women" from "men" so as to create complementary moral roles that are also hierarchically ordered, and by excluding from moral personhood those who live and act outside of the prescribed moral roles of either "gender" because of race, class, or sexuality. So, for example, those men historically excluded from manhood on the basis of race or class position can be excluded from the polity without threatening the claim that all "men" are created equal. In this economy, to be within the realm of normatively appropriate activity for females or males is also to perform prescribed moral labor. To act outside that realm is to fail in that moral labor, and hence to lose the moral right to claim appropriate female (or male) identity—womanhood or manhood. Those who live and act within the category "women" are ascribed moral agency as long as it is contained within the structure of complementarity, while those living and acting outside of appropriate "gender" are excluded from moral agency altogether. So, white, middle-class[5] women's activities can be restricted by pinning them to the identity woman—the complementary partner of man—and proscribing activities outside the bounds of that role, while those women not dependent on men, for example, those who work in public or paid employment or who do not accept the necessity of a partner who is their complementary opposite—can be excluded from womanhood and moral agency altogether. This exclusion places these women in a position particularly vulnerable to state intervention and control.[6]

The naturalization of this division of appropriate moral labor into complementary and exclusionary oppositions as a gender difference, which is then normatively protected, also accomplishes the exclusion of the private sphere—as a realm in which materiality, nonrationality, and particular differences could be enacted—from the modern public sphere—as a realm of autonomous and equal individuals. The existence of public individuals is maintained and reproduced by labor that is divided so as to extract material and moral labor from all those persons who are not white, middle-class, and male without according these persons the rights necessary to participate in the public sphere.[7] Thus, for example, not only has white women's labor been directed toward maintaining and reproducing the public lives of white men, but those African-American women providing domestic service in white households (whether historically in slavery or through wage labor) are also directly enlisted in the project of maintaining and reproducing white men's ability to participate in public sphere discourse.[8] An analysis of this structure of moral labor implies that an adequate feminist ethics must challenge gendered complementarity and the moral economy that structures it, including the division between public and private spheres.

Justice and Care:
The Ethics of Gender Complementarity

Given the gendered division of moral labor, it is not surprising that the division between justice and care, a division that articulates gender complementarity, has been a dominant concern in feminist ethics. The language of justice articulates the modern public sphere of reason, rights, and equal opportunity, while the language of care has until recently been taken to articulate private concerns with interpersonal relationships. Carol Gilligan's groundbreaking text, *In A Different Voice: Psychological Theory and Women's Development*, challenges the hierarchy that devalues women's private-sphere concerns by validating those very concerns as part of a fully developed ethical voice that should be heard in public.[9] This challenge might not be ultimately successful, however, because it fails to challenge the complementarity that structures gender hierarchy. Moving the voice of caring from the private sphere into the public sphere might be subversive, but it might also play out the same division in a new way—women are now responsible for caring in both private and public.

Moral reasoning from the traditional justice perspective of the Enlightenment deduces moral decisions by reference to universal norms intended to ensure impartiality. It is oriented toward protection of the rights of individual, autonomous moral agents, and its primary norms are equality and fair treatment. The care perspective highlights the creation of understanding among people in the context of their relationships, rather than justification of their individual rights. It represents a synthetic and inductive mode of reasoning that focuses on the particular relationships in any given moral situation. From the perspective of care the moral self is understood as fundamentally connected to others, while from the justice perspective the self and others are seen as autonomous beings who might or might not choose to connect. The primary norms of the care perspective are nonseparation and nonviolence. Thus, the women in Gilligan's studies place a high value on the maintenance of relationships despite apparent conflicts. In order to promote and maintain relationships, care perspective moral decisions are undertaken so that "no one should be hurt."[10] When faced with conflict, these women are concerned not to claim their rights, but to negotiate mutual responsibilities among the affected parties. Thus, practitioners of the care perspective are more likely to revise a given moral problem so that everyone's concerns can be creatively included, rather than to justify recognizing one party's concerns over another's. These norms are not rigid, however, as concerns of care exist in tension with concerns for personal integrity.[11] In articulating a model of moral development, Gilligan recognizes that to reach maturity women must be able to include themselves in the circle of care, sometimes separating from "false attachments," for the sake of their own well-being and integrity.[12] Nonetheless, in Gilligan's model, concerns regarding attachment and separation are always primary.[13]

Although the care perspective as articulated by Gilligan revalues women's moral labor in creating and maintaining caring relationships, it still has the potential to reinscribe the dominant gendered division of moral labor. In particular, the view of relationships described by Gilligan focuses on networks of individual relationships, without accounting for the implication of these networks in social structural relations of power. Thus, while women might make the most caring choice within particular relationships, from the care perspective alone they do not have a means of articulating the social context that establishes the structure of those relationships. For example, in her study of women who were considering abortions, Gilligan often refers to the ways in which the crisis of the situation in conjunction with moral development led women to recognize the "truth" about their particular relationships—often that the men with whom they were involved mistreated them. Yet the women did not articulate questions regarding the truth of social relationships that form the broader context of this mistreatment.[14] This lack of political awareness can lead women to value the maintenance of the very relationships that inscribe both their own subordination and that of others. For example, Adrienne Rich suggests that for white women to be antiracist is primarily to be disloyal to the civilization of white men.[15] How do the norms of nonseparation and nonviolence support such disloyalty? Is it enough to call implication in the social relations of white racial domination "false attachment"?[16] Furthermore, caring does not articulate communal or collective forms of agency. Although women might reconfigure the particulars of a moral dilemma in order to meet the needs of more individuals, the possibility of participating in social movements to change the structural conditions of a dilemma is not necessarily included in such reconfigurations. While the relationalism of caring is distinct from the individualism of justice, it does not articulate the multiple levels of relationships, including the moral economies, that form the context of women's moral agency.

After the publication of *In a Different Voice*, many of the concerns I have articulated were raised by feminists, often within arguments on behalf of the necessity of some form of justice language in order to be able to articulate power relations. Gilligan responded to these criticisms by considering the relationship between care and justice in *Mapping the Moral Domain*.[17] Gilligan argues that the two perspectives cannot be simply integrated, because each organizes the elements of the moral situation differently. In fact, her research indicates that women and men are generally aware of both perspectives, but they tend to "focus" on only one in order to cut down on the ethical ambiguity entailed in recognizing both at once.[18]

Gilligan goes on to argue that both perspectives are necessary to describe adequately any moral situation, adopting an analogy between the two perspectives and two dimensions of moral thought (hence the mapping metaphor of the title).[19] The mapping metaphor tends to naturalize the two perspectives, however, implying that the perspectives exist prior to articulation and enactment, waiting to be discovered and then mapped.[20] Once the perspectives are naturalized, the ties to the supposedly natural division of gender complementarity can reassert themselves.[21] Indications of a reinscription of gender-divided moral labor are particularly apparent in the claims by Gilligan and some of her colleagues who discuss women's entrance into male-dominated professions, such as medicine and law, as if women will save these professions from their uncaring structures.[22] Once again, women are expected to ameliorate the corrosive effects of capitalist structures.

Just as much as gender complementarity, the naturalization of care and justice as two distinct, but necessary, dimensions of moral reasoning can elide diverse moral voices. Since the publication of *In A Different Voice*, there has been significant research to support the conclusion that the moral perspectives of women and men vary with both race and class. Anthropologist Carol Stack has argued that the norms of both

African-American women and men in her studies of family migration interweave caring and justice concerns. Rather than establishing care and justice as alternative dimensions of morality, this interweaving suggests the possibility of an alternative perspective that does not maintain the dominant understandings of either.[23] Similar evidence is available in *Mapping the Moral Domain*. One of Gilligan's colleagues, Janie Victoria Ward, interviewed urban youths of various races with regard to their understandings of violence.[24] Several of the youths expressed both justice and care concerns, but rather than simply integrating the two perspectives, they took them apart, placing elements of each in an alternative perspective that could be read as a politicized car-ing, an awareness of connection and separation that did not lose sight of power relations.[25] This interwoven perspective is not a simple integra-tion (and Ward does not subject it to the focus critique), but a reorgani-zation of the moral context itself, one that challenges the coherence of both justice and care.

In arguing that both perspectives are important dimensions of the moral domain, Gilligan misses the radical implications of her analysis by implying that the ethical ambiguities of these two different modes of organizing moral perception underlie a single map of the moral domain. Rather than arguing for the necessity of both perspectives, I will argue that an adequate feminist ethics needs to break up the coherence of both the justice and care perspectives, a coherence based on the division of gender complementarity and the hierarchies and exclusions that this di-vision entails. A move to break up binary opposition and its suppos-edly coherent parts will continue to take women's moral experiences of relationality seriously, but will open the "moral domain" to diversity and complexity that cannot be articulated by a two-dimensional map.

H. Richard Niebuhr's Responsible Self

H. Richard Niebuhr uses "responsibility" to break open a moral field delineated by the opposition between deontology and teleology. I will argue that it can be used in a similar fashion to open the field delineated by the opposition between justice and care. In one sense, this effort con-tinues the articulation of Gilligan's project. While she labels the moral perspective "care," she recognizes that "responsibility" is an aspect of care, in the same way that "rights" are an aspect of justice.[26] Using Niebuhr's work, I will, however, attempt to articulate a version of re-sponsibility that does not reinscribe gendered complementarity or the gendered division of moral labor.

H. Richard Niebuhr raised the possibility that responsibility could become a major symbol for moral agency. Contrasting his image of responsibility as "man-the-answerer, man engaged in dialogue, man acting in response to action upon him," to the teleological symbol, "man-the-maker," and the deontological symbol, "man-the-citizen," Niebuhr emphasized the specifically relational aspects of morality.[27] Value is determined "in the experience of actual and potential interrelationships."[28] As a fundamentally relational being, the moral agent responds to actions upon "him" by first interpreting these actions, then considering the effect of "his" actions within structures of accountability and accepting the consequences of action. In particular, the responsible agent acts within continuing communities, social solidarities that form the context of both existence and action. Niebuhr uses the focus on material realities and social relations to critique moral perfectionism and the search for personal purity. Niebuhr argues that the search for the perfect or pure ethical act is likely to lead one to deny the actual parameters of ethical choice. Thus, Niebuhr's ethic implies a complex epistemology that includes experiential knowledge created in relationships and communities, reasoned interpretation, and social analysis. Although it maintains a place for reason, response in relationships is at the center of the ethic. While Niebuhr's androcentric formulation is obviously problematic from a feminist perspective, his emphasis on relationality resonates with many feminist ethics.[29]

Particularly useful for feminist ethics is a version of Niebuhr's paradigmatic ethical question, "In light of what is happening (as determined by social analysis) who is responsible to whom for what?"[30] This paradigmatic question emphasizes relational positioning as crucial to determinations of appropriate agency. The question is particularly useful in interrogating divisions of moral labor. By asking, in light of the social situation, "Who is responsible to whom for what moral labor?" it is possible to illuminate divisions of moral labor and to question whether these divisions contribute to domination. In addition, this question allows for differences in responsibility depending on one's position within various sets of social relations and in different historical moments. Thus, responsibilities can change as historical situations and social relations change. Responsibility, therefore, establishes the ethical import of historical context, present situation, and future hopes.[31]

Despite its correlation with many feminist ethics, there are also aspects of Niebuhrian responsibility that must be criticized from a feminist perspective. In particular, the direct reference to relationships is undercut in Niebuhrian responsibility when responsible relations are secured by radical monotheism.[32] Radical monotheism maintains certain androcentric aspects of traditional, patriarchal conceptions of God and, thus, is insufficient to claims for resisting the domination of women. Moreover, I will argue that the insurance that radical monotheism is intended to provide is unnecessary and misplaces the site of radical critique.

Niebuhr's radical monotheism establishes God as the One center of value that guarantees appropriate agency in the world of many competing values. This hierarchical relationship between the central and singular One and the multiple "other(s)" mirrors the structure of gender complementarity, however. Rebecca Chopp has argued that monotheistic ordering tends to recognize at most two subject positions—the inside or central position of "order" and the outside or marginalized position of "disorder."[33] As with the binary opposition of gender, this binary opposition of order—between the "One" and the "other(s)"—is also hierarchical and subjugating. Disorder (often signified by "woman") becomes the "difference" upon which order depends for its dominance. As with gender, too, this opposition excludes true diversity as "difference" becomes a collective singular that only reflects the One to which it is opposed.

This hierarchical ordering is not necessary to ground responsible ethics, however. The appeal of radical monotheism is that it ensures the value of each person through a relationship to God, the center of value. Because God remains outside the structure of any particular human relationship(s), [h]e can ensure a person's value no matter how that person is treated by those around her. Yet, the placement of God, as the center of value, outside the structure of relationships fails to recognize the ways in which God is embodied through human community. For any person to come to know a God who values her, this God must be embodied through a community that enacts God's commitments through community formation—in story, ritual, and social practices. If God is in this way dependent on human relationships, then the critique of domination is enabled through the possibilities created by multiple relationships, including possible relationships with a community that knows a God who opposes domination.

Radical Relationalism and Moral Labor

Given this analysis, I would like to suggest that in order to build an adequate feminist ethics starting from Niebuhr's delineation of responsibility, feminists should adopt a radical relationalism—radical in the sense of Niebuhr's radical monotheism, in that it locates relationships at the center of value; and radical in a political sense, in that it provides for a radical critique of domination.[34] Just as Niebuhr used the language of responsibility to challenge binary opposition, so feminists using the language of responsibility in the context of radical relationalism can effectively break apart the opposition between justice and care and the coherence of each perspective that makes them appear to divide moral labor "naturally". Once this opposition is broken, feminists can (without unnecessarily restricting moral ambiguity) make use of the moral concerns raised by each perspective, but these concerns are transformed by placing them in a radically relational context. Because the language of responsibility is not a moral perspective but a language of interaction, it allows for recognition of partiality and openness to others without having to protect its coherence. As a result, a responsible ethics can be open to moral diversity without undermining the possibility of effectively making moral claims. Reformulating moral claim-making as asking and response can also reconfigure understandings of appropriate moral labor by valuing the moral labor necessary to build communities and by providing a means to question how that labor is divided.

What does it mean to situate moral claim-making completely within the structure of relationships? Radical relationalism confirms many women's experience of morality in which relationships, rather than principles, provide the impetus for moral action. The question, "Why should I be moral?" is answered "Because we are in relationships; because we have to live together." Simply validating women's experiences of relational ethics is not sufficient to resist domination, however. A feminist relational ethic must provide a basis for critique of domination, and in order to do so, it must recognize multiple levels of relationship. Feminist, womanist, and *mujerista* scholars have identified at least three levels of relationality.[35] Relationality as understood by the women in Gilligan's study is grounded in particular relationships between individuals. Womanist scholar Katie Cannon, however, stresses the connections between the moral agent and moral communities, between subjective experiences and political realities. Thus, personal responsibility is interstructured with responsibility to a community and to inclusive struggles for human dignity and integrity.[36] Ada María Isasi-Díaz also confirms that *mujerista* agency occurs *"en la lucha,"* in the fundamental context of communal struggle.[37] Other feminists, such as Catherine Keller, have emphasized the fundamental relatedness of all things.[38] All three of these levels of relationality are necessary for an adequate understanding of responsibility.

These various and complex (because interrelated) meanings of relationality indicate the possible sites for critique of any given relationship or relational structure. For example, individual relationships can be questioned or criticized from the perspective of communities of struggle that articulate how personal relationships are implicated in social structural relations. The strength of the feminist slogan, "the personal is political," comes from the recognition that purportedly personal relationships such as familial bonds are implicated in social structural gender relations. Similarly, friendships among women across lines of race, class, or sexual identity are implicated in social structures. For this reason writers like Mary Hunt and María Lugones and Elizabeth Spelman have emphasized the importance of friendship as a catalyst of feminist political resistance to dominations among women. Mary Hunt argues that friendship "takes the power away from an external authority and relies on committed bonds to prevail."[39] Lugones and Spelman argue for friendship as the principal motivation for political work such as antiracism.[40] Yet, women are also implicated in relationships with persons whom they may not befriend or even know personally. For example, while a commitment to cross-racial alliances may be sparked by particular friendships across racial lines, this commitment also includes a recognition of how any woman's actions are intertwined with those of women she may not ever know. These "political" relationships generate moral claims just as do the sets of "personal" relationships named as morally generative by the women in Gilligan's studies.

An understanding of responsibility as embedded in multiple layers of relational networks and social structures distinguishes this feminist ethic from the notion of responsibility currently used as a right-wing buzz word. Responsibility is used in discussions of "welfare reform" to imply that "welfare recipients" need to take responsibility for their own lives and "work" rather than depending on the government. "Reform," then, actually refers to punitive programs and welfare cuts. These arguments are accomplished by narrowing the field of responsibility to focus only on individuals. The moral labor generated by such an ethic is once again the production of individuals who fit into a capitalist economy and liberal (in its most conservative sense) polity. This public moral economy erases the value of the labor necessary to produce and maintain communities, which, as Carol Stack has documented, is often the labor performed by urban poor women who sometimes receive welfare payments from the state.[41] In response to such arguments, the broader understanding of responsibility can be employed to interrogate the moral economy and social structural conditions within which responsibility is enacted.

Because moving back and forth across different levels of relationships provides various sites for critique, an ethic focused on relationality can make use of those concerns traditionally associated with the justice perspective. It locates these concerns differently, however, taking apart the justice perspective as the framework of good relationships and placing the pieces within the context of those relationships it supposedly framed. With this shift, the subject of concern and action is no longer the autonomous individual of liberal justice, but is instead persons and communities located in diverse and complex structures of relationship.

The source of knowledge about domination and resistance is no longer universal principles. Rather, such knowledge is constructed through communal activity. Finally, taking on appropriate moral labor does not make it the duty of the individual alone to act in response to moral problems, but requires the on-going and communal work of *creating* relationships and social systems.[42]

Responsibility, then, is a social process of asking for and undertaking moral labor in response to claims made within the structure of relationships. The central question of responsibility, articulated as "Who is responsible to whom for what?" considers what labor is necessary to create moral relationships and communities and how responsibility for this labor is to be shared. Moral claim-making can then be understood as a request to take on moral labor within the structure of particular relationships. The responsible self, as a self that is both individual and relational, cannot be separated from her material and communal needs.

Responsibility implies the possibility of negotiation between aspects of individual and communal agency. If responsibility is understood as asking each other to take on moral labor, then a space for negotiation of responsibility is opened that can take into account "each woman's knowledge of herself and her situation."[43] The multiple dominations faced by women, and the multiple mechanisms by means of which these dominations are effected, imply that no single practice will be either adequate or correct. Response can take a number of forms, and it is here that the process of negotiation enters in. When responding to others' request that we participate with them in processes of change, we bring to that interaction our own knowledge of what we value in ourselves and how we understand resistance and transformation. To recognize the multiplicity, partiality and even possible contradictions of these various strategies does not vitiate the need to challenge each other to consider the impact and effectiveness of our choices. Problems arise when these challenges are enacted as presumptions for correctness, rather than as a part of social processes for change that require multiple responses.[44]

Philosopher Nancy Fraser has provided a good example of this relational process in her analysis of women's movements in resistance to "domestic violence." Fraser argues that feminists have effectively used moral discourse to change interpretations of "domestic violence," from a private matter to one of public concern: a crime, worthy of public action.[45] The epistemological change in the United States from an acceptance of domestic violence to the knowledge that violence against women is wrong was not a sudden apprehension of a universal principle, but was built through the development of new types of relationships among women. Women began to talk to each other about their experiences, and through this relating they were able to create the knowledge that they were not alone in their situation, that violence against women was a social phenomenon, not the result of an individual deserving to be beaten.[46] By treating each other as people of value, women were also able to build the knowledge that they did not deserve abusive treatment. These women were then, through collective action, able to demand that others, including the society that had sanctioned their abuse, treat them as persons of value. It was the process of women's building relationships with each other that allowed them to relativize and critique the structure of relationships that were abusive to them. Through this process women have also been empowered to develop new organizations and structures that enable them to act on this truth and resist violence. Creation of alternative practices, institutions, and values is another means for feminists to enact power without the requirement of universal claims.

Moral Diversity and Responsible Ethics

The movement away from universal claims implied in the focus on particular relationships is not necessarily a move toward relativism, at least not in the strong sense usually implied when relativism is opposed to universalism.[47] While moral claims may be "relative" to particular relationships and situations, this relativism is not the same as a loss in the ability to make moral claims or an acceptance of any type of claim as moral. Rather, moral claims are made in a complex field of relationships, a field not defined by any single perspective. Competing claims cannot be simply adjudicated but must be worked out through interaction. This does open the field of moral action to ambiguities that the respondents in Gilligan's studies attempt to control through the use of the focus phenomenon. Niebuhr's critique of moral perfectionism would suggest, however, that ambiguity may be part and parcel of moral interaction, and attempts to control ambiguity may lead the moral agent away from the responsible act. Perhaps most importantly, as Gilligan argues, attempts to control ambiguity can lead to a fundamental denial of diverse moral voices. A focus on multiple types of moral labor can recognize and respect the diversity and complexity of moral voices, while the language of responsibility can help to articulate a response that is self-critical with regard to structures of moral labor.[48]

Given this focus on claims that are "relative" to one another, a relation-specific understanding of responsibility allows for different responsibilities depending on social location and historical context, thus opening the moral field to multiplicity, while the structure of specific relations militates against simple relativism. Different responsibilities are articulated by considering the moral labor necessary to address effectively the problem of creating transformed relationships. The moral labor necessary to build heterogeneous communities cannot be accomplished without recognizing power relations developed through histories of domination. A focus on building better relationships does not necessarily imply that now "we all" have to take the same actions for the good of the whole. The very structure of responsibility itself may differ depending on the historical development of moral communities. Chandra Mohanty has argued that while persons are implicated in shared histories across social divisions, they do not necessarily stand in the same position with respect to those histories.[49] Rather histories, specifically those histories structured by dominations, create "asymmetrical and incommensurate social spheres."[50] Thus, Mohanty argues that politics in relation to history is not a simple matter of "identity" but is rather a matter of questioning location as one "inherits it," in relation to "self-conscious, strategic location" in the present.

If norms are produced within historically specific communities, then these communities will also produce specific traditions and structures of responsibility. For example, Marcia Riggs has indicated how the language of responsibility is useful in elucidating the ethics used by the Black women's club movement of the late nineteenth and early twentieth centuries.[51] Riggs brings "the understanding of responsibility in traditional religious ethics as represented by H. Richard Niebuhr's ethic of responsibility . . . into critical engagement with the ethical insights of the black female reformers." Riggs "examine[s] how the black female reformers' socioreligious ethical understanding of responsibility . . . extends the meaning of responsibility in Niebuhr's ethic and serves as the basis of a mediating ethic for black liberation."[52] Riggs uses the language of responsibility in the specific tradition of liberationist African-American Christianity in order to address the various responsibilities of a diverse black community, which is itself stratified by social structural differentiations, including class and gender.

Within the ethic articulated by Riggs, God's liberating justice, "the justice of God and justice for Blacks as a command of God," forms the center of value.[53] This center of value allows for mediation between "a religious ethical and social contextual meaning for Black liberation," between the teleology of racial uplift and self-determination for the black community and the deontology of racial obligation and duty to the community, and between black religious liberation and womanist thought.[54] Thus, the language of responsibility takes on a distinct meaning within the context of black liberation. This meaning extends the understanding of God from Niebuhr's white androcentric formulation to that of a liberating God; it establishes social contextual understandings and emphasizes communal rather than individual relationships; and it implies a specific teleology and deontology of social responsibility toward a diverse black community. Thus, while the language of responsibility may be useful to various social movements, the specifics of that responsibility will depend on particular movements and traditions.

Moral Language/Moral Labor

The model of responsibility does not determine who is responsible for what, who has what type of relationships with whom, etc. Rather, it provides a language for actively questioning and contesting these features of moral life. It denaturalizes these questions, no longer accepting the supposedly natural division of moral labor that the categories of "gender" are meant to supply, and thus effectively challenging the moral perspectives based on this division. In sum, the care perspective emphasizes relationships but does not provide a means of articulating mechanisms of domination; nor does it articulate the historical or social context of particular relationships, contexts that create certain connections and separations, while eliding and even violently denying others. The import of the justice perspective is that it ensures a point of reference outside relationships from which to say that relations of domination are wrong. Yet the costs of such insurance are high, leading to a fundamental denial of diversity. From the point of view of responsible agency, it is the very diversity of relationships and the creativity of persons as they build different relationships that make possible the type of critique justice is meant to ensure.

In denaturalizing the gendered division of moral labor, responsibility also abandons the assumption that the moral agent knows "his" duty by reasoning alone to a coherent moral universe, without asking anyone. Responsibility also challenges the assumption that the main questions of moral life are to be decided by objective parties who stand in equal (non)relation to the issues at hand. Responsibility is enacted among interested parties who make claims within the structure of their relationships. In considering questions of responsibility the moral agent can ask herself and others: What work are you doing? What is its place in moral economies? How did you come to understand this work as moral? Whose norms are you responding to? Whom did you ask about it? Whom does it benefit or harm? What value are you creating? These questions are part of social processes that create moral knowledge by articulating rather than naturalizing "the politics of ethics."[55] In this sense ethics works to enable rather than foreclose political struggle. The priority of ethics shifts from resolution of conflict to creation of new possibilities for communities and relationships. Yet, ethical language is always limited by social conditions. Thus, constructing feminist ethics is only one part of a complex set of resistances addressing the nexus of discourse, political practice, and social conditions.

Notes

I would like to thank Dr. Gardner for his help and support during the time that I was at Emory. He was, to me, always a gentle-man. The seed for this essay was a paper that I initially wrote for Dr. Gardner's "Ethical Methods" class, and that eventually formed the basis for my dissertation topic.

[1] Chandra Talpade Mohanty, "Cartographies of Struggles: Third World Women and the Politics of Feminism," Introduction to *Third World Women and the Politics of Feminism* (Bloomington: Indiana University Press, 1991), 33.

[2] Thus, this ethico-political commitment to resist the domination of women is not a universal justice claim simply derived from a principled moral universe. It is, however, indebted to the *tradition* of enlightenment-based emancipatory politics, even as it transforms this tradition. For more on the relationship between enlightenment traditions and feminist ethics, see, Janet R. Jakobsen "Deconstructing the Paradox of Modernity: Feminism, Enlight-enment, and Cross-Cultural Moral Interactions." *Journal of Religious Ethics* 23/2 (Fall 1995): 333-363.

[3] Angelika Bammer, *Partial Visions: Feminism and Utopianism in the 1970s* (New York: Routledge, 1991).

[4] Charlotte Perkins Gilman, *His Religion and Hers: A Study of the Faith of Our Fathers and the Work of Our Mothers* (New York: The Century Company, 1923; reprint Westport, Ct.: Hyperion Press, Inc., 1976).

[5] Nancy Fraser argues, "[Critical theory of actually existing democracy] should render visible the ways in which social inequality taints delibera-tion within publics in late capitalist society." Nancy Fraser, "Rethinking the Public Sphere: A Contribution to the Critique of Actually Existing Democracy," *Social Text* 25/6 (1990), 77. The gendered division of moral labor is one of these mechanisms.

[6] I use the term "middle-class" broadly to represent the dominant ideal class position in United States society. The authors of *Habits of the Heart* trace the development in the United States of the term "middle-class." In the nineteenth century the term "middle-class" developed as the "concept of an all-encompassing process of escalation that will eventually include everyone [which] gives us our central, and largely unchallenged, image of American society." Robert N. Bellah, et. al., *Habits of the Heart: Individualism and Commitment in American Life* (Berkeley, Calif.: University of California Press, 1985), 119.

[7] These divisions can also be reversed in the service of domination, creat-ing a number of contradictions. For example, African-American women have

often been denied their position as women, since their labor and activities have not necessarily been aligned with the roles prescribed by dominant gender. Such narrow and exclusionary definitions of gender have led to important challenges to the category itself, such as Sojourner Truth's question "Ar'n't I a Woman?" Yet African-American women have also faced exclusions enacted by pinning them to the identity of women, as occurred when the Fifteenth Amendment to the Constitution barred denial of the right to vote on account of "race, color, or previous condition of servitude," but left African-American women disfranchised on account of gender.

[8]Gwendolyn Mink indicates the economic mechanisms that restricted women's access to the public sphere, including lack of access to, or full control over, property and earnings and denial of the right to contract. See Gwendolyn Mink, "The Lady and the Tramp: Gender, Race, and the Origins of the American Welfare State," in *Women, the State, and Welfare*, ed. Linda Gordon (Madison: The University of Wisconsin Press, 1990), 94.

[9]Gemma Tang Nain, "Black Women, Sexism and Racism: Black or Anti-racist Feminism?" *Feminist Review* 37 (Spring 1991): 3.

[10]Carol Gilligan, *In A Different Voice: Psychological Theory and Wom-en's Development* (Cambridge, Mass.: Harvard University Press, 1982).

[11]Ibid., 174.

[12]Ibid., 157.

[13]On moral integrity see Gilligan, *In A Different Voice*, 164. On false attachments see Gilligan, "Moral Orientation and Moral Development," 32.

[14]The final chapter of *In a Different Voice*, "Visions of Maturity," begins with the statement, "Attachment and separation anchor the cycle of human life, describing the biology of human reproduction and the psychology of human development" (151). Gilligan has carried the emphasis on connection throughout her work. In *Making the Connections*, the book on the study of the Emma Willard School for Girls, she describes how girls become disconnected from their experiential knowledge during adolescence as they are inducted into western cannons of objectivity, and the liberating effects for those girls who resist and maintain or rediscover a connection to experiential knowledge. Carol Gilligan, et. al., ed., *Making the Connections: The Relational Worlds of Adolescent Girls at Emma Willard School* (Troy, N.Y.: Emma Willard School, 1989).

[15]Gilligan also quotes one of the women in the abortion studies as stating, "somewhere in my life I think I got the impression that my needs are really secondary to other people's." Gilligan, *In A Different Voice*, 92-3. While the developmental stages that Gilligan delineates valorize women's caring for self as well as others over women's "conventional" devaluing of the self, the care perspective and Gilligan's stage theory do not provide any means of questioning how self-sacrifice became the conventional women's morality or why women should go through a stage of devaluing the self.

[16]Adrienne Rich, "Disloyal to Civilization: Feminism, Racism, Gynephobia," in *On Lies Secrets and Silence: Selected Prose, 1966-1978* (New York: W. W. Norton & Co., 1979), 275-310.

[17]It is possible to read Gilligan as if political perspectives are implicit in the ethics of care. Gilligan has something like this in mind in her reading of Ruth First's life as depicted in the movie "A World Apart." In responding to critics who read First's life as that of an "uncaring" mother because her political commitments to justice in South Africa lead to her arrest, taking her away from her children, Gilligan argues that in order to be a caring mother, First would have to "care" about social conditions in South Africa. Gilligan does not develop these political implications in her theoretical texts, however. See Carol Gilligan, review of "A World Apart," in *Tikkun* 4, no. 1 (Jan-Feb. 1989): 78.

[18]Carol Gilligan, "Remapping the Moral Domain: New Images of Self in Relationship," in *Mapping the Moral Domain: A Contribution of Women's Thinking to Psychological Theory and Education*, ed. Carol Gilligan, Janie Victoria Ward, and Jill McLean Taylor with Betty Bardige, (Cambridge, Mass.: Harvard University Press, 1988), 3-20.

[19]For more on the focus phenomenon, see also Gilligan, "Moral Orientation and Moral Development," in Kittay and Meyers, *Women and Moral Theory*, 22.

[20]Gilligan's argument against integration of the two perspectives need not imply a simple acceptance of both, however. Cheshire Calhoun, for example, has criticized simple integration of the two perspectives in so far as integration obscures the particularities of oppression, just as Gilligan's claim about the universality of experiences of oppression and abandonment does. Cheshire Calhoun, "Justice, Care, Gender Bias," *The Journal of Philosophy* LXXXV, no. 9 (September 1988): 451-63.

[21]This naturalization is further based on the problematic claims about the universality of early childhood experiences of abandonment and oppression. Gilligan, *Mapping The Moral Domain*, 4-5. Even if we are all subject to oppression and abandonment, are we subject to these experiences equally and in the same way? Does a girl who suffers racial oppression but is protected by her family have the same experience as a girl who experiences racial privilege, but is abused within her family?

[22]Gilligan initially described the two perspectives as complementary opposites, which "both sexes" needed to integrate in order to reach moral maturity:

> Development for both sexes would therefore seem to entail an integration of rights and responsibilities through the discovery of the complementarity of these disparate views.

Gilligan, *In A Different Voice*, 100.

[23]At the end of "Moral Orientation and Moral Development," for example, Gilligan states, "the promise in joining women and moral theory lies in the fact that human survival, in the late twentieth century, may depend less on formal agreement than on human connection" (32). See also Carol Gilligan and Susan Pollack, "The Vulnerable and Invulnerable

Physician," in *Mapping the Moral Domain*, where the authors state, "If women currently articulate a perspective which links achievement with attachment, women physicians may help to heal the breach in medicine between patient cure and scientific success" (262).

[24]Carol B. Stack, "Different Voices, Different Visions: Gender, Culture, and Moral Reasoning," in *Uncertain Terms: Negotiating Gender in American Culture*, ed. Faye Ginsburg and Anna Lowenhaupt Tsing (Boston: Beacon Press, 1990), 19-27.

[25]Janie Victoria Ward, "Urban Adolescents' Conceptions of Violence," in *Mapping the Moral Domain*, 175-200.

[26]Ibid., 194-5.

[27]In the opening chapter of *In A Different Voice*, Gilligan states clearly that one of the main characteristics that distinguishes the "care perspective" from the "justice perspective" is a focus on responsibility rather than rights:

> When one begins with the study of women and derives developmental constructs from their lives, the outline of a moral conception different from that described by Freud, Piaget, or Kohlberg begins to emerge and inform a different description of development. In this conception, the moral problem arises from conflicting responsibilities rather than from competing rights and requires for its resolution a mode of thinking that is contextual and narrative rather than formal and abstract (19).

In presenting a strict parallel, she focuses on "care" in contrast to "justice," responsibility representing an aspect of care, just as rights are an aspect of justice. My constructive ethic will shift the focus to make responsibility primary to caring.

[28]H. Richard Niebuhr, *The Responsible Self* (New York: Harper and Row, 1964): 55-56. Niebuhr describes teleology and deontology as follows:

> Those who consistently think of man-as-maker subordinate the giving of laws to the work of construction. For them the right is to be defined by reference to the good; rules are utilitarian in character; they are means to ends. All laws must justify themselves by the contribution they make to the attainment of a desired or desirable end. Those, however, who think of man's existence primarily with the aid of the citizen image seek equally to subordinate the good to the right; only right life is good and right life is no future ideal, but always a present demand (55).

[29]Niebuhr, quoted in Marcia Riggs, 178.

[30]For a survey of feminist ethics, many of which emphasize relationality, see Barbara Hilkert Andolsen, Christine Gudorf, and Mary Pellauer, eds., *Women's Consciousness/Women's Conscience* (San Francisco: Harper & Row, 1987). For an indication of the centrality in feminist ethics of questions regarding relationships, see the Introduction, xvi.

[31]Niebuhr, *Responsible Self*, 68.

[32]In contrast, the main focus of deontological ethics is the present situation, often obscuring historical context, while teleology emphasizes the future, often obscuring contemporary questions of how a future goal is to be accomplished.

[33]H. Richard Niebuhr, *Radical Monotheism and Western Culture* (San Francisco: Harper & Row, 1943).

[34]Chopp specifically criticizes Niebuhr as follows:
What I am calling a monotheistic ordering—the securing of and by a primal referent "God" or "Man" by casting woman always as other and under—became, it seems to me, the hidden ordering of patriarchy in Christianity. While I have great respect for radical monotheism like H. Richard Niebuhr's and I understand it to be a claim about God's transcendence, it still seems the case that if the logical-rhetoric-linguistic argument of monotheistic ordering as it has developed in many forms of Christianity is followed, then the "one" and the ones it guarantees tempts self-protection by way of denying and oppressing the many.
Rebecca Chopp, *The Power to Speak: Feminism, Language, God* (New York: Crossroad, 1989), 26-27, n. 43.

[35]This radical relationalism may be theological by including relationships with God, but it is not necessarily so. Thus, the ethical is not necessarily dependent on the theological.

[36]These various meanings of relationality contradict those scholars, such as Sandra Harding who have emphasized "relationality" as the common component in ethics of the oppressed. Harding for example claims a similarity between colonizers and "the rest of us" based on this relational emphasis. Sandra Harding, "The Curious Coincidence of Feminine and African Moralities: Challenges for Feminist Theory," in Kittay and Meyers, *Women and Moral Theory*, 305. The Afro-centric texts to which Harding refers are Vernon Dixon, "World Views and Research Methodology," *African Philosophy: Assumptions and Paradigms for Research on Black Persons*, ed. L. M. King, V. Dixon and W. W. Nobles (Los Angeles: Fanon Center Publication, Charles R. Drew Postgraduate Medical School, 1976) and Gerald G. Jackson, "The African Genesis of the Black Perspective in Helping," in *Black Psychology*, ed. R. L. Jones, 2nd ed. (New York: Harper and Row, 1980), 314-331.

[37]Katie Cannon, *Black Womanist Ethics* (Atlanta: Scholars Press, 1988).

[38]Ada María Isasi-Díaz, *En la Lucha/In the Struggle: Elaborating a Mujerista Theology/A Hispanic Women's Liberation Theology* (Minneapolis: Fortress Press, 1993).

[39]Catherine Keller, "Feminism and the Ethic of Inseparability," in *Women's Consciousness/Women's Conscience*, ed. Barbara Hilkert Andolsen, Christine E. Gudorf and Mary D. Pellauer, 251-263.

[40]Mary Hunt, *Fierce Tenderness* (New York: Crossroad, 1991), 76.

[41]María Lugones and Elizabeth Spelman, "Have we Got a Theory for You! Feminist Theory, Cultural Imperialism and the Demand for 'The

Woman's Voice'" *Women's Studies International Forum* 6, no. 6 (1983): 573-581. Lugones and Spelman make the strong claim that friendship is the only reason for undertaking this work (581). I am hesitant to rule out the importance of other reasons along with friendship, since motivations are often complex and prescribing a single motivation as appropriate seems to deny this complexity.

[42]This reconfiguration of moral concern does not erase the importance of the past. We live with the past in the present, particularly since contemporary moral perspectives develop out of particular histories. Understandings of history articulate how we came to the type of relationships in which we currently find ourselves, and the active work of memory can make important contributions to building relationships in the present and future. A proactive sense of responsibility does, however, shift the field of action from ascribing guilt and obtaining compensation for the past to using our understandings of the past to create better relations in the present and the future. For more on moral labor in relationship to memory and history, see Jakobsen "Deconstructing the Paradox of Modernity."

[43]Marilyn Frye, "History and Responsibility," *Women's Studies International Forum* 8, no. 3 (1985): 216.

[44]This opposition to perfectionism also militates against "political correctness," if correctness means the possibility of adopting a position that successfully overcomes social problems, e.g., which is not racist in any way. I want to distinguish my criticism of a perfectionist "correctness" from the current right-wing campaign against political correctness, which is directed against any attempt to hold each other responsible for resistance to structures of domination. Thus, to hold professors responsible for refraining from blatantly racist comments is seen as the harbinger of enforced correctness rather than as a claim for responsibility on the part of members of a diverse community. For a helpful discussion of the distinction between correctness and mutual responsibility see Frye, "History and Responsibility," 215-217.

[45]Nancy Fraser, "Struggle over Needs: Outline of a Socialist-Feminist Critical Theory of Late Capitalist Political Culture," in *Unruly Practices: Power, Discourse and Gender in Contemporary Social Theory* (Minneapolis: University of Minnesota Press, 1989), 175-181. Enactment of power through discourse is neither uncontested nor unproblematic, however. Despite the power gained by women in articulating a discourse of domestic violence, the now public nature of "domestic violence" also opens the avenue to more state intervention in the lives of many women.

[46]Nelle Morton calls this process of women developing new knowledge and perspectives on reality "hearing into speech." The relational act of women listening to one another allows for new articulations that would not have been possible for individuals to think, much less speak, outside of the interactive process. Nelle Morton, *The Journey Is Home* (Boston: Beacon Press, 1985).

[47]The need for universals is often invoked when legitimation of the feminist cause is required to make claims on persons who act as oppressors and

who stand outside the bounds of feminism. For example, Susan Thistlethwaite makes such a claim in favor of absolutes in relation to a feminist suspicion of post-critical theories. Thistlethwaite argues that the multiplication of moral voices (or regimes of truth), while providing necessary leverage to loosen the hold of a falsely universalized dominant male experience in modernist ethics, can also loosen the claims that women and others make on those same men:

> What concerns me is that as I employ poststructuralism to loosen the absolutist hold on "women's experience" that I have held as a white feminist (that is, as a dominant) I may be opening the door to a denial of the truths of my experience in the movement to end violence against women (as a nondominant). I find that the postcritical theory does not always allow me to declare that violence against women is wrong in all circumstances.

Thistlethwaite, *Sex, Race and God: Christian Feminism in Black and White* (New York: Crossroad, 1989), 14-15. Hasn't the door to a denial of the truths of women's experiences been standing wide open for much longer than feminists have considered poststructuralist claims to relativism, however? In this book Thistlethwaite also delineates a tool, "truth-in-action," which can effectively be employed as the basis of women's claims on their oppressors (Thistlethwaite, 12).

[48]For more on ambiguity and moral agency see Janet R. Jakobsen, "Agency and Alliance in U.S. Public Discourses about Sexuality," *Hypatia*, 10, no. 1 (Winter 1995): 133-154.

[49]Chandra Talpade Mohanty, "Feminist Encounters: Locating the Politics of Experience," *Copyright*, Vol. I (Fall 1987): 30-44. Mohanty argues that there are a number of different histories in relation to imperialism, yet we cannot "afford to forget the co-implication of histories with [a more general] History" (31). By establishing this distinction between histories and History, she questions how one's location in relation to one's history and to the shared History of imperialism or racism affects one's politics. While the concept of History with a capital "H" may appear monolithic and lacking internal contradictions, it is not necessary that a shared history be a monolithic one.

[50]Chandra Talpade Mohanty, "On Race and Voice: Challenges for Liberal Education in the 1990s," *Cultural Critique* (Winter 1989-90): 181.

[51]Marcia Riggs, "Toward a Mediating Ethic for Black Liberation: Ethical Insights of Black Female Reformers of the Nineteenth Century," (Ph.D. diss., Vanderbilt University, 1991).

[52]Ibid., 20-21.

[53]Ibid., 177.

[54]Ibid., 169, 177 and 185.

[55]Margaret Urban Walker developed this term to describe the ability to interrogate how traditional ethical systems such as justice can be employed to serve systems of domination.

When we construct and consider representations of our moral situations we need to ask: what actual community of moral responsibility does this representation of moral thinking purport to represent? Who does it actually represent? What communicative strategies does it support? Who will be in a position (concretely, socially) to deploy these strategies? Who is in a position to transmit and enforce the rules which constrain them? In what forms of activity or endeavor will they have (or fail to have) an application, and who is served by these activities?

Margaret Urban Walker, "Moral Understanding: Alternative 'Epistemology' for a Feminist Ethics," *Hypatia* 4, no. 2 (Summer 1989): 14-28.

Chapter 3

The Gospel As Tragedy:
On Moral Collisions, Tragic Flaws,
and the Possibility of Redemption

Louis A. Ruprecht, Jr.

> There is no true science of religion, any more than there is a science of culture. Scholars are still debating about which cult Greek tragedy should be ascribed to. Were the ancients correct in assigning tragedy to Dionysus, or does it rightfully belong to another god? Undoubtedly this is a genuine problem; but it is also, I think, a secondary one. Far more important, but far less discussed, is the relationship between tragedy and the divine, between the theater in general and religion.
>
> René Girard, *Violence and the Sacred*[1]

It is surely a little jarring, in this cultural and linguistic environment, to speak of "the *tragedy* of the Gospel." It is probably even more jarring to speak of the Gospel as itself a "tragedy."[2] Reinhold Niebuhr, for instance, popularized the notion that the Gospel stands "*beyond* tragedy,"[3] and he was clearly speaking to some widespread assumptions in saying so—ironically so, since what he said seemed otherwise so often to cut *against* the North American grain. He was neither the first nor the last Christian theologian to have thought of the Gospel in these terms. Yet this is precisely the presupposition—that "tragedy" lies in one place, and that the "Gospel" lies somewhere else, somewhere "beyond" it—that I wish to call into question. This is not an assumption that can be borne out by the history of the early church or the history of its devotional literature. By beginning biblically, I will try to make the "Gospel," a word that *seems* so close to us (too close, in my judgment), a bit more foreign and strange. It is often worthwhile to stop and pause over such a word, a word that is used far too unreflectively, in order to interrogate it for its fuller meaning "Gospel" is one such word. "Tragedy" is another. What I want to do is to suggest a deep connection between the two words, and then to explore briefly what that intriguing relationship might mean.[4]

What relates these words, initially, is the fact that they are both— *tragôidia* and *euangelion*—Greek words. More than this, they are both Greek *ideas*. They are, in fact, *related* Greek ideas. In this essay, I would like to explore that connection, sketching out along the way some of the implications of this connection for talking about responsibility in Christian, and in other, contexts.

In modern English, we tend to think of "tragedy" as a word connoting disaster, pure and simple.[5] Our newspapers and television news reporting alike are full of the word. In a word (if you will pardon the pun), 'tragedy' connotes a bad ending, whereas 'comedy' connotes a happier one. We have taken to distinguishing the Shakespearean canon between those plays that end in multiple deaths (they are the tragedies) and those that end in multiple marriages (they are the comedies).[6] In this sense, Byron's comments are whimsically representative and appropriate:

> All tragedies are finished by a death,
>   All comedies are ended by a marriage;
> The future states of both are left to faith,
>   For authors fear description might disparage
> The worlds to come of both, or fall beneath,
>   And then both worlds would punish their miscarriage;
> So leaving each their priest and prayer-book ready,
>   They say no more of Death or of the Lady.[7]

But Byron knew that he was joking; we, by contrast, no longer get the joke. This simple assumption—which, by the way, makes nonsense of the Shakespearean canon just as surely as it does the Greek[8]—helps to explain the Anglophone quandary. If tragedies end in disaster and comedies end happily ever after, then clearly the Gospels *cannot be* tragedies. They are excluded from this genre almost by definition.[9] After all, the Gospel is supposed to embody the paradigmatic happy ending (I wonder whether it really is quite that, just as I wonder why the excruciation of the Passion would have been "necessary" if that were the case).[10]

What if we are wrong about this? What if tragedies are "tragic" because of something in the nature of their presentation? And what if it has little, finally, to do with how the plays end? The word 'tragedy' is, as I say, a Greek word. It derives from the Greek *tragôidia*, a word which seems to have meant something like "goat-song."[11] There are debates about the meaning of this, but little scholarly agreement, just as there is little clarity about how the dramatic festivals in Athens originated sometime in the early part of the sixth century BCE.[12] What *is* clear is that the "tragedies" were a part of an elaborate three-day religious festival dedicated to the god of theater and of wine, Dionysus.[13]

And here we happen upon a second problem. After the Alexandrian conquests in the fourth century BCE,[14] the entire eastern Mediterranean was "speaking Greek"—both as a second language, but more importantly as a second, and a potentially unifying, set of cultural codes and symbols. It was a pagan culture, polytheistic to a fault, and this raised particular problems in the Palestinian crescent, soon to be the Roman province of "Palestine." In olden times, *scriptural* times, the line on pagan literature and culture had been clearer: burn it down.[15] And what you cannot burn, be sure not to touch.[16] Now, I am not suggesting that this scriptural mandate was ever widely practiced. There is *no* archaeological evidence for the massive destructions described in the book of Joshua. What I am suggesting is that a scripturally committed Jew of the fourth century BCE (let's say) would, in all likelihood, have paid lip-service to this widely understood religious obligation, the obligation to abhor pagan culture absolutely. The Canaanites may have been a temptation, but they, and their culture, were consistently viewed as a *negative* temptation, a temptation to be avoided wherever possible (it was *not* possible, of course, in diaspora). So, too, for the peoples and the cultures of Moab, Philistia, Ammon, to a lesser degree Egypt, and especially Amalek.

With the coming of the Greeks (and then the Romans), that all changes. With really astonishing suddenness, if we reflect theologically upon the matter, the Jewish community becomes emphatically pluralistic. Judaism itself, in the Dispersion, becomes a multinational and multicultural phenomenon. Now, the Jewish community not only reads Greek, and participates quite deliberately in that broader Alexandrian umbrella-culture, but it even sees its way clear to translate the holy scriptures into Greek—in, of all places, Alexander's city of Alexandria, on the coast of north Africa. And it is out of this remarkably fertile crucible—*the crucible of Hellenistic Judaism*—that the traditions of Rabbinic Judaism and Christianity were born.

How is it that a committed monotheist, with a clear historical sense of the biblical mandate *against* cultural assimilation, could so suddenly fall under the sway of another culture, Greek culture, in this way?[17] Be it noted: not viewed in the *old* way, as "temptation," as "falling away"—in a word, as "sin"—but rather viewed in a *new* way, as syncretism and mutual spiritual enlightenment. What ultimate relation can there be between monotheism and polytheism? Between Athens and Jerusalem? How can a committed Jew or Christian read an emphatically pagan literature with such evident (mono)*theological* profit?

Clearly, a great many religious persons in a variety of historical periods—and in all *three* of the monotheistic scriptural religions—have done so, have seen their way clear to live in this unusual kind of double-mindedness. *How* they have done so is another matter. In a sense, the classicists of the nineteenth century in Germany and in England had an answer to that question (and the departments of "classical studies" in western universities are testimony, still, to the longevity of that answer's intellectual appeal). They believed that classical Athenian society was congenial to *their kind* of (moral, textual) Protestantism.[18] They felt that classical Greece was a remarkable *moral* moment, and that Greece's greatest legacy was to be found in its moral-philosophical literature. That is why they gravitated to Plato and Aristotle and even more so to Socrates, who was responsible for putting moral issues on the front burner[19] ("philosophy" in the generation prior to Socrates had been involved in very different sorts of speculation, indeed).

It was Hegel, and then even more emphatically Nietzsche,[20] who called that assumption into question. I think that they were right to do so. For the remarkable cultural complex that we call "Greek antiquity" was arguably far *more* remarkable for its tragic and erotic literature than for its moral philosophy.[21] The tragedies, and the lyric poetry, are more probing in their own ways even than Plato (save in the *Symposium* and the *Phaedrus*, where he turns his attention to precisely these genres). The tragic and erotic vision of the Greeks in the so-called Classical Age laid the intellectual foundation upon which their moral thinking was built.[22] They are the "Greece"—an emphatically *older* Greece, as Nietzsche was quick to remind us[23]—to which we might still profit-ably return.

The Greek Vision of Tragedy

Yet all of this begs the question, the Socratic question: "What is it?" What is tragic, or erotic, poetry? What is the connection between the two? There are no simple answers to these questions. Yet tragedy and the erotic seem to be intimately linked in Greek thought—for a reason. Both speak to the essential question of what it means to be a human being—finite, limited, locked in a very peculiar kind of longing, and all of this in a comparatively limit-less universe. They speak of the indivisibility of pleasure and pain. They speak of the hard necessity of loss, especially the loss of those things we hold most dear. *Risk* is part and parcel of the tragic and erotic life—the risk of harm and the risk of emotional distortion implicit in such inevitable limitations. Since this is so, risk is an essential ingredient in every responsive human life. As Martha Nussbaum frames the matter, in a defense of Aristotle's moral point of view:

> There is a beauty in the willingness to love someone in the face of love's instability and worldliness that is absent from a completely trustworthy love. There is a certain valuable quality in social virtue that is lost when social virtue is removed from the domain of uncontrolled happenings. And in general each salient Aristotelian virtue seems inseparable from a risk of harm.[24]

In saying this, and in saying it this way, Nussbaum is suggesting that these tragic, or lyric, or Platonic, or Aristotelian texts are as "unmodern" as they could possibly be.

An excellent source for beginning to reflect about what "tragedy" entailed among the Greeks is Aristotle,[25] from whom we have a fairly full discussion of this dramatic genre, the *Poetics*.[26] That discussion breaks off in midstream, presumably just before the discussion of "comedy" began.[27] Now, Aristotle's is a rich and influential discussion, especially influential after its rediscovery in the Italian Renaissance and its use as a source (in what now appears to be ludicrously rigid fashion) for the canons of French neoclassicism.[28] Each one of us, presumably, has heard many of the essential Aristotelian claims, even if we were not immediately aware that they come from Aristotle. We all know that tragedy involves the feelings of "pity and fear."[29] We all know that it involves us in the "catharsis" of these same emotions.[30] We have all heard of the "tragic flaw."[31]

It is this last term that has been most often (and most egregiously) mistranslated and misconstrued. The Greek word is *hamartia,* and the verb is *hamartanein.* In the New Testament this word is consistently translated as "sin." It is this word, or rather this essential tragic concept, that I would like to interrogate at some greater length.

Aristotle mentions the *hamartia* (I hesitate to call it the "tragic flaw" for reasons that will become obvious) in the thirteenth chapter of the *Poetics*.[32] He does so in connection with his further discussion of the tragic emotions—pity and fear—and the manner in which they are developed in either simple or complex plots. It is a rather interesting discussion, if for no other reason than because Aristotle's style of thinking and organizing are so clear there. In a dramatic version of the doctrine of the mean,[33] Aristotle lays out the dramatic extremes that he feels the good poet (who is primarily good at plot-construction) will avoid.

First, we do not wish to see a virtuous person fall from good fortune to ill fortune, because there is nothing particularly fearful or pitiable in that. The only emotions that result from witnessing such a reversal are visceral horror before a morally repugnant event.

Conversely, we do not wish to see the wicked person rise from ill fortune to good fortune. Such a dramatic reversal is, Aristotle insists, "the most untragic [*atragôitaton*] form of all," presumably because the presentation of virtue's irrelevancy in the universe lacks precisely the moral assumptions and values the theater is supposed to provide. Such plots inspire neither pity nor fear nor even the basic feelings of human sympathy [*philanthrôpon*], he says.[34]

Thirdly, we do not wish to see the really wicked person fall from good fortune to ill fortune. Such dramatic reversals may inspire common human sympathy [*philanthrôpon*], but never pity or fear. In explaining why, Aristotle tells us explicitly what he thinks pity and fear entail. Pity, he says, results from the dramatic observation of undeserved suffering, from suffering out of all proportion to the nature of the transgression. And fear, he adds, results from our feelings of communion with those characters who are, however roughly speaking, like us.

Ho metaxu ara toutôn loipos, "what remains is the man in the middle," Aristotle tells us now. Having sketched out the dramatic extremes to be *avoided* in plot construction, Aristotle tells us now what to look for, especially in tragic plots.

> The man in the middle is neither a paragon of virtue and justice, nor does he suffer the reversal into ill fortune because of some evil or wickedness in him. He suffers it because of some *hamartia*.[35]

There are, naturally, endless debates about how best to translate this latter term. Is Aristotle saying that tragic heroes and heroines suffer because of some mistake?[36] There is much to commend this view, especially given Aristotle's interest in the moral meaning of the theater in this same passage. But I think that Aristotle is telling us something more difficult than the seductive rhetoric of morality will allow. Morality, so Nietzsche would later remind us, is the last great temptress of Art.[37]

Aristotle begins by speaking of the tragic character as someone "in the middle" [*metaxu*]. Now this is an extremely loaded philosophical term. Plato had galvanized the word in his *Symposium*,[38] arguing there that *erôs* is a semidivine mediator between mortals and immortals. *Erôs* is himself an "in between" sort of being, child of Resource and Poverty, and this genealogy positions him to be uniquely benedictory to humankind--humankind, which is itself another sort of "middling" creature. Tragedy, it seems to me, is thus intended to deal not with the moral caricatures who people the stages of our morality plays (as well as the hallowed corridors of the Attic Old Comedy), but rather with those who are in between, which is to say, those who are much like us. The tragic flaw is no "flaw" at all; it is rather a mode of being, a *necessary* mode of being, of being *human*,[39]in the appropriately human way.

> How curious it is that we should see Prometheus suffering because he has transgressed a law of heaven and Antigone suffering because she has not! Tragedy's span of vision would seem to be wide enough to admit strange contradictions. . . .
>
> In general, we have fastened ourselves to the flaw because we were looking for an explanation of the disastrous end that overtakes tragic figures. We thought we saw death everywhere and we searched for a weakness or an error or a sin that might account for it. We sought a beginning negation in order to explain an ultimate negation. But neither negation is uniformly present. Tragedies do not all end in disaster, or death;. . . a number of tragic figures seem wholly uncorrupted.
>
> We are forced to look elsewhere for a term that will describe the nature of the tragic action while accommodating its extraordinary range of gestures.[40]

The Greeks had several such words, I think. Aristotle intends *hamartia* to be one such word. Another was *sophrosunê*, a term that appears quite often in tragic discourse and that might best be translated as "skill at being human" or "skill at playing with limit."[41] It is a knowledge of place, a knowledge of the limits implicit in having a place—a modal place—in the cosmos. Our mode of being is a mode of "in-between-ness." And that is a position that proves to be as ripe with possibilities for redemption as it is with invitations to disaster. For in the midst of our really excruciating limitations, we are also radically, almost unbearably, free.[42]

Hegel's Tragic Theory

Of all those who grappled with the Greeks' tragic legacy, especially in its erotic permutations (*philosophia*, for the Greeks, being itself a kind of passionate attention), none probed the territory more meaningfully than Hegel. His "tragic theory," if we can call it that, has an occasional character about it, since he did not write, as Nietzsche did, any extensive treatise on the Greek theater. Yet the Athenian tragic theater, and its imagery, was a subject to which he constantly returned, from the opening chapters of the *Phenomenology of Mind,*[43] through his *Lectures On The Philosophy of Religion*[44] and the *Lectures On The Philosophy of Fine Art,*[45] even into *The Philosophy of Right,*[46] his final published work. These various and varying discussions have been helpfully compiled and edited into a single volume,[47] which makes an assessment of what Hegel's tragic ruminations achieved far more accessible to the general reader. Of equal assistance is the remarkable essay by the noted Shakespearean scholar, A. C. Bradley,[48] "Hegel's Theory of Tragedy," reprinted in the same volume.[49]

Of what, then, does Hegel's tragic theory consist? First and foremost, Hegel accepts the Aristotelian dictum that tragedy cannot play solely in the realm of ideas; it is always and emphatically involved in a certain kind of staged dramatic *action.*[50] More specifically, the tragic action is what he calls a "collision," a collision between opposed moral forces.[51] What is most essential to (and most creative about) Hegel's analysis, however, is the nature of this tragic collision. Tragedy involves the collision between two systems of value, each of which lays a legitimate claim upon our sympathy.[52] That is an important point for Hegel, because it takes tragedy immediately and emphatically out of the realm of the morality play. What we witness on the tragic stage is never the easy collision between good and evil, in which our moral sympathies are clear. Rather, tragedy involves us in the infinitely more complex collision between two forms of right. An opposition between conflicting spheres of value, tragedy involves us in the inescapable conflict of good with good, not the pedantic conflict of good with evil. Tragedies are *not* apocalypses. If tragic drama be concerned with moral matters, it is not conversant with the "ethics of the obvious." Instead, it challenges us, tempting us into an ever-widening moral vision, insisting upon an ever-more-dizzying moral compass.

Hegel's concluding observation about the nature of such tragic collisions is perhaps his subtlest and, for me, his most supple point. Tragic collisions—despite the intractable nature of the collision, and despite the necessity upon which they seem to rely—are not *necessarily* beyond redemption. In a discussion of Sophocles' *Antigone,* he makes this quite clear, by making a really crucial distinction between fate and destiny:

> Fate is what is devoid of thought, of the Notion, something in which justice and injustice disappear in abstraction; in tragedy, on the other hand, destiny moves within a certain sphere of moral justice. We find this truth expressed in the noblest form in the Tragedies of Sophocles. . . . .Blind destiny is something unsatisfying. In these tragedies justice

is grasped by thought. The collision between the two highest moral powers is set forth in plastic fashion in that supreme and absolute example of tragedy, "Antigone.". . . Creon is not a tyrant, but really a moral power; Creon is not in the wrong; he maintains that the law of the State, the authority of government, is to be held in respect, and that punishment follows the infraction of the law. Each of these two sides realizes only one of the moral powers, and has only one of these as its content; this is the element of one-sidedness here, and the meaning of eternal justice is shown in this, that both end in injustice because they are both one-sided, though at the same time both obtain justice too. . . . It is only the one-sidedness of their claims which justice comes forward to oppose.[53]

Such comments might be endlessly recapitulated from Hegel's published and unpublished works. Perhaps one further example will suffice to make the point, since it again invokes the Greek stage explicitly, and attempts to grapple with the curious (curious especially to modern sensibilities) dramatic fact of the Greek Chorus.[54]

The final result, then, of the development of tragedy conducts us to this issue and only this, namely, that the twofold vindication of the mutually conflicting aspects is no doubt retained, but the *one-sided* mode is cancelled, and the undisturbed ideal harmony brings back again that condition of the Chorus, which attributes without reserve equal honor to all the gods. The true course of dramatic development consists in the annulment of *contradictions* viewed as such, in the reconciliation of the forces of human action, which alternately strive to negate each other in their conflict. . . . And it is only in so far as we retain such a view securely that we shall be in a position to understand ancient tragedy.[55]

Now this rhetoric of redemption—Hegel's privileged term is "reconciliation" [*Versöhnung*]—is easy enough to recognize, but enormously difficult to understand. Understanding it would, in all likelihood, take us some long way toward understanding Greek tragedy—and the Gospels—more fully.

What, then, is Hegel attempting to say? What, then, does tragic reconciliation entail? Some clue to the answer to that question may be found in the essential distinction between fate and destiny that Hegel uncovered from his earlier reading of the *Antigone*. For Hegel, as for Aristotle, Sophocles' *Oedipus* is one of the paradigmatic tragic presentations, just as his *Antigone* is another. The plot is so well known that we often skip over it too easily. Yet there is a parable in this dramatic story and its Sophoclean presentation. Oedipus' fate is what we see enacted, or rather realized, on the stage. He is fated to kill his father and to marry his mother. His is a regicide, a parricide, an incest. If he does not do these things, then he is not Oedipus. *How* he manages to fulfill this cruel fate, however, involves himself and the audience in his own very singular character and no other. We know that Aeschylus and Euripides each wrote an Oedipus-play. We can assume that they *performed* Oedipus' fate quite differently. What we see in Sophocles, then, is the marriage between a wholly singular character—Oedipus, the intransigent king—and a fate not of his own making, inescapable on the one hand, yet decidedly personal and his very own. *We see a man participate in his own undoing.* No one save Oedipus, we realize, would have been so self-certain, so confident that he could flee his decreed fate. No one save the hot-blooded child of Laius would have killed an anonymous older man at a crossroads, or have married a queen so much older than he. What we see on stage, to say it simply, is the dramatic *enactment* of a fate. What we see on stage is Oedipus' *destiny*.

For tragedy emerges necessarily and inescapably from the fact that there is more than one will in the world. That is the essential source of tragic collisions. Fate is what the gods will. Our character determines what we will. Out of their collision, their *necessary* modal conflict, something new and really singular emerges—the tragic destiny of the character or characters whom we witness on the stage. In Gethsemane, Mark will make much this same point, by portraying a collision between what God presumably wills and what Jesus cannot will— namely, his own death. Out of that collision, the Gospel's tragic vision emerges clearly for the first time.

Now, such collisions are not, as I say, necessarily beyond redemption. Oedipus is, after all, redeemed in the end, reconciled with the very gods who had conspired in his destruction. He is even brought into their august company in another play, the *Oedipus at Colonus.* Indeed, tragedy speaks of the only redemption that is humanly possible, one that emerges on the far side of such conflict. "Salvation," as Hegel observed in a private letter, "is *through* suffering, not *from* it."[56] And here we are returned to the modern muddle that results from equating "tragedy" too easily and unreflectively with "disaster." The dramatic facts could not be farther from this posture. "Tragedy is the form that promises us a happy ending," Walter Kerr reminds us. "It is also the form that is realistic about the matter."[57]

The Gospel as Tragedy

Now what does all of this have to do with the Gospel? It has *everything* to do with the Gospel.

The early evangelists who preached the new way charted out by Jesus, and who then wrote their narrative accounts of that way in what we call "Gospels," needed first to learn Greek. To do so they went to school and learned the language with the assistance of elaborate Greek primers, several of which have recently come into our ken.[58] We know that the evangelists learned how to write much as grade-school children learn to read and write today. And we know that they would have been taught to read Homer and the tragedians, excerpted from the same anthologies that helped to determine which plays survived into the present day. So the classical Athenian tragedies could not be more relevant to the early Christian evangelists who groped for literary and philosophical models in the mapping of their own theological arguments.

Speaking philologically, the Gospels are one among several Jewish intertestamental genres that look for all the world like classical Attic drama. Certainly *Job*, in its finally redacted form, looks like a tragedy,[59] much as *Ecclesiastes* looks like the Epicurean and Stoic collections of sayings so popular as modes of reflective moral discourse. The Gospels look, and feel, like tragedies.

Immediately there is a difference, however—above and beyond the obvious difference implicit in the fact that staged drama has a number of speaking parts and the Gospels are narrative recitations without such plurality of "character." That is a relatively minor point in comparison with the major point Hegel helps us to clarify. Hegel distinguished quite clearly between tragic collisions that take place in a *vertical* dimension versus those that take place in a *horizontal* dimension.[60] A horizontal tragedy is one in which "moral" matters, traditionally so called, are paramount. Here we see the collision, the *necessary* collision, between two forms of "right," two appeals to the law and to moral obligation. The paradigm for such a collision, according to Hegel, is Sophocles' *Antigone*, with its modal contrast between the written law of the state and the unwritten law of heaven. He is surely correct in this assessment, and no student of the New Testament can fail to notice this same dynamic in the Gospel. Jesus is depicted in almost constant conflict, horizontally, with the proponents of the written Law. There was a long-standing prophetic tradition to which Jesus could appeal in this conflict.

A vertical collision is not "moral" in the traditional sense of that term. Here we are witnessing a collision between two wills in the world, the will of a god or the gods on the one hand, and the will of the tragic hero or heroine on the other. These are plays in which fate and destiny are distinguished, and Sophocles' *Oedipus* is the paradigm. Here we see the necessary and inescapable collision of the will of heaven with the alternate vision of the hero, who is beaten down (but not broken) by such a fate. What we see is the performative enactment of something we call "destiny." Again, Hegel is quite right to see Oedipus as paradigmatic here. Yet this same dynamic animates the crucial scene in Gethsemane, at least in the three Synoptic performances (John is altogether different, here as elsewhere).

Hegel suggested that Greek tragedies traditionally operated in one dimension or the other, but not in both. Such multidimensional dramas tend to lack focus, he felt, as if they are trying to do too many things at once. They are infinitely more difficult to stage. Yet the Gospels *do* operate in both horizontal and vertical dimensions, and they seem to manage this with considerable grace and dramatic power. Hegel suggests as much, given his own deep appreciation for the dramatic power of the Gospels. So the Gospels are tragedies, generically to be sure, but also and more importantly in terms of the moral vision they commend.

Implications of the Tragic Vision

I have cast a wide net in this essay and have doubtless brought in a confusing variety of fish. Let me begin—as a way of concluding, tentatively—to sort through several of the insights we may have captured, and thus to reflect briefly upon what the implications of this tragic perspective might be.

First and foremost, I have been viewing Christianity as a primarily Greek, not a Jewish, religion. Indeed, the process whereby what we now know as Christianity detached itself from Judaism was a complex one, having as much to do with culture and geography as with theology *per se*. To be sure, theological matters—of a curiously cultural sort (curious from a Protestant point-of-view)—were at stake. We see this matter amplified in the first Church Council in Jerusalem.[61] Once the argument was made—namely, that this new "way" was open to Greeks as well as to diasporic Jews—a whole new set of questions was foregrounded, questions that had not been asked so forcefully before: about circumcision; about the Mosaic Law; about the continuity of one covenant with another; about the contemporary relevance of the Judean Kingdom and the future of the Jerusalem Temple; about the appropriate level of cultural assimilation to the Greco-Roman environment in which Judaism now found itself embedded. To be sure, many of these questions had been asked before; in one sense, they were simply questions in the air in the Hellenistic Jewish environment of the eastern Mediterranean at the time. Yet the change of audience, and the change of venue, served to change the fundamental focus of these questions.

To these vaguely recognizable questions, the Jesus movement added an essential and altogether novel one: *the question of who Jesus was*. The remarkable genre of the Gospels was designed to answer that troublesome question. And the material answers the Gospels provided led,

after subsequent philosophical speculation, to the doctrinal pronouncements of Nicaea (325 CE) and Chalcedon (451 CE), creeds designed to
answer yet again that same troublesome question of Jesus' identity, but
in a different, far more esoteric, idiom.

Clearly it is the question of who Jesus was that is new, and different,
about the religious phenomenon we now call Christianity. Answering
it involved tacking a vertical dimension on to the chronicle of religious
conflicts that had been taking place for quite some time in the horizontal arena of Roman Palestine. The Christian tragedies called "Gospels"
provided an additional, and determinative, explanation of what was going on. Clearly it was in the manner that one answered this latter question—the question of who Jesus was—that determined whether one was
Jewish or had left Judaism behind. The Incarnational answer to that
question did leave the monotheism of the first-century Hellenistic
Jewish world behind. And this was the *theological* heart of the matter.

Yet there is geography, and culture, lying equally at the heart of these
difficult disputes. And that fact, too, bears further reflection than it
normally receives. After all, "responsibility" implies answerability; to
answer the call of being a Christian certainly requires some careful attention to the historical and cultural genesis of the religious tradition of
which one claims to be a part. The most cursory glance at the New
Testament tells the tale I wish to tell. There are Gospels, four of them,
designed to address the complex mystery of who Jesus was. There is an
historical narrative of the way in which "the way" was expanded, and
the sorts of theological and cultural resistance it met along that way.
There is theology here, complex conflict, and high drama. There is also
one long narrative apocalypse, representative of a hugely popular *genre*
in the Hellenistic Jewish world, and in this case, the only *anti*-Roman
document in what is otherwise a shockingly apolitical canon.

But most strikingly there are letters—personal letters to friends, letters ascribed to the early leaders of the movement, letters to religious
seekers and to fellow travelers along the way. Most of these letters bear
the names of the major *metropoleis* in the eastern Mediterranean basin
to which they were sent. Thus the letters present an interesting picture
of the expansion of this new religious movement: one letter to Rome
(Italy), two to Corinth (mainland Greece), one to Galatia (Asia Minor),
one to Ephesus (Asia Minor), one to Philippi (northern Greece), one to
Colossae (Asia Minor), and two to Thessaloniki (northern Greece).
There is no letter to anyone in Jerusalem that we know of, or to Syrian
Antioch, or even to Alexandria, as we might expect. The canonical
shape of the New Testament broadcasts loudly and clearly that
Christianity took off, not in Roman Palestine, where it began, but in
Greece and Asia Minor—then, in the next generation, in Italy, Spain,
France, and North Africa.

Combining these geographical and theological facts tells us something significant. As the preachers of "the way" spent extended periods in the Greek-speaking Aegean basin, their message was naturally tailored to its audience.[62] The message was, itself, assimilated. Yet that process of syncretism[63] was simultaneous with one of the most formative developments in the early Church, the discovery of a new question that began to displace the older Hellenistic Jewish questions and threatened to detach this religious movement from Judaism altogether. The question, as I say, concerned who Jesus was. The Gospels were designed to answer this question. Yet precisely because of *where* Christianity had gone in the interim, and precisely because of *whom* Christians were now addressing, the Gospels took the form of the most accessible genre in the ancient Greek-speaking world: the classical tragedies that were taught in school and staged in all the major sanctuaries on all the major religious festivals (festivals that Christians, be sure to note, in Asia Minor had come to believe they might attend. In north Africa, a different view would prevail).

To be sure, there is more to the genre question than just a genre. That has been my point all along. To say that the Gospels are tragedies is to say far more than that these texts took a generic shape we recognize as vaguely "tragic." There is a world view implicit in certain genres and in certain cultural environments. The tragedies spoke often and eloquently of the *apotheosis* of the hero or heroine, the person who achieved his or her fullest humanity, a sort of divinized humanity, in the ritual context of suffering that was thought to be somehow redemptive. "God was made a man," said Saint Athanasius, "so that we might be made gods."[64] That, too, is an essential part of the story the Gospel tells. And that is what is new about it. In trying to articulate an answer to the crucial question of who Jesus was, the Gospel charted out a new path along the way, a path leading inexorably, if vaguely, to the later doctrine of God's Incarnation. The creeds of Nicaea and Chalcedon are the next chapter in Christianity's essentially tragic—which is to say, redemptive—ruminations.

Implications for Christian Responsibility

In order to come to terms with the notion of Christian "responsibility" resident in such complex Christian texts, it is imperative to examine the world view, and the cultural environment, that gave birth to those texts. It is not immediately clear that there is a Greek word that accords very well with our notion of "responsibility." There are clearer notions of culpability (Peter's, for instance), and probably complicity as well (Judas', to be sure), but not responsibility. One must dig deeper.

There is a profound awareness in the tradition of Greek moral enquiry—a tradition of which the tragic stage *and* the Socratic-Platonic-
Aristotelian traditions are *both* essential ingredients—that certain questions must come first. A sense of human being—a sense of human possibilities, of essential human limits, and of the fundamental matter of
human "in-between-ness"—is fundamental to the Greek analysis of
moral obligation and moral responsibility. "We are only geometricians
of matter," as Simone Weil observed; "the Greeks were, first of all, geometricians in their apprenticeship to virtue."[65] What, then, does the
Greekness, the *tragic* Greekness, of the Gospels imply for a coherent
notion of Christian responsibility?

Several things, I think. First, it means that our own way of distinguishing moral matters from aesthetic matters will not do. I have
stressed this repeatedly in this essay. The tragic stage was a rich locus
of *both* moral *and* aesthetic experience. The two would have been inseparable to the tragic mind. We, by contrast, live in a world—after
Kant, we think, although Kant was far more aware of the linkage than
we realize[66]—that wants to distinguish radically between the realms of
epistemology and ethics and aesthetics. Three modes of human enquiry, three critiques. Such a tripartite view of human understanding,
while suggestive, probably creates more problems than it resolves.
There is, after all, a unity in the plurality of human understanding, such
that the realms of knowledge are trinitarian rather than tripartite.
Blurring lines that have been far too sharply drawn—between philosophy and literature,[67] between history and fiction,[68] between reason and
emotion[69]—has been one essential task of contemporary moral thinking. I have offered two additional lines for our blurring: that between
tragedies and Gospels, on the one hand; that between pagan and
Christian, on the other.

Careful attention to these matters might, I think, helpfully blur another essential *disciplinary* boundary that is so close to most of us that
we seldom question it—the line separating philosophy from religion.
Socrates was executed on a charge of *religious* impiety, and there was
something essentially *political* (if not cultural) about the execution of
Jesus by the Roman establishment. The knife of speculation clearly
cuts in a variety of ways. Indeed, when one examines the major
Hellenistic schools that grew out of the Socratic-Aristotelian main-
stream—whether Stoic, Epicurean, or Skeptic[70]—it becomes rather difficult to say whether we should call them philosophies, or religions, or
psychological therapies. They are, quite simply, all three. And
Christianity, in the second and third centuries of the Common Era, was
contending that it belonged to that same discipline of speculative enquiry. Our inherited way of dividing these disciplines into three or

more separate university departments conceals these deeper and subtler connections. Seeing the Gospels for the Greek dramas that they actually were might help us to see in them rich resources for philosophical, religious, and even therapeutic speculation. Jesus was portrayed, after all, as teacher, prayer, and healer.

Socrates made a career out of asking the most deceptively simple question: "What is it?" I have tried to participate in this same moral discipline in this essay. H. Richard Niebuhr made a career out of asking an equally troubling, because equally complex, question: "What is going on?"[71] E. Clinton Gardner has quietly and compassionately devoted his life with *Christocentric* (Incarnational?) attention to such fundamental moral questions.[72]

It is my contention that taking the tragicness—which is to say, the *Greekness*—of the Christocentric story seriously would contribute helpfully to a deeper understanding of the full complexity of such superficially simple questions. There is a world view bound up in a simple attestation of genre, especially when that genre is tragic, and Greek. It is my further contention that the tragedy of the Gospel disrupts in most illuminating ways—disrupts, precisely, by blurring lines that have become entrenched and reified in Christian, and other, accounts of the moral life.

To ask the question one last time: In what, then, does "the tragedy of the Gospels" consist? How is one to extract an "ethic" from the New Testament, an enormously diverse canon in which any number of competing claims are made on behalf of Jesus and his message? Does seeing the Gospels as tragedies help us to extract a moral meaning from them at all?

Naturally enough, I think that viewing the Gospel as tragedy does help, in all of these ways. Using Hegelian categories, we see that the Gospels operate in both a vertical and a horizontal dimension. Indeed, it is one of my surest convictions that the vertical informs the horizontal, that the finer awareness of what Jesus' ultimate destiny involved— Gethsemane, and the Cross—deeply informs the way in which we are invited to think about the moral (and even legal) matters that he debates earlier in the Gospel.[73] His horizontal collisions with the religious and political authorities inform the way in which we are asked to read the ultimate collision—with God's will—in Gethsemane.[74]

And *vice versa*. In a sense, the vertical collision of Gethsemane calls us to a reevaluation of Jesus' earlier collisions with scribes, Pharisees, and his own endlessly misunderstanding disciples. Now, really quite suddenly, we become aware of just how many times Jesus warned us that the only way to save a life is to lose it, first.[75] Such a theology informs his politics; the vision of being in the world has a priority over the ethics. The responsible way of being human involves attending to our frustrating position "in the middle."

For human beings exist—the disciples first of all, and each of us who read or hear this story—in the mode of being divided, of being in-between [*metaxu*]. Coming to terms with that kind of double-mindedness is an important first step in coming to terms responsibly with our life in the world. Each of us—passionately committed to our lives, to our loves, and to certain social responsibilities—must come to terms with the radical incompleteness of all such precious labors as well. We live amid fragments, unfinished tasks, incomplete relationships, insecurity, and the constant risk of real harm. We live in the valley of the shadow of death. As Ecclesiastes knew well,[76] God has placed eternity in our minds but has given us no way outside of our embodiment, outside of time. *There is more than one will in the world.* And tragedy bears forth the inevitable fact of being caught between such disparate spheres of value.

That, in a word, is *hamartia*—a *fact of life*, not simply a "flaw." The doctrine of "original sin"—so troublesome to mainline and off-line Protestantism—is not a Synoptic idea. In the Sermon On The Mount, we are told unabashedly to be perfect, even as our Father in heaven is so.[77] The notion of *hamartia* as "sin" owes more to the Pauline vision than it does to the tragic vision of Matthew and Mark. Tragedies hinge on the notion of responsibility, presupposing human agents who are neither utterly depraved nor entirely salutary.[78] The tragic hero or heroine stands radically in-between, standing between heaven and earth much as the patristic saints are depicted. We suffer because of where we stand—which is, precisely, in-between, and thus potentially nowhere. A legalistic account of the moral life asks us to embody a kind of moral one-dimensionality that the Gospel, in its richer moments, knows is impossible. Dealing with the complexities of moral failure, not moral perfection, is the primary concern of the Christian way.

Yet this is not the last word—not for Oedipus, not for Antigone, not for Jesus, not for us. Redemption is always possible. *At least* as many Greek tragedies end well as end poorly.[79] It is only a flat misunderstanding of the Shakespearean canon, coupled with the fact that Dante called his epic a *commedia*, that invites us to read tragedies as disasters in which meaninglessness wins out in the end. The tragic posture, an emphatically modern posture, bears no resemblance to the tragic vision, classical or Christian. Tragedies end in any number of ways—happily, unhappily, ambivalently. Tragedies are not defined by the manner in which they end at all, but rather by the nature of the conflicts that come in the middle.

Redemption, as I say, is always possible—else it is no tragedy. Redemption is not *necessary*, of course. Tragedy is deeply realistic about the matter. The suffering is necessary; without it a human life would not be human, and a drama portraying such a life would not be a tragedy. Salvation is through suffering, not from it.

That there is good news, even and especially here, is remarkable news indeed. It makes being and remaining undistortedly human possible even when embedded in the necessary collisions of every life, no matter how carefully constructed. More finely aware of this fact of human life, the moral life—a genuinely responsible life, a genuinely love-informed life—becomes possible, arguably for the first time.

That, in any case, is something of what the Gospels have to teach us. And tragic conflict is their bracing way of teaching it.

Notes

[1] René Girard, *Violence and the Sacred*, trans. Patrick Gregory (Baltimore, Md.: Johns Hopkins University Press, 1982), 351.

[2] For an initial stab at this same thesis, see my "Mark's Tragic Vision: Gethsemane" Religion *and Literature* 24, no. 3 (1992): 1-25.

[3] See the collection of Reinhold Niebuhr's sermons, *Beyond Tragedy: Essays On the Christian Interpretation of History* (N.Y.: Simon and Shuster, 1937).

[4] The work that most explicitly addresses this connection is my *Tragic Posture and Tragic Vision: Against the Modern Failure of Nerve* (N.Y.: Continuum Press, 1994).

[5] This clearly was not the Greek view of the matter. See John Gassner's "Aristotelian Literary Criticism" in S.H. Butcher's classic *Aristotle's Theory of Poetry and Fine Art* (N.Y.: Dover Publications, 1951), lxiii-lxiv. For more in this vein, see Butcher's own contribution, "The Ideal Tragic Hero," 304-308.

[6] I leave to one side the more complicated idea of the "histories," which were clearly not seen as "historical" in any modern sense, but were rather more akin to the sort of historical reconstruction we get in the Gospels. I am indebted to Gary Hauk for this important qualification. For more on this see note 7 below.

[7] Lord Byron, *Don Juan* III, ix, edited with an introduction and notes by Leslie A. Marchand (Boston, Mass.: Houghton Mifflin Company, 1958), 109.

[8] In the formal Patent under the Great Seal of England issued to Shakespeare's company at the outset of James I's reign, on 19 May 1603, the entire group was granted permission "freely to use and exercise the art and faculty of playing comedies, tragedies, histories, interludes, morals, pastorals, stage plays, and such others" [as quoted by S. Schoenbaum, *Shakespeare's Lives* (Oxford: Clarendon Press, 1991), 18].

Clearly, the Shakespearean canon permitted of much finer distinctions in his own day than it does in ours. So, for that matter, did Plato's:

There are kinds of poems and stories which are told entirely by means of imitation: tragic and comic plays, among them, as you pointed out.

There is another and contrary kind in which the poet recites in his own person, best exemplified, I should think, by lyric narrative. There is still a third kind that employs both techniques, epic poetry, for example, and a number of other poetic forms, if you follow me (*Republic* 394b-c).

[9]George Steiner, *The Death of Tragedy* (N.Y.: Hill and Wang, 1961), 8-13.

[10]See the remarkable rejoinder to Steiner's thesis in Walter Kerr, *Tragedy and Comedy* (N.Y.: Simon and Shuster, 1967), 36-56. See also Ruprecht, *Tragic Posture and Tragic Vision*, i-xxv.

[11]Gerald F. Else, "The Origin of TRAGOIDIA" *Hermes* 85 (1957) :17-46.

[12]One of the "classics" in this domain is still A. W. Pickard-Cambridge's *Dithyramb, Tragedy and Comedy* (Oxford: Clarendon Press, 1927). See also Steiner, *The Death of Tragedy*, 351-355.

[13]See the collection of essays edited by John J. Winkler and Froma Zeitlin, *Nothing to Do With Dionysus? Athenian Drama In Its Social Context* (Princeton, N.J.: Princeton University Press, 1990).

[14]See Arrian, *The Campaigns of Alexander*, translated by Aubrey de Sélincourt (N.Y.: Dorset Press, 1971). For a classic modern biography, see William W. Tarn's *Alexander the Great* (Boston, Mass.: Beacon Press, 1948, 1962), and Peter Green's *Alexander of Macedon, 356-323 BC* (Berkeley, Calif.: University of California Press, 1991). Finally, see Lionel Pearson, *The Lost Histories of Alexander the Great* (Atlanta, Ga.: Scholars Press Reprint, 1983).

[15]*Deuteronomy* 20; *Joshua* 6:21, 8:24-29, 10:28-43, 11:20.

[16]*Joshua* 24:14-24; *Judges* 2:1-5,11-23.

[17]For a fuller discussion of this problematic, see my "On Being Jewish or Greek in the Modern Moment" *Diaspora* 3, no. 2 (1994):199-220.

[18]For a powerful elaboration of this essential insight, see Vassilis Lambropoulos, *The Rise of Eurocentrism: Anatomy of Interpretation* (Princeton, N.J.: Princeton University Press, 1993).

[19]Francis M. Cornford, *Before and After Socrates* (N.Y.: Cambridge University Press, 1966), ix, 32ff.

[20]Both men received considerable classical training. Nietzsche was, for his part, a professor of Classics for a decade before the period of his mature philosophical writings began. For more on the philosophical implications of this, see William Arrowsmith's excellent introduction to the notes for an unfinished 1876 essay titled "We Classicists" in *Unmodern Observations* (New Haven, Ct.: Yale University Press, 1990), 307-320.

[21]This comment is directed especially against Alasdair MacIntyre's claims in *After Virtue*, 2nd Edition (Notre Dame, Ind.: The University of Notre Dame Press, 1984). For more on this see my "After Virtue? On Distorted Philosophical Narratives" *Continuum* 3 (1994) :1-25.

[22]For a longer explication of this complex relationship, see my

Symposia: Plato, the Erotic, and Moral Value (forthcoming).

[23]See my "Nietzsche's Vision, Nietzsche's Greece" *Soundings* 73.1 (1990) :61-84, and "We Classicists," 3[70] (Arrowsmith, 342).

[24]Martha Nussbaum, *The Fragility of Goodness: Luck and Ethics in Greek Tragedy and Philosophy* (N.Y.: The Cambridge University Press, 1986), 420.

[25]Invoking the name of Aristotle almost immediately calls to mind the names of Alasdair MacIntyre in moral philosophy and Stanley Hauerwas in Christian ethics. Part of my disagreement with their approach is grounded in the claim that Aristotle may be read quite differently than they do, precisely by paying closer attention to the tragic dimension of his thinking. I am deeply indebted to Martha Nussbaum in making this point. For more specific criticism of MacIntyre and Hauerwas, see my *Afterwords: Hellenism, Modernism, and the Myth of Decadence* (Albany, N.Y.: SUNY Press, 1995).

[26]I have used two excellent translations of the *Poetics*—one by Gerald F. Else (Ann Arbor, Mich.: University of Michigan Press, 1967), and the other by Samuel Butcher (*op. cit.*)—in consultation with the Greek text in Rudolf Kassel's *Aristotelis: De Arte Poetica Liber* (Oxford: Clarendon Press, 1965). For more on the *Poetics*, see Gerald F. Else's masterful commentary, *Aristotle's Poetics: The Argument* (Cambridge, Mass.: Harvard University Press, 1957).

[27]For a discussion and partial reconstruction of this lost manuscript, see Richard Janko, *Aristotle On Comedy: Towards A Reconstruction of Poetics II* (Berkeley, Calif.: University of California Press, 1984).

[28]See Else, *Aristotle: Poetics*, 89, note 49, and Steiner, *The Death of Tragedy* , 45-105.

[29]*Poetics* §9; 1449 b27; Kassel, *Aristotelis: De Arte Poetica Liber*, 10; and Else, *Aristotle's Poetics*, 221-237.

[30]*Poetics* §9 1449 b28, and Kassel, *Aristotelis: De Arte Poetica Liber*, 10.

[31]*Poetics* §13; 1453 a7-10, and Kassel, *Aristotelis: De Arte Poetica Liber*, 20. See also Else, *Aristotle's Poetics*, 375-399.

[32]See Butcher, *Aristotle's Theory of Poetry and Fine Art*, 317-325; and Else, *Aristotle's Poetics*, 375-399.

[33]Aristotle, *Nicomachean Ethics*, 1106 a26-1109 b27.

[34]One wonders what Aristotle made of Euripides' *Medea*. It would *seem* that he would not consider her to be a wicked person, however wicked her final actions may indeed have been. This bears directly on the issue of *moral failure* to which I will return.

[35]Aristotle, *Poetics* §13, 1453 a7-10, and Kassel, *Aristotelis: De Arte Poetica Liber*, 20.

[36]This is the way Gerald F. Else translates the term here, *Aristotle: Poetics*, 38. See also his *Aristotle's Poetics: The Argument*, 376.

[37]For a wonderfully creative presentation of this view and some of its

moral-political implications, see James J. Winchester, *Nietzsche's Aesthetic Turn: Reading Nietzsche After Heidegger, Deleuze and Derrida* (Albany, N.Y.: SUNY, 1994).

[38]Plato, *Symposium* 202 a-b. See also my "A Funny Thing Happens On The Way to Mantinea: Diotima and Martha Nussbaum On Love's Knowledge" *Soundings* 75.1 (1992): 97-127, esp. 108-109.

[39]How far the modal language of necessity stands from the language of sin may be seen in some rabbinic discussions of the Eden-story, where we are told that Adam's and Eve's great sin was not the transgression of eating the fruit (this was necessary, *modally* necessary), but rather the refusal of their freedom and the implicit denial of responsibility. See Elie Wiesel, *Messengers of God* (N.Y.: Summit Books, 1976), 27.

[40]Kerr, *Tragedy and Comedy*, 118-119. See also 120-143.

[41]I am indebted to William Arrowsmith for this suggestion, which was made to me in personal communication, and which seems the more apt the more I reflect upon the matter. For eloquent posthumous testimony to his fertile views of tragic characterization, see "The Heroic Voice: Letters to Stephen Berg" in *Arion, Third Series* 2, nos.2/3 (1993): 209-215.

[42]Kerr again:
"Tragedy seems to me to be an investigation of the possibilities of human *freedom*. . . ." This freedom can be measured only in the doing and only in the dark. . . ." Tragedy proposes that the door is open and that man may walk through it. It does not say what is on the other side until it sees what is on the other side. . . ." Tragedy seems to me an exploratory form, not an illustrative one. . . ." [For] he is freer still. Beyond knowledge, beyond memory, beyond reason, he can still act. Man has a vast freedom to know and then—when he does not know— to choose. A kind of terror enters here. When he has not knowledge, man has choice. Blinded, he can yet move, over Dover cliff with Gloucester or into the heart of God with Oedipus." [*Tragedy and Comedy*, 121-123].

[43]Originally published in 1807, G. W. F. Hegel, *The Phenomenology of Mind*, translated by J. B. Baillie (N.Y.: Humanities Press, 1910, 1966).

[44]Hegel, *Lectures On The Philosophy of Religion*, 2 Vols., translated by E. B. Spiers and J. Burdon Sanderson (London: Routledge and Kegan Paul, 1976).

[45]Translated and edited in an abridged version running to only one sixth of the original manuscript by Henry Paolucci, *Hegel: On The Arts* (N.Y.: Frederick Ungar Publishing Company, 1979).

[46]Originally published in 1821. Hegel, *The Philosophy of Right*, translated by T. M. Knox (N.Y.: Oxford University Press, 1952, 1967).

[47]Anne Paolucci and Henry Paolucci, eds., *Hegel: On Tragedy* (San Francisco: Harper & Row, 1962).

[48]Bradley is probably best known for his masterful *Shakespearean Tragedy* (London: MacMillan and Company, 1950), which applies many of Hegel's better insights to the four "canonical" tragedies of Shakespeare's

so-called "middle period"—*Hamlet, Othello, King Lear,* and *Macbeth.*

[49]Paolucci and Paolucci, *Hegel: On Tragedy,* 367-388.

[50]Ibid., 1-22.

[51]Ibid., 112-152.

[52]Ibid., 318-327.

[53]Ibid., 325. This passage originally appeared in the lectures published posthumously as *The Philosophy of History.*

[54]The latest edition of *Arion, Third Series* 3 (1995) and 4, no. 1 (1996), entitled "The Chorus in Greek Tragedy and Culture," are devoted to the creative analysis of the role of the chorus in Greek drama and its primitive ritual enactments.

[55]Paolucci and Paolucci, *Hegel: On Tragedy,* 71. This passage originally appeared in the posthumously published *Lectures On Fine Art.*

[56]Clark Butler, ed., *Hegel: The Letters* (Bloomington: Indiana University Press, 1984), 57.

[57]Kerr, *Tragedy and Comedy,* 36.

[58]For one such primer, see the edition of Theon's *Progymnasmata* by Ronald F. Hock and Edward N. O'Neil, *The Chreia in Ancient Rhetoric,* Volume I (Atlanta: Scholars Press, 1986). The essential classical model is, of course, Aristotle. See George A. Kennedy, *Aristotle: On Rhetoric* (N.Y.: Oxford University Press, 1991). Two excellent secondary sources for this material are George A. Kennedy, *New Testament Interpretation Through Rhetorical Criticism* (Chapel Hill, N.C.: University of North Carolina Press, 1984) and Burton L. Mack and Vernon K. Robbins, *Patterns of Persuasion in the Gospels* (Sonoma, Calif.: Polebridge Press, 1989).

[59]Horace M. Kallen, *The Book of Job As a Greek Tragedy* (N.Y.: Hill and Wang, 1918, 1959).

[60]Paolucci and Paolucci, *Hegel: On Tragedy,* 186-187.

[61]*Acts* 15:1-33.

[62]Paul's behavior in Athens is indicative, I think. See *Acts* 17:15-33.

[63]See the fascinating work of Charles Stewart, *Devils and Demons: Moral Imagination in Modern Greek Culture* (Princeton, N.J.: Princeton University Press, 1991) and, with Rosalind Shaw, *Syncretism/Antisyncretism: The Politics of Religious Synthesis* (N.Y.: Routledge Press, 1994).

[64]Athanasius, "On the Incarnation of the Word," §54, translated by Archibald Robinson in Edward R. Hardy's *Christology of the Later Fathers* (Philadelphia, Pa.: Westminster Press, 1954), 107.

[65]Simone Weil, "The *Iliad,* or, The Poem of Force," translated by Mary McCarthy (Wallingford, Pa.: Pendle Hill Publications, 1956), 15.

[66]I am indebted for this insight to my good friend Jeffrey Wilson, who is currently completing a dissertation that develops this reading of Kant's complex *Critique of Judgment.*

[67]Martha Nussbaum, *Love's Knowledge: Essays On Philosophy and*

Literature (N.Y.: Oxford University Press, 1990).

[68]Gregory L. Jones and Stanley Hauerwas, eds., *Why Narrative? Readings In Narrative Theology* (Grand Rapids, Mich.: William B. Eerdmans Publishing Company, 1989).

[69]Suzanne K. Langer, *Philosophy In A New Key: A Study in the Symbolism of Reason, Rite, and Art*, Third Series (Cambridge, Mass.: Harvard University Press, 1942, 1957).

[70]Martha Nussbaum, *The Therapy of Desire: Theory and Practice in Hellenistic Ethics* (Princeton, N.J.: Princeton University Press, 1994).

[71]See H. Richard Niebuhr, *The Responsible Self: An Essay In Christian Moral Philosophy* (N.Y.: Harper & Row, 1963), 60.

[72]E. Clinton Gardner, *Christocentrism in Christian Social Ethics: A Depth Study of Eight Modern Protestants* (Washington, D.C.: University Press of America, 1983).

[73]For example, see *Mark* 7:1-23, where the things of God are contrasted with all human things.

[74]That is the working thesis of Ched Myers's remarkable book, *Binding the Strong Man: A Political Reading of Mark's Story of Jesus* (Maryknoll, N.Y.: Orbis Books, 1988).

[75]*Mark* 8:35, ff.

[76]*Ecclesiastes* 3:11.

[77]*Matthew* 5:48.

[78]E. Clinton Gardner, *Christocentrism in Christian Social Ethics*, 108-111.

[79]Ruprecht, *Tragic Posture and Tragic Vision*, 89-99.

Chapter 4

Responsibility and Moral Betrayal

Christine D. Pohl

"What is going on?" seemed like a most appropriate question to ask a seminary student who had responded to a discussion of the moral implications of euthanasia with intensity and anger. He had argued that no person had a right to address the dangers of killing innocent human life if he or she had never been in a situation that called for such a decision.

Uncomfortable with any strong moral claims, the student was equally troubled by recognition of moral ambiguity. In fact, for him, the whole project of ethics was suspect and problematic. Moral reflection was dangerous when it was not entirely irrelevant. Moral authorities had failed him grievously in the past and he was very restless in a required course in Christian ethics.

I would have considered this episode odd and the student idiosyncratic were it not for two factors. First, he was extraordinarily articulate about his experience of moral betrayal in Vietnam. Second, in my short tenure of teaching ethics, he was the third Vietnam veteran who had verbally exploded in response to a class discussion on Christian ethics.

Between fifteen and twenty-five years had passed since their service in Vietnam, but the war is still with these veterans. They are Christian men, uncertain of whether or how to make sense of what they had done or had been asked to do in war, struggling to forge a personal identity centered in fidelity, trust, and love. These are men headed toward ministry yet still quite unsure of issues of responsibility; they trust in God yet seem to lack any assurance that human existence has moral coherence or meaning.

More carefully documented accounts of the moral struggles of Vietnam veterans suggest that my experience with these three seminarians was not exceptional.[1] The legacy of the Vietnam experience is not ethically intense for all veterans, perhaps not even for most. But for some, the most adequate way to describe the fallout is in terms of loss of confidence in moral authority and in a coherent moral universe, an abiding sense of betrayal and violation, and struggles with responsibility and trust.

Disconcertingly similar responses are emerging from a very different segment of the American population. In listening to women's actual accounts of their abortions, one hears themes of irresponsibility, betrayal, violation, and lostness with alarming frequency. Again, not all women respond this way, but a significant number do, and their struggles challenge us to think more deeply about what these two experiences have in common and what they might suggest about the nature of the moral life and of human relationships.

Why Reflect on Selected Experiences from Within These Two Groups?

No American sociomoral conflicts during the past twenty-five years have been more acrimonious than the disagreements over the war in Vietnam and over abortion. The discussion of each issue has been deeply polarized and dependent on highly inflated rhetoric. Neither debate has sufficiently attended to the actual experiences and insights of those young men and women who were participants in the fighting or in abortion. The polarization of the societal discussion has deepened the silence of those persons who "know" from experience the profound ambiguities of life and death, of those whose moral identities and moral frameworks have been challenged.

The wounds from abortion and war strike at the heart of human community and moral identity because they involve the destruction of human life. Although for some men and women there seem to be no lasting effects from the experience, others are deeply troubled. For a variety of reasons, these persons have come to understand their own past acts as immoral, though legal and even sanctioned by significant moral authorities.

The troubled accounts are the most morally compelling ones.[2] Such stories suggest that making moral and religious sense of those legally-sanctioned actions that destroy life is very problematic for several reasons. One cannot interpret one's own behavior as "killing innocent life" and simultaneously not feel compelled to question the larger moral authorities that permitted such behavior. To conclude that such moral authorities were mistaken, malevolent, uninterested, or incompetent undermines confidence in social institutions and in a coherent moral universe and threatens the meaning of one's own sacrifice and moral identity.

Questions of personal responsibility are particularly acute for some of these men and women. Accepting responsibility for their actions is required for moral maturity as well as for healing, yet accepting responsibility for what one defines as killing is very traumatic. Issues of guilt and grief, remorse and regret, can be overwhelming. Furthermore, assuming personal responsibility for such wrongdoing is complicated by a social context that at least in part lent moral approval to the action.

The most frequent individual response to such moral difficulty is to "not think about it." Internal shutdowns are as common as is the absence of conversation about the experience that seems to accompany both events. Neither Vietnam veterans nor women who have had abortions talk about their experience much; this response is particularly ironic given the enormous public debates about both issues.

Many of those who are most troubled describe themselves as having been betrayed —betrayed by the moral authorities of government, law, religion, or family—betrayed by institutions whose roles include keeping people from wrongdoing. For both men and women, silence, rage, flight from responsibility, and fragile, troubled, or absent intimate relationships accompany the experience of betrayal.

Defining and Describing the Experience of Moral Betrayal

Moral betrayal involves a breach of trust or confidence, especially by persons or institutions that function as moral sources or moral authorities. It is a "unilateral breaking of faith . . . or trust with another."[3] The moral authority of institutions is derived from their role in shaping a community's ethos and protecting the common and individual good. Institutions routinize societal values and shape individual understandings of virtue, roles, responsibility, and meaning. Because of this, institutions (government, military, law, family, church) can demand loyalty.

The betrayal of individuals by institutions with moral authority occurs when such institutions ask or permit persons to do what, at least in other contexts, is considered wrong; when they ask for trust but are not trustworthy; or when they demand loyalty but are disloyal. Betrayal occurs when institutions do not take seriously the moral implications of actions for the actors, and when they intentionally mislead or define reality and particular actions falsely.

Individuals experience a betrayal of the institution's very reason for existence. Especially in a liberal society, law is expected to provide a minimum standard of morality and to proscribe killing. If government asks for the sacrifice of soldiers' lives, citizens and soldiers expect governing authorities to be sure that the cause is just and that the means are right. Daughters do not expect parents to urge them toward actions that undermine their very moral identity. Persons trust their clerical leaders not to sanction or ignore significant wrongdoing or to dismiss the personal moral implications of troublesome acts. Moral betrayal thus threatens the foundations of social life—shared commitments, respect for moral sources, maintenance of social bonds, and personal responsibility.[4]

Betrayed by moral authorities, these men and women feel they also betrayed their own instincts about life. They feel they were betrayed into acts that they cannot undo, into courses of action from which there is no return and only a difficult recovery. These men and women understand themselves as having killed innocent human life. Institutions allowed, sanctioned, demanded, or even encouraged action that undermined basic moral identity. Often, the process of undermining was subtle, because the reality of the acts was hidden behind abstractions like freedom, duty, choice, and patriotism. It was often in the midst of the act that the abstractions collapsed, but it was not until much later that the experience could be processed.

Robert J. Lifton describes the multiple layers of betrayal experienced by some Vietnam veterans who felt that they had been "victimized" and "badly used" "in having been sent to Vietnam": "They spoke about having been misled, put in a situation where they both slaughtered people and suffered for no reason, and then [were] abused or ignored on their return." One veteran's response captures the experience of moral betrayal: "You get stuck in Vietnam . . . expecting that you're doing the right thing, and all along you're doing the wrong thing."[5]

A disturbing combination of entrapment and personal responsibility haunts these accounts of betrayal by institutions.[6] Women who regret their abortions sometimes also reflect on their circumstances using the vocabulary of betrayal. They wonder how they could have been so misled, how laws that should protect life could have allowed them to "kill their own child." Describing her confused feelings in the midst of her abortion, one woman comments, "All along I was told it was the right thing to do, but then why was I feeling like it was so wrong and terrible? I hated myself so much."[7] Some find themselves unable to cope with the moral impact of something that large segments of the community maintain is a morally neutral act. Some feel betrayed by partners who did not resist their decisions to abort or who abandoned them upon learning of the pregnancy. Abandoned, they feel they then abandoned their own responsibility to life, and betrayed the life inside them. Their pathos is suggested in one woman's account that reflects the complex intertwining of betrayal, responsibility, remorse, and guilt: "I grieved for my lost baby but I had to push it down and out of my mind because I was the cause of my baby's death."[8]

Some men and women feel acutely betrayed by the institutions that claim particular responsibility for moral, spiritual, and emotional well-being. "Guardians of the spirit"[9] who rationalized or justified acts that were experienced by the actors as morally troublesome effectively cut off any significant moral conversations within the structures where such reflection traditionally would take place. Some comments reveal a deep level of betrayal experienced because chaplains blessed troops, guns, missions, and killing but ignored the spiritual and moral implications of the action, and because clergy suggested abortion was a responsible solution to unexpected pregnancy. Clergy and psychiatrists who attempt to help women and veterans "adjust" to war and abortion tend to interpret moral difficulty as an individual psychological problem that needs a cure.

Some women feel deeply betrayed by the women's movement that has so closely allied women's right to an abortion with women's autonomy and well-being. Until recently, it was rare for pro-choice women to admit that a woman might be troubled by abortion. Even now such a troublesome feeling is interpreted as a spiritual or emotional problem rather than as a moral one.[10]

Some of the ambivalence in interpreting troubled responses is related to the society-wide conflict over interpreting the meanings of the Vietnam War and of abortion. In both situations, alternate interpretations of actions are available to participants, and yet they experience their decisions or participation as grave wrong, at least after the fact. The larger society is ambivalent about listening to the experience of persons "caught in the act," because those accounts often render the community responsible in some way for the wrong. The individual hesitates to speak from experience about betrayal because her or his experience raises profound moral questions about earlier commitments and key institutions, and because it requires the individual to admit personal responsibility for wrongdoing.

Interpreting Moral Betrayal

The potency and continuing impact of moral betrayal suggests that a covenantal approach to ethics is experientially sound, even though much contemporary moral thinking is framed in terms of contract. Both betrayal and covenant are deeply relational concepts. The moral language of covenant involves responsibility, fidelity, trust, and loyalty. People for whom covenant would not be a first language still feel profoundly betrayed when commitments that have been made, promised, or demanded fail. At their deepest level, persons' relations to the institutions of law, family, government/country, and church are heavily embedded in covenant. The moral authority of such institutions runs deeper than contractual arrangements, and when it falters, the moral universe can seem uncertain, and responses can become ambiguous or cynical.

Neither contractual interpretations nor the moral orientation arising from expressive individualism[11] can adequately explain the moral intensity and pain of the betrayal accounts. Only a covenantal understanding of human relationships can capture the profound loss of moral identity and coherence. E. Clinton Gardner, reflecting on H. Richard Niebuhr's thought, writes that the "fundamental form of human society is covenant, i.e., the making and keeping of promises." He continues, "the presence of community—even in its negative forms of fear, suspicion, injustice, and violence—points to a universal moral order which monotheistic faith makes intelligible." Covenant, he suggests, "represents the acknowledgment of mutual responsibility and accountability to and for each other under God."[12]

In developing Niebuhr's responsiblist ethic, Gardner offers insight into the significance of betrayal in human relations.

> Human communities, then, are fundamentally faith communities. Insofar as they are human, all communities are bound together by bonds of trust and loyalty. . . . [T]he existence and authority of the state rest upon the allegiance of its subjects, upon their oath of obedience to its laws and their promise to defend it against its enemies. Significantly, however, the structures of faith—of trust and of loyalty—appear in human community largely in negative form as distrust and unfaithfulness to one another. Such negative manifestations do not, however, point to the absence of faith, but rather to the distorted forms in which the latter is present even in broken community. Thus treason, for example, presupposes faith. Treason is not the mere absence of trust and fidelity; rather, it is distrust and disloyalty, which reflect the brokenness of community rather than the absence of the latter.[13]

Betrayal experiences confirm the covenantal structure that undergirds societal relations. Betrayal, like treason, presupposes faith; in the experiences of betrayal under consideration, institutions with moral authority depend on the loyalty and the responsibility of the community but are experienced as disloyal and irresponsible by some members of the community.

Covenant understandings are "based in the experience of the self as a responsible moral agent, in the perception of trust and faithfulness as the basic moral bonds in human relationships, and in the apprehension of a transcendent moral order which makes human moral life intelligible."[14] Responsible action requires a continuing conversation and a universal community for reference. Human action is responsible, Niebuhr suggests, "when it is response to action upon us in a continuing discourse or interaction among beings forming a continuing society." He suggests that the task of ethics is to help persons understand and conduct themselves as responsible human beings, to help them structure, clarify, and interpret human action in the direction of responsibility.[15]

The experiences of betrayal recounted by veterans and by women who had abortions underline the significance of every component of the above definition of responsibility. The accounts reveal the difficulty of discerning the fitting response to action that is contested or unclear. The comments also underscore the significance of personal accountability, the consequences of defining the boundaries of community, and the necessity of ongoing conversation and relationships.

In many of the accounts, it appears that the preferred response to moral difficulty is to not think about it. People deliberately avoid reflection and interpretation. They deny personal responsibility, claiming to have had no choice. There is no conversation and no community of reflection; however, often there is present an undefined sense of guilt and ongoing difficulties in sustaining intimacy. A common response to betrayal is further betrayal and a flight from responsibility.

A seminary student's reflection on her abortion captures many of the features noted above.

> I knew it was wrong when I did it, but I never put it in terms of killing my child because then I would have to justify it. It was an answer to a dilemma. It was legal. It was easy. I always said I'd never have an abortion. I always knew it was wrong. Abortion was my choice when the guy said he wouldn't be responsible. Once I made my decision, I wouldn't budge. I had to keep focused and not think about right or wrong.[16]

After the abortion she did not think about it, but carried with her what she called "nebulous guilt" for several years; she could not name the trouble but said it kept surfacing in bad and failed relationships. She never talked about the abortion with anyone. Years later, she interpreted her experience when she was confronted by a direct question about being "good" before God. She comments, "I realized I wasn't good; I had killed my own child." In defining her previous action and in taking responsibility, she experienced freedom and relief. In a new community context that assured her that forgiveness was possible if responsibility were acknowledged, she found the moral support needed to interpret her own experience. Now she is troubled by laws that are supposed to protect persons from doing wrong but instead permit it. She finds healing in sharing her story with others because they have found it helpful in dealing with their own unresolved guilt. Their common question to her is, "How do you ever get to the point where you don't feel guilty anymore?"

Some of the women and veterans later concluded that the boundaries of community were drawn too narrowly when they excluded fetuses or Vietnamese civilians from the protection due human beings. In the struggle to deal with this, in their silence, pain, and sometimes anger, they placed themselves outside of significant human communities as well.

The theoretical definitions of responsibility and the morally troubled accounts offered by some veterans and some women who have had abortions intersect in three areas that will structure the rest of this discussion. They are (1) the relationship between interpretation and integrity, (2) the relationship of responsibility, choice, and guilt, and (3) the relationship between conversation and covenant.

Interpretation and Integrity

Arthur Egendorf, author of *Healing from the War*, writes,

> What do you do with an experience that touches your core? Bury it? Run from it? Stalk it like an enemy? Charge into it with full force? Surrender to it? Some vets try a variety of approaches, keeping silent about it at one time, talking to anyone who'll listen at another. Those intent on healing keep coming back to one question in particular: "What happened over there?" In asking this, they are struggling to come to grips with what took place, to mourn and hopefully move on.[17]

To find wholeness, veterans needed to find a way to interpret their experience; interpretation and ethical reflection were required to recover an integrity of self.[18] The yearning to experience themselves once again as "in one piece" graphically suggests the loss of that integrity. Only with the interpretation of their war experiences could they later find meaning and purpose in civilian life.[19] Robert J. Lifton observes,

> This inability to find significance or meaning in their extreme experience leaves many Vietnam veterans with a terrible burden of survivor

guilt. And this sense of guilt can become associated with a deep distrust of the society that sent them to their ordeal in Vietnam. They then retain a strong and deeply disturbing feeling of having been victimized and betrayed by their own country.

He continues, "as a result many continue to be numbed as civilians, the numbing now taking the form of a refusal to talk or think about the war."[20]

A deep sense of meaninglessness runs through numbers of the accounts given by veterans and by women who have had abortions. Egendorf notes that the most pervasive problem among the Vietnam veterans is the feeling of hopelessness, a sense that life is meaningless and empty, without purpose. Neither the public nor the mental-health community, he contends, has recognized that "the primary psychological burden among veterans is a profound emptiness."[21] In attempting to interpret an experience in which death was all around them, they are plagued with the "gnawing suspicion that 'it was all for nothing.'"[22]

These comments suggest that the fundamental problem is not psychological so much as it is moral. The tendency has been to respond to veterans' struggles in therapeutic, individual categories and with therapeutic, individual approaches. But such approaches tend to overlook the socioethical dimensions of veterans' struggles. These are fundamentally struggles of meaning and integrity. The troubled veterans sense that the moral order and their personal feeling of human connection have been fundamentally broken by the war in Vietnam."[23]

Egendorf concludes, from his own experience with the war, that the trauma often experienced by Vietnam veterans is not so much individual and personal as it is cultural: "Trauma takes place when . . . we see there's no terrain, nothing to believe, nothing to know, nothing to profess that will make us inviolate."[24] Egendorf's words suggest the total breakdown of meaning and interpretation experienced by some veterans. Stripped of the possibility of believing and knowing, they find integrity of self profoundly elusive.

The important relation between interpretation and integrity is also evident in some of the women's accounts. The legality of abortion-on-demand is confusing for women who "know" that the life inside them is growing. Law is expected to proscribe wrongdoing, but, in this case, matters of life and death become matters of personal choice.[25] Only in recognizing this confusion is it possible to make sense of the remarkable phenomenon of a woman being in the midst of an abortion and starting to worry that the procedure was hurting the fetus.[26] One woman commented, "At the back of my mind I kept thinking, 'It can't be true that this is a baby—elsewise, how could abortion be legal?'"[27] In these situations, women with basic moral commitments face the challenge of making sense of their voluntary role in a form of violence that is legal, but often apparent only after it is too late to interrupt the procedure.

Part of the problem is that women faced with an unexpected pregnancy often feel pressured to make decisions quickly. Once committed to a course that ends in abortion, they stop moral reflection to avoid conflicting input. Most interpretation is done after the fact. In the midst of combat, soldiers had neither the time nor the permission to reflect extensively on the meaning of their experience. It was afterwards, removed from combat, when the issues of meaning and interpretation surfaced. They surfaced especially, though not exclusively, when soldiers changed communities, particularly when they returned to civilian life. In instances of abortion and war, once one is involved in the process it is very difficult to change one's mind. Both experiences suggest the enormous importance of moral formation and reflection before the act.

Interpretation and integrity are closely tied to fitting one's actions and identity into culturally valued roles and virtues. For some of these men and women, their actions violated particularly important organizing heroic images—the good soldier and the good mother/woman. One soldier wistfully reflects,

> Sometimes I would remember and feel sad about the thoughts I used to have before the war. It felt as though I had been deceived by the older generations. They led me to believe that war was an honor to participate in, and that it is something that every young man needs to do to prove his manhood.[28]

His experiences left him feeling not like the heroic warrior but rather like one who had been deceived by those myths.

During an abortion a woman worried that her child felt pain; later she had recurring dreams about a baby boy. Another woman felt as though she had abandoned her daughter, that "she just went down the tubes," and regretted the decision to abort.[29] In both cases, these women had other children and sensed that they had violated their maternal role by terminating an unexpected pregnancy.

Maternal and warrior identities remain important organizing definitions of self; however, interpretations of the good mother and the good soldier are highly contested today, and this conflict is reflected in the individuals themselves. Interpretations that view veterans as heroic for their efforts and women as responsible in their decisions to terminate unexpected pregnancies exist side-by-side with interpretations that view war and abortion as profound wrongs.

Soldiers faced with the task of making sense of killing and death depend on moral and societal justifications for those acts. When these are absent or contested, soldiers are left to struggle alone with how to interpret their acts of killing, and their own sacrifices. Feeling betrayed, some conclude they gave their trust, health, morality, innocence, and friends to a war that was a mistake. Difficulty in interpreting one's actions and roles leaves persons with a deep distrust of authority and institutions and with an undefined feeling of shame.[30]

Responsibility, Choice, and Guilt

Conflicting larger interpretations of war and abortion and a sense of having been betrayed by moral authorities undermine a person's capacity to face his or her own responsibility. In both cases, it is possible to have acted responsibly, even to have "done one's duty," but then later to regret one's decisions and acts. Although struggles about responsibility, guilt, and regret are acute, their very difficulty discourages persons from addressing them.

Personal responsibility, freedom, and guilt are closely interwoven but are also much more ambiguous within the context of moral betrayal. Guilt is an appropriate moral response to failures in responsibility; guilt and forgiveness are essential to the sustaining and reconstructing of moral bonds. Understanding oneself as a responsible human being and as responsible for particular acts is closely connected to freedom and choice.

It is within this mix of responsibility, freedom/choice, and guilt that one can identify some of the most complex difficulties with experiences of war and abortion. Both war and abortion involve death—death that is intended yet violates human bonds at their most fundamental level. If the ultimate structure of responsible human action is that which is fitted into the life-giving action of God,[31] choices for death strike at the order of being. Lifton, quoting Martin Buber, suggests that guilt involves a "wound in the order of being."[32] The wounded in war and abortion include more than the immediate victims; those who are the actors also experience themselves as hurt.

Lifton describes the difficulty of giving definition to guilt when the larger social and moral structures have collapsed.

> The kind of evil encountered in Vietnam has little place in anyone's cosmology; it is unformed, chaotic, inchoate, and on a number of levels, unspeakable. . . . [T]he sense of absurd evil, then suggests a relationship to a realm that is incongruously bad and deadly, and the guilt derived from that sense, at least initially, has a parallel absence of structure, a chaotic nakedness. Unlike guilt that has a clear place

within a religious or cultural system, this guilt must be supplied with form and direction. The men provide such form and direction first by placing themselves in the categories of both victims (thrust into an atrocity-producing situation deadly to all) and executioners (who dealt with their situation as expected, by killing) and then by moving beyond and rejecting both of these roles.[33]

Lifton distinguishes between two forms of guilt—static and animating. Static guilt results in numbness or a deadened state, a self-lacerating guilt that allows one to keep killing oneself; but animating guilt moves a person toward connection and integrity. He notes that animating guilt "is inseparable from the idea of being responsible for one's actions."[34]

Taking responsibility for one's actions is complicated when there is truth to understanding oneself also as a victim. An army psychiatrist observed that almost every GI he encountered in Vietnam "acted like a victim."[35] The claim to victim status cuts both ways—soldiers did experience a victimization that was related to their role in a war whose purpose was highly contested and unclear. In claiming to be victims, however, they also gave up any empowering notions of autonomy and personal authority. Egendorf notes that holding oneself accountable for the killing one was involved in, whether or not it was legitimated by ideology, religion, or state, was an essential component of every veterans group's successful moves toward recovery.[36]

The ambivalence about responsibility and guilt often results in denials of having had a choice. This is a recurring theme in women's accounts of abortion, although there is almost always some choice involved in abortion. Although legalized abortion is portrayed as fundamental to women's choice and autonomy, numbers of women who have had abortions describe themselves as having had "no choice" in the matter.

Choice and responsibility are closely related moral notions, and claims of having had no choice suggest several different issues. Some women offer the claim as a despairing response to a situation that allowed no good choices. Others, faced with a decision they felt or feel ambivalent about, deny choice and responsibility in order to fend off guilt. One woman comments, "It was like I knew what I had to do and I was dead set on doing it, but I didn't want to. It was like I was being forced to do something, but that I didn't want to."[37]

Mary Zimmerman notes that only fifteen percent of the women interviewed in her study explicitly stated a belief that "the fetus was *not* a person or human life." Often they explicitly related abortion to killing. Thus, most felt in some way that they, who generally were not committed to lives of moral irresponsibility, were engaging in an immoral act. To resolve this tension between their action and their self-perceived character, they denied choice and responsibility.[38]

The pathos of choice and guilt comes through clearly in the following statement by an actress who uses this piece as part of a one woman show:

> I don't remember feeling bad. Well no, I do. I remember not letting myself feel bad. That'd be like giving in, you know? If I let myself feel bad, it might make those people who are so against it think that they're right, like I'd be proof, a chance for them to say: "you feel awful; therefore, you shouldn't have done it. You're wrong" . . . so you don't think about it, because if you think about it, you might feel bad or guilty and have to give up your choice. So no, I don't remember feeling bad. It was too scary for me to feel, because then maybe they would seem right? And they're not right.
>
> See, when you do something like that, you do it because for you it is your only choice. The sad thing is you really want to be able to feel bad about it without feeling wrong.[39]

Denying choice may be a rejection of responsibility, but it is also a way of coping with guilt and grief. Women who "know" that the life inside them is growing yet abort the pregnancy are forced into a position of having to interpret their action as choosing against life. Often their response is to deny choice.[40]

Denying choice sometimes takes the form of describing the fetus as aggressor and suggesting that the only choice was to act in self-defense, quite like accounts offered by soldiers who described unarmed civilians as aggressors. Rarely were persons' lives actually endangered by these "aggressors," yet such claims provide a moral structure within which to account for one's actions.[41]

Understandings of responsibility are sometimes reduced to the notion of making a choice and living with it. When the choice is defined as killing, the moral reasoning or its absence can be quite startling. Commenting on her late abortion, one woman stated,

> I struggled with it a whole lot. Finally, I just had to reconcile myself—that, yes, life is sacred, but the quality of life [of the mother and fetus] is also important, and has to be the determining thing in this particular case. . . . And I had to be able to say, "Yes, this is killing. There is no way around it, but I am willing to accept that, but I am willing to go ahead with it, and it's hard." I don't think I can explain it. I don't think I can really verbalize the justification.[42]

A fuller understanding of responsibility requires a framework of meaning, community, and conversation.

Issues of responsibility are made more complex when the larger society has a stake in not addressing the responsibility and guilt that individuals experience. One of the ironies of the interpretation of abortion as a woman's choice is that it allows the larger society to avoid addressing the social issues that help to structure such a dilemma and allows it to avoid the responsibility and guilt associated with choices that destroy life. Abortion constructed as a woman's choice offers a convenient social and economic solution whose moral implications are experienced only by the woman who makes the "choice." Sometimes, however, the woman experiences herself as having been betrayed, coerced into a choice she did not make or will not own. When the society denies the moral significance of the destruction of human life, it leaves the persons who were most immediately involved with no way to interpret their subsequent moral difficulties. By interpreting the problematic actions and responses of women and soldiers as individual aberrations, the larger society (or military) can avoid owning any responsibility.

Carrying a sense of guilt but finding no social context in which to process and resolve it allows no mechanism for persons who understand themselves as guilty to reenter the moral community. Their only penance is self-inflicted, and in some cases it knows no boundaries. Some persons who understand themselves as having violated covenantal community by killing then place themselves outside of community, its responsibilities, and its comforts.

Issues of responsibility are also made more complex by technological approaches that allow distance or disconnection between decisions, actions, and consequences. When technology hides the victims from view, as when warfare is conducted at a distance through air strikes, the task simply becomes a technical job that needs to be done well. In technological warfare "men are freed from the hatred, doubts, greed or rationalizations that killing usually entails."[43] Ground-war veterans struggle with guilt, but when warfare is at a distance, separating the act from the idea of killing,

> the avoidance of guilt is built into technology. To call forth guilt, and to achieve an animating relationship to it, requires at least an opportunity and sometimes a concerted effort to reconnect the act and the idea of killing.[44]

Without the sight of flesh and blood, killing can become clean and impersonal. Lifton reports that there was a correlation between the altitude of air strikes and the potential for guilt; the farther the soldier was from the target, the less guilt he experienced, and the more he focused on professional performance and skill.[45]

A highly technocratic approach to war or to abortion hides the covenantal character of human experience by removing the destruction of life from view and by excising individual persons from responsibility. A culture of nonresponsibility[46] is nurtured when technology separates act from consequence. Breakdowns in technology can result in unexpected personal confrontation with the brutal reality of death, and persons caught in these situations feel the responsibility and betrayal most acutely.

Often those most troubled by war and abortion are those for whom the experience has involved personal or face-to-face interaction in which the "other" is recognized as human. The soldiers who had the most difficult recovery from Vietnam were those engaged in direct combat. Women who aborted a fetus with whom they had developed connection, those who had other children, and those who were somehow exposed to the aborted fetus experienced the impact of the abortion in a highly conflicted way.

When responsibility, guilt, and meaning are excised from killing, any sense of tragedy and loss are denied. In some of the accounts of veterans one does find a "joy in killing," and in some of the women's accounts abortion is described as exhilarating and empowering. Any death has a tragic dimension; to protect the value of life whatever the problem it poses, one must also protect the horror of death. Recovery from abortion and war seems to require an acknowledgment of personal responsibility and an ability to articulate some minimal social critique. Lifton notes that as veterans recognized personal responsibility, they also found the freedom to criticize the war and to seek fundamental change in the society that had produced produced it.[47]

Conversation and Covenant

The definition of responsibility includes situating oneself and one's actions in an ongoing moral conversation within a universal community,[48] but veterans and the women who had abortions are frequently silent about their experiences. The community itself often indicates an unwillingness to hear their stories and effectively cuts off discussion by defining their action and moral ambivalence as not morally significant or as an evil from which there is essentially no recovery. Self-imposed silence allows the person to silence his or her own internal struggles. One veteran noted, "We would talk about R&R and basic training and Europe and buddies—but not about combat and not about killing."[49]

Breakdowns in conversation and in significant relationships characterize most of the troubled accounts of Vietnam veterans and the women who had abortions. One veteran, in recounting his experience of returning home, remembered,

> I did not feel like a movie hero or a baby killer. And I was deeply hurt by the horrible misconceptions of the situation in Vietnam by both supporters and opponents of the war. But I was still an inarticulate teenager, confused and exhausted by my years in combat. There was no way that I could express what I had seen and knew to be true. So for ten years I said nothing.[50]

Another veteran observed,

> When I returned to the United States . . . I did not meet any hostility. . . I did meet confusion, ambivalence, and—most of all—indifference. That was painful enough. . . .
>
> I know many Vietnam veterans. . . . None of them has ever told me that he was spat upon or called a baby killer. . . . Only that he was ignored and felt abandoned and betrayed.[51]

For many women, the process of abortion involves breaks in significant "conversations." Persons who are significant but not supportive of the decision are excluded. Conversation often ceases with mates who participate in the decision.[52] The woman herself stifles internal conversations. One woman, in describing her interaction with her doctor, said, "[W]e never talked about the fact that he was doing an abortion. He didn't and I didn't, though we both knew exactly what was happening."[53] Another woman who was very ambivalent about her decision to have an abortion reflected,

> My husband and I decided not to talk about it, and it worked. I regret the abortion even though I know it was right. It's hard. I admitted to my husband last night. I still have doubts. He told me not to think about it. He's sure it was a boy.
> Sometimes I blame him for having let me go through with it. I think he should have said we could have made it with another baby. We made a selfish decision.[54]

These breaks in conversation subtly etch persons out of the covenant community. Lifton writes,

> There is a bitter paradox around the whole issue of wrong-doing that is neither lost on these men nor fully resolved by them. Sent as intruders in an Asian revolution . . .they return as intruders in their own society, defiled by that war in the eyes of the very people who sent them as well as in their own. Images and feelings of guilt are generally associated with transgression—with having crossed boundaries that should not be crossed, gone beyond limits that should not be exceeded.[55]

Problems with love and commitment are common in the accounts of veterans and women who had abortions. Some veterans find themselves so alienated that they commit "relational suicide"—sabotaging relations with anyone to whom they grow close.[56] Lifton notes the extreme precariousness of all intimacy in Vietnam and the veterans' subsequent difficulty with intimate relationships.[57] Fearing the disillusionment that might follow the risk of intimacy, they avoid the risk.

Intimacy and trust are difficult because persons fear being betrayed again, fear another mistake or another loss. Intimacy can be seen as dangerous dependence, or as counterfeit. Some suggest, as one veteran does, "'I don't let nothing get to me.'. . . as if their lack of feeling is a great achievement."[58] Others recognize the loss, however, as is evident in the statement of a woman who anticipated how she would get through the abortion.

> Probably what I will do is I will cut off my feelings . . . . So that I don't feel anything at all, and I would probably just be very cold and go through it very coldly. The more you do that to yourself, the more difficult it becomes to love again or trust again or to feel again.[59]

If silence and breakdowns in relationships are so characteristic of the responses, then what is it that allows some men and women to process their experience, come to grips with responsibility and betrayal, and find forgiveness and meaning? If both the personal and corporate nature of responsibility and betrayal, interpretation and guilt, are not addressed, individuals cannot make sense of their own experience and cannot move beyond it. Dealing only with personal guilt and responsibility does not necessarily allow a person to address questions of meaning and the moral coherence of the universe. Movement in the direction of responsibility requires a reinterpretation of the past; it also requires a reinterpretation of the future. General understandings of the fitting response are not radically altered unless an understanding of one's ultimate context or community is also revised.[60]

These reinterpretations take place within a community, a safe place in which persons are given permission to speak by others who take their moral struggles seriously, who do not deny responsibility or recoil from some of the pain and horror. Some veterans find effective help in rap groups with other veterans.[61] In the context of being able to tell their stories, veterans are allowed to mourn and to restore broken community. Egendorf suggests that the troubled veteran needs the "freedom to be appropriately upset by what he has seen and done." After that, his reactions "subside quite naturally, and he experiences himself as 'more himself.'"[62] Women's groups made up of women who have had abortions also provide a safe context in which to reflect on the experience.

Socioethical analysis within a moral community can help persons sort out both individual responsibility and the responsibility of the larger community. Some veterans who have told their stories publicly have found it essential to expose the "atrocity-producing situation within which these acts were committed."[63] Reflections on the abortion decision that recognize that individual choices are made in a larger social and moral context have been helpful to some women who regret their decision to abort.

The ability to develop a morally satisfactory interpretation of the experience usually required some distance from the actual experience and a rootedness in a moral community.[64] Such communities help persons interpret the larger experience and their place within it. These communities are safe places insofar as their members recognize and address their own ever present capacity for irresponsibility and betrayal, and their own need for forgiveness. Communities that offer a point of orientation within an ordered but broken universe, that help persons to view life as a trust from God, that hold out to troubled men and women a call to responsibility and a promise of forgiveness, are communities that offer the hope of healing from deep wounds and deeper disillusionment.

Notes

[1] See Robert Jay Lifton, *Home from the War* (New York: Simon & Shuster, 1973), and Arthur Egendorf, *Healing from the War* (Boston: Houghton Mifflin, 1985).

[2] My approach has been informal, anecdotal, and dependent on interviews done by others. There exist, in published form, numerous collections of personal accounts from Vietnam veterans and from women who have had abortions. Not all of the accounts are troubled or conflicted; however, I have chosen to focus on the troubled ones because they so regularly raise issues about identity, betrayal, meaning, and responsibility.

My study and conclusions are preliminary and exploratory. A more systematic and comprehensive approach to interview questions and a more rigorous analysis of the accounts would be needed in order for these reflections to be generalizable. This study is an attempt to bring theoretical moral reflection to some of these stories.

Books used in this study of Vietnam veterans include: Arthur Egendorf, *Healing from the War* (Boston: Houghton Mifflin, 1985); Peter Goldman and Tony Fuller, *Charlie Company* (New York: Wm. Morrow & Co., 1983); Bob Greene, *Homecoming* (New York: G. P. Putnam's Sons, 1989); Robert Jay Lifton, *Home from the War* (New York: Simon & Shuster, 1973); Al Santoli, *Everything We Had* (New York: Random House, 1981); Al Santoli, *To Bear Any Burden* (New York: E. P. Dutton, 1985).

Books used as sources for women's accounts of their abortions include: Angela Bonavoglia, ed., *The Choices We Made* (New York: Random House, 1991); Linda Bird Francke, *The Ambivalence of Abortion* (New York: Random House, 1978); Carol Gilligan, *In A Different Voice* (Cambridge: Harvard University Press, 1982); Sumi Hoshiko, *Our Choices: Women's Personal Decisions about Abortion* (New York: Haworth Press, 1993); Pam Koerbel, *Does Anyone Else Feel Like I Do?* (New York: Doubleday & Co., 1990); Katrina Maxtone-Graham, *Pregnant By Mistake* (New York: Liveright, 1973); David C. Reardon, *Aborted Women, Silent No More* (Chicago: Loyola University Press, 1987); Mary K. Zimmerman, *Passage through Abortion* (New York: Praeger Publishers, 1977).

[3]Aaron David Gresson III, *The Dialectics of Betrayal: Sacrifice, Violation and the Oppressed* (Norwood, N. J.: Ablex Publishing Co., 1982), vii.

[4]Part of the complexity of this discussion arises because institutions are not monolithic. Institutions and the persons acting with authority in them can offer conflicting interpretations and make conflicting demands. While institutions can betray, they can also be essential in providing a moral context for healing. Some families, churches, lawmakers, etc., were deeply concerned about the moral implications of particular acts. In this paper, however, the focus is on the experience of betrayal.

[5]Robert Jay Lifton, *Home from the War*, 140, 117. The accounts from Vietnam veterans that are noted in this paper tend to come from soldiers who saw direct combat and who killed civilians.

[6]Frequently, there are particular persons within the institutions who act out the betrayal. However, it is their role within the institution, however, that gives them authority. Other betrayal experiences by institutions with moral authority come to mind: clergy sexual misconduct with parishioners that is often ignored by the larger church or denomination; incest; sexual harassment by teachers; etc.

[7]Pam Koerbel, *Does Anyone Else Feel Like I Do?*, 3.

[8]Ibid., 26.

[9]Lifton, 166.

[10]See Mary Otto, "Women Finding Spiritual Help Dealing With Abortions," *Lexington Herald-Leader* (April 28, 1994), p. A1; and Sarah Buttenwieser and Reva Levine, "Breaking Silences: A Post-Abortion Support Model," in *From Abortion to Reproductive Freedom: Transforming a Movement*, ed. Marlene Gerber Fried (Boston: South End Press, 1990), 122-23, 127.

[11]"Expressive individualism holds that each person has a unique core of feeling and intuition that should unfold or be expressed if individuality is to be realized. . . . [I]t shows affinities with the culture of psychotherapy" (*Habits of the Heart*, 333-34). See extended discussion of the significance of expressive individualism for contemporary American society in *Habits of the Heart*, by Robert N. Bellah, Richard Madsen, William M. Sullivan, Ann Swidler, and Steven M. Tipton. (New York: Harper & Row, 1985).

[12]E. Clinton Gardner, *Christocentrism in Christian Social Ethics* (Washington, D. C.: University Press of America, 1983), 213, 202.

[13]Ibid., 153-54.

[14]Ibid., 155.

[15]H. Richard Niebuhr, *The Responsible Self* (New York: Harper & Row, 1963), 87, 65, 18.

[16]Personal interview with the author, June 1994.

[17]Arthur Egendorf, *Healing from the War*, 47.

[18]See Niebuhr, 16.

[19]See Egendorf, 77, 88-89.

[20]Robert Jay Lifton, "Existential Evil," in *Sanctions for Evil*, ed. Nevitt Sanford and Craig Comstock (San Francisco: Jossey-Bass Inc., 1971), 47.

[21]Egendorf, 141.

[22]Lifton, *Home from the War*, 36.

[23]Ibid. Lifton makes use of the work of Murray Polner in *No Victory Parades: The Return of the Vietnam Veteran* (New York: Holt, Rinehart, and Winston, 1971).

[24]Egendorf, 158-59.

[25]Mary Ann Glendon, in her study of abortion in Western law, notes that United States law is singular in providing "no protection of unborn life at any stage of pregnancy." See Mary Ann Glendon, *Abortion and Divorce in Western Law* (Cambridge: Harvard University Press, 1987), 24.

[26]See Linda Bird Francke, *The Ambivalence of Abortion*, 3-7.

[27]Koerbel, 7.

[28]Chuck Dean, *The Book of Soldiers* (Mountlake Terrace, Wash.: Point Man International, 1991), 7.

[29]Francke, 96-100.

[30]See Lifton, *Home from the War*, 35.

[31]Niebuhr, 144-45.

[32]Lifton, *Home from the War*, 126.

[33]bid., 124.

[34]bid., 126, 127.

[35]Ibid., 336.

[36]Egendorf, 135.

[37]Mary K. Zimmerman, *Passage Through Abortion*, 193.

[38]Ibid., 194-95.

[39]Kathy Najimy, in *The Choices We Made*, 185.

[40]In Zimmerman's study, she found that "two thirds of the women made statements in which they portrayed themselves as having 'no choice' in the matter of abortion, being 'forced' to have the abortion." (p. 193)

[41]Certainly the perception of danger is present in these situations. Unexpected pregnancies do threaten women's life plans, and soldiers found

it difficult at times to distinguish between enemy soldiers and "sympathetic" civilians.

[42]Carol Gilligan, *In A Different Voice*, 58.

[43]Lifton, *Home from the War*, 347. Lifton is quoting from the work of Fred Branfman.

[44]Lifton, *Home from the War*, 347.

[45]Ibid., 347-49.

[46]Lifton, "Existential Evil," 39.

[47]Lifton, *Home from the War*, 327, 287.

[48]Niebuhr, 64, 89.

[49]Bob Greene, *Homecoming*, 227.

[50]Al Santoli, *To Bear Any Burden*, xviii.

[51]Greene, 140.

[52]Linda Bird Francke, *The Ambivalence of Abortion*, 162, 170, 202.

[53]Kristin Luker, *Abortion and the Politics of Motherhood* (Berkeley, Calif.: University of California Press, 1984), 103.

[54]Francke, 100.

[55]Lifton, *Home from the War*, 100-101.

[56]Chuck Dean, *The Book of Soldiers*, 59.

[57]Lifton, *Home from the War*, 79.

[58]Egendorf, 70.

[59]Gilligan, 90.

[60]Niebuhr, 104-5.

[61]See discussions in Lifton, *Home from the War*, 303, and Egendorf, 115, 118.

[62]Egendorf, 69.

[63]Lifton, *Home from the War*, 147.

[64]Ibid., 401.

Chapter 5

A Womanist Model of Responsibility: The Moral Agency of Victoria Way DeLee

Rosetta E. Ross

From the period of slavery in the United States through modern times, black religious women's activism has been guided by a perspective that views duty to God and calling by God as the origin of their work. Sojourner Truth, for example, described herself as called by God to speak against slavery.[1] After emancipation, many educated black women felt "a strong conviction of duty" to go South to teach newly freed persons.[2] Around the turn of the century, the National Baptist Convention's Women's Convention felt it was their duty to link social generation, racial advancement, and spiritual regeneration.[3] Under the leadership of Nannie Helen Burroughs, these Baptist women worked well into the early twentieth century, seeking to live their response to God through work for the community of African Americans.[4]

Because their everyday circumstances included conventional and institutional repression of black people, these women's ordinary activities, which otherwise may have developed as easy, mundane tasks, became hard work. Relying on and responding to what they understood as God's provisions in their lives, the women demonstrated fidelity by routinely working hard and taking risks as they sought to change repressive traditions, institutions, and social conventions that hampered the well-being of African Americans. Responding to God through routinely working hard has been the historic form of black religious women's activism.

In South Carolina, near the beginning of the United States civil rights movement, Victoria Way DeLee, another black woman activist, responded to what she felt was God calling her to "help those who can't help themselves."[5] DeLee participated in voter registration campaigns, school desegregation efforts, and an array of other activities, as she tried to improve life for black people in Dorchester County, South Carolina. The moral practices of Victoria DeLee reflect a type of responsibility evident in the tradition of religious black women activists. DeLee, like the others, regularly worked hard in the face of repression while she responded to needs in her community as a means of responding to God. This essay examines Victoria DeLee's activities as a part of the moral tradition of resisting, survival, and sustaining practices by religious black women activists. The discussion begins by exploring the circumstances of subjugation that DeLee faced and her early experiences of repression within this context. Coupled with DeLee's religious upbringing and opportunities for public activism, these experiences shaped her response to local class and racial oppression. After discussing interaction of these factors, the essay explores how DeLee's understanding of Christian duty influenced her to work with voter registration and school desegregation. The final section of the essay explores DeLee's activity as expressing moral responsibility.

Everyday Circumstances of Racial Oppression.

Victoria DeLee registered to vote in 1947. With this, she participated in the arduous work of breaking down barriers to black social and political participation, especially the state-sanctioned practices of black disfranchisement, which had been the norm in South Carolina since the first formal statute restricting voting to "every white man (and no other)" in 1716.[6] During the period when DeLee registered to vote, despite full suffrage in the United States generally, voting rights for African Americans still were obstructed, particularly in the South, by the racist, classist, and sexist perspective demonstrated in the statute cited above, as well as by repressive post-Civil War ideologies, conventions, and legislation. Barriers to black enfranchisement and full political participation were initiated with Reconstruction in South Carolina and throughout the South. By the turn of the century, these barriers had been consolidated. The legacy of their impediment to black political participation continues through some contemporary court battles over state and local redistricting.

After the Civil War, South Carolina's provisional governor Benjamin Franklin Perry, convened an 1865 Reconstruction Constitutional

Convention that "adopted laws limiting voting and office holding to free white men at least twenty-one years of age." During that same year the state legislature adopted "an elaborate Black Code," which relegated African Americans to a status similar to that during slavery. The 1866 Voting Rights Act, one means by which Congress responded to such politically regressive action in South Carolina and across the South, did not long abate the building of such barriers. By 1868 the Ku Klux Klan became active across the state, and political violence for the purpose of intimidation was common.[7] This backlash against Reconstruction gains established the political climate that paved the way for election of "Pitchfork" Ben Tillman as governor in 1890.

Tillman entered office with an agenda to secure white supremacy. He stated this pledge in his inaugural address saying, "The whites have absolute control of the government, and we intend at any hazard to retain it."[8] Under Tillman's administration, the state legislature abolished election of local government officials, replacing election with gubernatorial or legislative appointments. The legislature also devised a new state constitution requiring a poll tax, a literacy test, and property ownership for voter registration. Finally, under Tillman the state's legislature instituted other laws specifically fashioned to disfranchise African Americans.[9]

When the United States Supreme Court struck down the all-white primary in Texas in 1944, South Carolina Governor Olin D. Johnson called a special session of the state's legislature to enact statutes that would ensure continued disfranchisement of African Americans.[10] Along with this renewed political exclusion, lynchings and other mob violence against African Americans were exacerbated.[11] Such severe conventional and legalized repression in South Carolina continued well into the 1950s and included repressive actions and laws against the National Association for the Advancement of Colored People (NAACP), which, from 1918 to 1956, was the primary organizational means through which African Americans addressed Southern repression.

In South Carolina this anti-NAACP tactic was seen in 1956 legislation that made "unlawful the employment by the state, school district or any county or municipality . . . any member of the National Association for the Advancement of Colored People, and to provide penalties for violations."[12] Further, during the same year the South Carolina legislature appointed a committee to investigate NAACP activity at historically black South Carolina State College.[13] During its next session, the legislature passed a bill requiring each organized NAACP chapter to file with the Secretary of State "a list showing the names and addresses of all its members."[14] The legislature also adopted acts sponsored by various county delegations, that further promoted the state's anti-NAACP provisions.[15] These legislative actions against the

NAACP were complemented by informal conventions consistently practiced in local areas. In 1957, for example, the South Carolina Council on Human relations reported that white citizens used economic pressure in Orangeburg and Clarendon[16] counties to discourage NAACP participation.[17] In addition to general southern repression, South Carolina's anti-NAACP sentiment resulted from the NAACP's judicial challenges to conventional and legal restraints in the state. In 1946, for example, Federal District Court Judge J. Waties Waring ruled, in two separate cases brought by the NAACP, that the state's white primary was unconstitutional.

The year after Waring's ruling, the Reverend R. B. Adams, an NAACP member and the young pastor of St. John Baptist Church in Ridgeville, urged members of his congregation to try to register to vote. One Sunday that year, Victoria and S. B. DeLee decided to follow Adams' recommendation, and the following Monday traveled by train to the county seat in St. George where Victoria registered. Although she was responding to Adams' prompting, Victoria DeLee's decision to register to vote also arose from her seeing in enfranchisement a possibility for changing local practices of repression that had long angered her. This decision to change the way things were was a determination DeLee made for herself as a child.

Social and Moral Influences in DeLee's Early Life.

Victoria Way was born April 8, 1925, to Essie Way in the town of Ridgeville, Dorchester County, South Carolina.[18] As a child Victoria, two sisters, a male cousin, her mother, and grandmother Lucretia, were tenants of a local white farmer. Essie worked as a maid for her landlord and other local white households to support the family. Lucretia Way reared the children, worked as a field hand, and further supplemented family income by taking in laundry.[19] Victoria was greatly affected by seeing her mother and grandmother labor relentlessly for as little as 25 cents per day. Remembering those times later, she said, "Well, really, we were treated like slaves,[20] because when the white people came in and said that you had to go to work, you had to work whether you wanted to or not. . . . [I]t was in my mind from a little girl when my grandmomma and them were being treated like that, I used to say 'well, one day I'm gonna fix it.'"[21]

In addition to the circumstances of her mother and grandmother, the customary treatment of African Americans in Dorchester County during this time had a profound influence on Victoria. She says, "We would overhear things. . . . They used to, back there in them days lynch people. They'd hang 'em. If a black person did something, they would take them in the woods and hang 'em."[22] What Victoria Way over-heard about lynchings was particularly graphic. She recounts a time when one white landowner, Bub Cummings, rode an ox by her grandmother's house specifically to tell Lucretia of his opportunity to have the first shot at a black man, a Mr. Fogle, who was to be killed in the nearby town of Dorchester for allegedly whistling at a white woman. "I can see it as if it was yesterday," DeLee says.[23]

> We were, my grandmomma had this beautiful flower yard in the front of her house, you know. And she had all these rose bushes and stuff. And we were out there in the rose bushes. I can remember that it was some-time in the year, that she was in, we was in the flower yard. And he call out to my grandmomma. And he say, "Mom Cretia." 'Cause they would call her Mom Cretia or Aunt Cretia. It was Mom Cretia. And, uh, he tell her, "Come here." He say, "I'm in a hurry. I got to go 'cause they done promise me that if I git there they gonna give me the first shot at that niggah. And I'm going to git the first shot!" He was go be in the group of the first people to shoot.

After the execution, she says, Cummings returned to intimidate her grandmother further by recounting the details of the event:

> And all she could do was just sit there and listen. She wasn't allowed to say nothing back to him. And when he was gone, she just cried, and she just prayed and was crying how awful it was. And they said they [castrated him] and stuffed them in his mouth while they shoot him. And they shoot him piece by piece. . . . That thing stuck in my mind. Here this man being killed, and I overheard. He didn't care. He talked right in front of us. "If you do so and so, we'll have you killed, you niggers this and that." That's all they would call us back there was niggers, you know, they didn't try to butter it up at all.[24]

Perhaps as significant as the oppression and violence Victoria saw meted out against her mother, grandmother, and other local African Americans was her personal encounter with the same repression and violence.

While she felt she must be an adult before she could take significant actions, Victoria began expressing dissatisfaction with her predicament as a child. When children in the Way family were old enough to work, they went to the fields with Lucretia. However, whenever possible, Victoria would rebel against having to do so at the bidding of whites. "[W]henever we would work in the field," DeLee says, "my grand-momma them tell us what to do. Soon as her back would turn, I'd go contrary to it, and let the white man see that I could, I wasn't gonna be doing it the way he wanted it." Seeking to assert her own will in this way caused another childhood event that left an indelible impression on her mind. DeLee says,

> One particular time, this white man he told me that I was nabbing the cotton, leaving it back there, and I said, "I didn't." And he said, "Yes you is." And he told my grandmomma what I was doing, and he hauled off and slapped me out. That man knocked me in my head 'til I fell out. . . . And my grandmomma had to beat me, had to beat me until this man was satisfied. . . . He said, "That's enough. That's enough." I'll never forget it.[25]

Seeking to protect Victoria from such violence through attempts to inculcate what Katie Cannon calls "functional prudence," Lucretia Way sought to curb Victoria's strong will in order to save her life.[26] Reflecting on the event, DeLee says, "My grandmomma just, had to just beat me, 'cause she know if not he could, would have killed me." At the time of this incident, however, DeLee was not able to accept or understand her grandmother's actions. "She told me afterwards, when we come home," DeLee says, "but I don't think right then I had ever forgiven her for beatin' me for that white man, 'cause I felt like she didn't had to do it. And I told her so. I said, 'I don't see where you had to beat me to satisfy him. I wouldn't beat one of my children to satisfy him.' She say, 'But you don't know. If I didn't, he would have killed you.'"[27]

Such oppressive circumstances and Victoria's militant perspective led to her early marriage, so that she could begin to "get what I wanted done." Living with her protective grandmother, DeLee felt doubly repressed. In addition to racial repression, DeLee says, "my grandmomma was so strict on me. She beat me all the time, and try to keep me straight." By the time she was fourteen, Victoria had developed a plan to run away from her grandmother's defensive severity in order to strike out violently against whites. "[White] people used to do a lot of fox hunting and coon hunting," she says, "and I was hoping when they ganged up together hunting foxes, somehow or another I would be able to kill a good many of them. That was my plan."[28] Fortunately, this plan was thwarted by Victoria's best friend who convinced her that getting married would provide freedom from her grandmother. Victoria thought this was a good idea, and at age fifteen, on 21 December 1940, she married her suitor, S. B. DeLee.[29] Once she entered civil rights activity, DeLee experienced a refocusing of her energy away from violent retaliation back toward her original goal "to fix it" for her people some day.

Religious Influences in DeLee's Early Life.

At Lucretia's insistence, regular church participation became a part of
Victoria's early life. Whenever Lucretia went to Bethel Methodist
Church, she took her four grandchildren with her. "[M]y grandmomma
was a church-goer," DeLee recalls.[30] Perhaps naming the origin of her
later attraction to the House of God holiness denomination, of her current church, DeLee also says her grandmother practiced holiness.
"[W]hen I was raised in the Methodist church, it was clean," she says.
"Really and truly my, my grandmomma and those, they was sanctified
people. They was so sanctified."[31] Regular family prayer also was a
part of DeLee's childhood since Lucretia prayed every evening.
However, Victoria struggled with and questioned the efficacy of entreat-
ing God for help. DeLee says:

> That's when I learned to pray. My grandmomma always taught me how
> to pray, but when— I didn't believe in God all the time. 'Cause, you
> see my grandmomma say God would fix it. He knowed how. 'N' she
> would be just prayin' and cryin' all in the night. 'N' then I went to
> wonderin' what kind of God is that? If he go fix it, why would He let
> the people do what they was doing to her? Whey she had to work so
> hard? Why she work for 25 cents a day? Why we had to go out there
> and bring a bag of those white people old clothes and stuff home and
> things like that? And, then, she think God would, she jus' believe in
> God. I didn't believe in Him. And she would have me down on my
> knees, she'd be prayin' in the night, teachin' me the Our Father prayer,
> you know. I'd quote the Our Father prayer with her. And then after we
> done say the Our Father prayer, then she would pray. Oh, my Lord, and
> my grandmomma just cry and pray. And I'd be down there jus' cussin'
> away in my mind. I was sayin', "Don't you worry, I'll fix it for my
> grandmomma. I'm gon' fix it."[32]

By the time she was a pre-teen, Victoria became attracted to the active
youth usher board at nearby St. John Baptist Church, which took trips
for singing programs in local towns. Although DeLee says she attended
church as a child only because her grandmother compelled her, she continued regularly attending church after her marriage and throughout her
life. S. B. DeLee also was a regular church member, and, in fact, the
couple met at St. John Baptist Church.[33]

DeLee did not immediately let go her idea of revenge in favor of social
and political action; however, changes dawned in her life that disposed
her to refocus her energy. Important among these changes were the birth
of her first child, Sonny B. DeLee, in 1942 and a compelling sermon
that DeLee heard when Sonny was a baby. Recalling her excitement
about their son, DeLee says:

[O]oh when that baby born, I had love that baby! You know how, your first baby, ooh. And I went to church that Sunday with my first new baby. And the preacher preached a sermon. I'll never forget that. . . . I think it was all for me. And he was saying, "You could git by, but you wouldn't git away." . . . And I listen at that message. And every time I look at that baby. . . . And he said that whatever them white people do to you . . . God had they number, and He right way they live. And if they didn't git it, they children children children would git it. . . . and then he brought out that whatever *we* do, we might git by, but our children would reap what we sow. . . . And he just went on. And every time I looked at that baby, and looked up, and that preacher jus' went on. And ooh, my God, for the first time I see myself. And I say, "Oh, Lord, way should I turn?" 'Cause I already did some things [to whites]. And I still had . . . planned on killin' 'em. I meant to go about and kill some white people just like they had kill all them black people. . . . and when that preacher preached that sermon that Sunday, I got converted to myself right in that church, right there. . . . And I say, "Ooh, there is another way. Uh huh, I can't do that, 'cause my baby gonna reap it. And I love my baby."[34]

Later that day, DeLee walked approximately three miles to Lucretia Way's home to seek her counsel. She says, "I walk and went to my grandmomma house that evenin' and tote that baby. And I told her, and I went and start tellin' her, and I went to cryin'."[35] Lucretia advised DeLee to seek forgiveness:

I went to my grandmomma, and she said that before God would convert my soul I would have to love the white people. She said, "You got to *mean* it." And, sure enough, the Lord answered my prayer and I started to love white folks. But I stand up all right. I let 'em know that they wasn't goin' to run over me.[36]

The DeLees continued to participate as members of St. John Baptist Church for at least thirteen years after their marriage. During the mid-1950s, however, "[t]hey had a big mixed-up in the church,"[37] and the DeLees left. When the family left St. John they attended Surprise Baptist Church for one year in the nearby town of Dorchester, where some of S. B.'s relatives also were members. During the course of their association with Surprise Church, Bishop James Ravenel, of the House of God Church (the Church of the Living God, the Pillar and Ground of the Truth, Inc.),[38] a "sanctified denomination," began a radio ministry in Ridgeville. His messages particularly appealed to the DeLees because he emphasized "holiness." DeLee says, like others attracted to Ravenel's message:

we just started one Sunday, everybody was going out to hear him. After he started revival, we went out there to go hear him. It was going on a good while. And we went out there, and he went to teaching in the scriptures. And he went to, and we went to reading, and we, then our eyes come open, then about holiness. And that you had to be holy.[39]

During one evening of this revival, DeLee asserts, "I got saved that night, and I was the happiest woman." The couple continued to attend the revival meetings and eventually decided to become a part of the ministry Ravenel started in their town. Consequently, Victoria and S. B. DeLee were founding members of the House of God congregation at Ridgeville.

Bishop Ravenel run [the revival] for seven weeks. . . . And then, we got busy. We just had meeting right there. So we decided to, that we was going to build a church. . . . We built, first, you know, we built it, I call it a little small sanctified church. 'Cause back yonder all sanctified churches used to be, you could pinpoint them out amongst all the rest, because it was just something put together. But, and then after years, we add on. And then a few years back ago, we tore the church down and built a real church. Now we really got a nice church up there now. But, that's how we got with the holiness. And that, as I say, when we find out it was right, we receive the baptism of the Holy Ghost, and then we built this church.[40]

Perhaps of great significance to the intensity with which DeLee carried out her activism was the combination of her natural militancy with the spiritual independence and compulsion she began to embrace after she entered the House of God holiness denomination.[41] Both of these were necessary to undergird her consistently expressing dissent against oppressive local laws and conventions.

DeLee's Early Community Activism.

DeLee entered the public arena as a local activist, seeking to make changes in conditions for people of her immediate community. As a community activist, Victoria DeLee sought to improve the welfare of African Americans or to maintain traditions integral to their survival. As early as 1948, for example, she expressed concern about the education of community children through her leading role in a protest against the county school board to prevent firing a teacher whom DeLee valued as someone who cared for "all the children."

JohnEtta Grant began her teaching career at Clay Hill Elementary School in Ridgeville. Grant, a native of Charleston, owned a car and commuted twenty-six miles from Charleston to Ridgeville to teach school. That Grant did not board in the town where she taught was unusual. It was even more unusual when other teachers from Charleston who had been boarding decided to commute with Grant. After this turn of events, Josephine Bannister, the town resident with whom teachers traditionally boarded, contacted local authorities who told Grant that she must move into the county or lose her job. Upon learning of this, DeLee organized parents who together traveled by train to the school board meeting in St. George.[42] DeLee recalls:

> [T]he trustee board went to try to fire one of our teachers because [she] wouldn't board out– Every teacher had come into Dorchester County then, we had the little schools out here, they would make them, they had to board in this area where they teach school at. And so this woman . . . she had a car and she would drive from Charleston here. And . . . Mrs. Banister didn't like it because the woman wouldn't board with Mrs. Banister. See she wasn't gon' board with nobody. That's why [she] bought a car. . . . her name was Miss . . . Johnetta Grant. Johnetta Grant was that black teacher. And, boy, she was one to stand up. She was the teacher that first started to teaching all my children. . . . So they went to fire this teacher. And I got all the parents to come together, and we had a meeting one night. And we baffled that school board. And that's the first time blacks ever stand up in this area to white people. And we got on that school board, and then they couldn't fire the woman. So that was the first thing that really, to me we accomplished.[43]

Perhaps equally significant as this protest is DeLee's memory of it as the first time African Americans of the area successfully challenged whites. Experiencing the success of African Americans working together in this instance surely influenced and helped sustain in DeLee the possibility of cooperative community activity during later years of her work. She saw the event as a success of the community. For her, as she says, it was the first thing that "*we* accomplished."

1. Voter Registration. Victoria DeLee's entrance into the civil rights movement resulted in large part from her desire to vent the anger she felt about racial repression. Although her faith challenged DeLee to reconsider the meaning of resistance, she also had a continuing desire "to fix" the oppressive circumstances under which African Americans lived. In view of her early rejection of the idea that God would make a real difference in her grandmother's life, it is perhaps ironic that after discarding plans for violent reprisals against whites, DeLee encountered a powerful and creative outlet for channeling her energy in a religious context through preaching about voter registration in a rural black church.

DeLee began civil rights work in 1947 at age twenty-two, after she obtained her own voter registration certificate. The pastor of St. John Baptist Church, DeLee says, preached about civil rights and urged his congregation to attempt registering to vote. When Rev. R. B. Adams's promptings caught DeLee's attention, she and her husband traveled fifteen miles by train to St. George, the Dorchester County Seat, where registration was held. DeLee recalls that when they arrived there was a room full of blacks who "were given permission to register." An attendant was moving the process along by calling out "Next!" whenever another person was allowed to go to the inner office for registration. The DeLees moved into the room and sat with the crowd. When the attendant said "next," Victoria rose to her feet. Upon seeing her rise, the person who should have been next sat down again because he thought he was out of turn. DeLee says,

> But I got on up. I went like I was next. When I went in there to register, he said, "Who brought you?" I said, "I brought myself." I had on a black overcoat because I was pregnant with Vicky. I'll never forget. I had both of my hands in my pockets.

Because she had come without "permission", the registration agent told DeLee that he could not register her. She insisted that he would, and the two argued back and forth. Finally, standing in front of the door and keeping one hand in her pocket as if she had a weapon, DeLee told the registrar that he would not leave the room if she were not given her "civil rights." The agent finally complied, telling DeLee not to let others know of her success; however, DeLee replied that she would not consent to such a thing, and upon leaving the room she "went right on out there and went to talking right loud to everybody" about the registration.[44]

Because of how empowered she felt as a result of her own success, voter registration immediately became for DeLee the major vehicle by which she sought to make a difference. "I'll never forget that day!" she says. "That was a good feeling day. I felt so good that I got, made that man registered me!"[45] She was so encouraged and enthused by her own success that she became tenacious in efforts to register other persons. She began voter registration activity at once. "Then I went out, and I start talking to people," she recalls. "I start tellin' 'em 'bout my registration certificate. I come back to the church, and I get up in the church and tell the preacher how I get my registration certificate. And the preacher went to telling everybody how they must do like I done."[46]

DeLee's remembering her pastor, R. B. Adams, telling others to follow her example indicates the importance of this acknowledgement.

Occurring so early in her career and life, it must have affirmed DeLee's developing sense of her self. Apparently Adams felt it was significant to encourage DeLee's activity. Noting DeLee's leadership, he further supported her work by introducing DeLee to South Carolina NAACP Field Secretary, the late I. DeQuincey Newman. Newman, who oversaw the NAACP's state registration drive, particularly promoted DeLee's activities. "So when I started working," DeLee says, "then they start to working with me. Oh, I had a lot of help from the outside, you know, to help me work with this."[47] In addition to persuading others to seek registration, DeLee transported persons to registration sites (and to polls), organized applicants for notaries public, and trained and organized other voter registration workers.

As DeLee continued to register black voters, she encountered frequent attempts to obstruct her. These attempts included various forms of harassment and sometimes use of physical force. Furthermore, presumably in reaction to DeLee's efforts through the NAACP, in 1956 the White Citizens' Council meeting at Ridgeville Elementary School asked South Carolina Governor George B. Timmerman, Jr., to stop NAACP activity in the state. More than two hundred persons attended this meeting.[48] During the next two years the state legislature and county legislative delegations enacted the restrictive statutes that significantly inhibited NAACP work.

Although DeLee continued to lead voter registration, throughout the decade state and local statutes and conventions severely limited success. At one point DeLee became so frustrated with obstacles to black voter registration that "she took two carloads of twenty people" to the Justice Department in Washington to seek assistance of the Federal Government. This trip occurred as an improvisation, since DeLee felt she had exhausted all other possibilities. She told one reporter:

> We had just enough money to buy gas and have one hamburger and a drink on the way there and back. I came to Washington, and brother, did I raise said(sic). I wanted them to send some federal men down to help register voters.
>
> They said, "go home Mrs. DeLee and we'll do something"; and I said "the only way I'll understand is if you send someone." They didn't come for a week so I went back myself and went from door to door in the Justice Department and told them if they didn't send someone I'd bring everybody up there.[49]

The Justice Department responded by sending in federal personnel to oversee voter registration activity of three South Carolina counties, including Dorchester, in which persons complained about opposition to black registration. Justice Department activity in the state caused reaction at the highest levels. Responding to the probes in South Carolina,

Governor Ernest Hollings (now United States Senator for South Carolina) sought to protect "the state's sovereignty and [said] that the 'harassment' that the people of Clarendon, Dorchester and Williamsburg counties have been put through by the FBI is going to stop."[50]

As DeLee persevered against repressive practice opposing her work, when needed, she improvised in other ways to achieve success. In 1960, for instance, responding to repression of the NAACP, DeLee founded the Dorchester Voters' League, a means by which she continued coordination of voter registration and other county civil rights activities. After years of persistence, there emerged meaningful differences in black voter registration statistics. By 1958, 412 African Americans of Dorchester County were registered to vote. This was only 7.2 percent of the county's total registered voters.[51] In 1968, however, 4,556 African Americans were registered. This represented an increase to 33.5 percent of the total county voters.[52]

2. School Desegregation. As DeLee continued to register voters she encountered varieties of civil rights activity in other places, including school desegregation efforts. DeLee initiated this work in Dorchester County. The major school desegregation activity in South Carolina began with the Clarendon County suit, one among the several decided in the 1954 United States Supreme Court ruling in *Brown v. Board of Education.* Initially filed in Federal District Court on 16 May 1950, the Clarendon County case primarily fought to improve the education provided for black children. The suit originated with an attempt to secure bus transportation for black students, a service provided for white students. Later, the case grew into an effort to improve education for blacks, generally. Because they were

> [d]istressed by the evident inferiority of the facilities provided for their children, Negro parents filed a petition with the county board of education in November, 1949, asking for equalization of educational opportunities. . . . As it became increasingly evident that no steps were being taken by the authorities to bring the Negro schools up to the standard of those maintained for white children, the decision was reached to make a frontal attack upon the segregated schools.[53]

Even though the Clarendon case was among those decided in the Brown decision, South Carolina continued to resist integration, and it was at least fifteen years later before any semblance of full desegregation occurred across the state.

The year following the Supreme Court's decision in *Brown v. Board of Education,* Governor George Bell Timmerman declared that the citizens of South Carolina were "determined to resist integration" of the races in the public schools: "There shall be no compulsory racial mixing in our state."[54] Furthermore, South Carolina's delegation to the 1955 White House Conference on Education presented a report from the state saying "public schools will not be operated in South Carolina on a racially integrated basis." The report reasoned that integration would disrupt the state's past progress in education.[55] In further contradiction of the Brown decision, the state's legislature appointed a special unit, the State School Committee of Segregation, headed by State Senator L. Marion Gresette, to ensure the continuation of segregation. By 1960, the Committee of Segregation recommended, and the legislature approved, a statute "repealing specific requirements for segregation in South Carolina." The strategy of this legislation was to eliminate "a major point on which school integration suits [had] been brought into Federal Court."[56]

Over the next five years, state officials took various legislative actions to circumvent desegregation. This occurred even though the state was under fire to have each of its 108 school districts submit integration plans to the United States Office of Education. By the 1965 school year, only thirty-eight districts had approved compliance plans, although 104 districts had submitted plans for approval. Dorchester County Districts One and Three were among four districts that had not filed any compliance plans by 1965. Moreover, Dorchester County Districts One and Three turned away thirteen parents who took their children for the opening day of school that year.[57]

In 1964 the DeLees initiated desegregation activities in Dorchester District Three when they attempted to enroll two of their children at Ridgeville Elementary School. Other parents later joined the DeLees. However, school district officials repeatedly resisted these efforts by disqualifying some black students from eligibility to attend the white schools or by allowing only a few students to be received at any given time. By March 1966, Dorchester County Three submitted an acceptable voluntary desegregation plan.[58] Dorchester's plan, like that of most other districts in the state, was called freedom of choice. Placing the burden of desegregation on the black community, the freedom of choice plan provided opportunities for parents to choose which schools in the district their children would attend. The effect of freedom of choice was to dilute the possibility of desegregation. Under the burden of full responsibility for initiating and carrying through desegregation efforts, black parents and children were placed between the nation's requirement and local segregationist sentiment, the latter of which caused economic and physical retaliation for desegregation activity. Freedom of choice began for Dorchester County District Three in Spring, 1966. Fearing severe reprisals, most black parents and children in Dorchester

County (and in other counties across the state) took the physically, financially, and emotionally safer route of leaving things as they were.

In March, 1966, DeLee, in behalf of her sons Van and Elijah, led the list of plaintiffs in a suit seeking to completely desegregate the district's schools.[59] The effort to desegregate Dorchester's schools took more than five years of court battles, strategizing, and protesting. While none of DeLee's activity was met with enthusiasm from white county residents, desegregation work proved to be extremely provocative to local whites.[60] It was during this period that the DeLee home was most frequently shot into and subsequently completely destroyed by fire. DeLee says, when

> we went to integrate the schools, that's when the whites really started trying to kill us, [even though] they were trying to kill me for the longest. Before that house burned down, it would look like a polka dot dress where the bullet holes from where they would shoot in the house. . . . One night I was sitting in the chair, and I was rocking the baby. When I rocked back like that, the bullet went right through by my face and went in the wall . . . and just missed me. . . . And the sheriff couldn't find nobody, couldn't catch nobody.[61]

In addition to initiating the court action, DeLee continued to lead demonstrations, encourage other parents to reject segregation, and frequently sought to meet with district superintendents and the school board.[62] She also engaged those organizations that could assist her work. After filing suit in behalf of her sons in March, DeLee attended the 2 April Conference on Education Desegregation sponsored by the South Carolina Advisory Committee to the United States Civil Rights Commission. This conference encouraged desegregation activists and suggested strategies for achieving school desegregation.[63]

As DeLee continued to resist school segregation, the scope of her activity expanded to include Native Americans. Encouraged by DeLee, Dorchester County Native American parents joined the desegregation activity.[64] Until that time Native American children attended a third county school system geographically located within District Three. While the district's 1966 approved desegregation plan asserted freedom of choice, when Native American parents sought to exercise choice, "those choices were uniformly denied[,] even though the choices of black children were uniformly granted."[65] When officials refused Native American enrollment by freedom of choice, DeLee organized "demonstrations against [their] having to attend [the] inadequate school." Following several days of protests, the district superintendent agreed to admit fifteen Native American children "on the basis that that number would not overcrowd the white school."[66]

The District Court's response to this action demonstrates corroboration of local and state agencies in maintaining racial repression. When the group sought an order requiring the district to admit all Native American children who chose to enter the white schools, presiding judge Robert Hemphill "announced that he had 'heard' that there had been some demonstrations and that he wanted to make it clear that 'there will be peace in the valley.' He stated several times his willingness to cite these people in contempt and to have a marshal sent down to arrest them."[67] Hemphill enjoined further demonstrations and issued an order upholding the superintendent's decision to admit only fifteen children.

Having visited his courtroom numerous times during the integration activity, DeLee apparently angered Hemphill through her persistent work. When she went with Native American parents to enroll children in Ridgeville Elementary School, marshals arrested her for disobeying the demonstration injunction. Judge Hemphill placed DeLee under a $10,000 bond and ordered her to show why she should not be held in contempt of court. DeLee and others continued desegregation work, however, and because it progressed so slowly they also took their demonstrations beyond the state.

By 1969, only 10 percent of black students attended white schools, and no white students attended black schools in District Three.[68] That year the United States Department of Health, Education, and Welfare set the fall as the deadline for full school desegregation. At the same time, news reports from the White House said school desegregation guidelines would be relaxed to give schools with special problems additional time.[69] Responding to these reports, South Carolina and Mississippi field workers for the American Friends Service Committee organized a multistate grassroots bus caravan to Washington to protest relaxation plans. Dissatisfied with desegregation progress in Dorchester County, DeLee joined the caravan.[70] As a participant in this protest, she expressed her disappointment with the federal government's slow down first to Jerris Leonard, Assistant Attorney General for Civil Rights, and later to Attorney General John Mitchell. The passionate posture through which DeLee presented herself to Mitchell was captured in a photograph that presented the protest as a reminder to the nation of the problems continuing in the South.[71] When she returned home, DeLee encountered threatening letters, phone calls, and other harassment as a result of her participation.[72] In spite of consistent attempts by DeLee and others, schools in Dorchester County District 3 were not completely desegregated until 1971.

Conclusion.

Seeing their responsibility to the community as religious responsibility, the women routinely presume divine intervention in support of their mundane practice. On this basis, their practice has persisted in spite of social oppression, which, in many instances, has precluded black women's being in charge of their lives and their bodies. When social barriers to the practice of moral responsibility arise, the women determine and execute methods to overcome the barriers.[73] This responsibility expresses a "take charge" attitude in the face of conventional obstacles to black community prosperity. Using their bodies and minds to fulfill this responsibility, these women routinely determine ways of transforming everyday life.

In the case of black religious women social activists, whether in resistance, survival, or sustaining work, dispositions that cause their practices reflect responses to what they conceive as duty to or calling by God. These women act out of their relationship with God, whom they understand as faithful to them, and, therefore, with them in all circumstances. They respond to God's faithfulness by practicing fidelity to God through consistent efforts to preserve their community while ultimately striving for a good society. This was no less true in the case of Victoria DeLee who says she persisted because she saw "God in front leadin' all of us" in the work.[74] The tradition of work by black religious women activists reflects this perspective of fidelity that governed DeLee's life as she worked in Dorchester County and the state of South Carolina.

Notes

[1] Sterling, Dorothy, *We Are Your Sisters: Black Women in the Nineteenth Century* (New York: Norton, 1984), 151.

[2] Ibid., 265.

[3] Evelyn Brooks Higginbotham, *Righteous Discontent: The Women's Movement in the Black Baptist Church, 1880-1920* (Cambridge: Harvard, 1993), 124.

[4] Loc. cit.

[5] Victoria Way DeLee, Interview by author, 8 August 1992, Ridgeville, South Carolina. Tape recording.

[6] Laughlin MacDonald, "An Aristocracy of Voters: The Disfranchisement of Blacks in South Carolina," in *South Carolina Law Review,* 37 (Summer 1986): 557. MacDonald notes: "Also denied the franchise were non-Christians, the poor (those either without a freehold of at least 50 acres or not liable to pay fifty pounds in taxes), apprentices, covenanted servants, 'any seafaring or other transient man,' and, of course, women."

[7]Alrutheus Ambush Taylor, *The Negro in South Carolina during Reconstruction* (Washington, D.C.: The Association for the Study of Negro Life and History, 1924), 188-89. Taylor reports of the Klan's "whipping and otherwise intimidating inoffensive Negroes and white men solely because of their political affiliations," often resorting to arson and murder. These included the 1868 murder of B. F. Randolf, a black state senator from Orangeburg; James Martin, a white Republican legislator from Abbeville; and freedmen Tabby Simpson of Laurenceville and Johnson Glascoe of Newberry.

[8]MacDonald, 569.

[9]MacDonald, 570-71. "Included as disfranchising offenses were those that blacks were thought especially prone to commit, such as larceny, adultery, wife beating, incest, house-breaking, perjury, fornication. Excluded were crimes that whites were thought equally inclined to commit, such as murder and fighting. A man could kill his wife and still vote; but if he . . . beat her, he was denied the franchise." Also see Francis Butler Simkins, *Pitchfork Ben Tillman: South Carolinian* (Gloucester, Mass.: Peter Smith, 1964), 297.

[10]I. A. Newby, *Black Carolinians: A History of Blacks in South Carolina from 1995 to 1968* (Columbia: University of South Carolina), 282.

[11]MacDonald, 572; George Brown Tindall, *South Carolina Negroes: 1877-1900* (Columbia: University of South Carolina, 1952), 239ff.

[12]South Carolina Code of Laws, *Statutes at Large* (1956) #741, 1747.

[13]Ibid., #920, 2182.

[14]"Propose Open NAACP Roll: Bill Would Require Group to File List," *The State*, January 25, 1957.

[15]South Carolina Code of Laws, *Statutes at Large* (1957), 216, 247.

[16]Several families from Clarendon County were among those participating in the coterie of cases argued before the United States Supreme Court by the NAACP and resulting in the 1954 Brown decision.

[17]"Monthly Report" (Columbia, S.C.: The South Carolina Council on Human Relations, March, 1957), Southern Regional Council Files, Atlanta University Center Special Collections.

[18]Five years after DeLee's birth, the population of Dorchester County was 18,956. In the town of Ridgeville, the population was reported as 418. Of the county's total inhabitants, 10,609, around 56 percent, were reported as rural farm population. *Fifteenth Census of the United States: 1930: Population* (Washington: Government Printing Office, 1932), Volume I, 990, Volume III, Part 2, 808.

[19]Mrs. Victoria Way DeLee, interview by author, 4 July 1988, Tape recording, Ridgeville, South Carolina. Dorchester was primarily a rural county without a population of black professionals. Until the late 1950s, black county school teachers were boarders from adjacent Charleston and Orangeburg counties. Unsurprisingly, in 1930 agriculture was reported as the largest employer of all African Americans in the state. Domestic work

was the second largest employer of black women. Manufacturing and mechanical industries were the second largest employer of white women. For the entire reported white population, manufacturing and mechanical industries and agriculture were almost tie as largest employers, with farming having a slight majority. Other employment options in the state included forestry and fishing, transportation and communication, public service, professional service, and clerical occupations. See *Fifteenth Census of the United States: 1930: Population,* Volume IV, (Washington, D.C.: Government Printing Office, 1933), 1483-85. By 1950, manufacturing was reported as twice as large an employer of whites as was agriculture, 36 percent to 16.4 percent, with textile mill production dominating the manufacturing area. For African Americans, farming continued to be the principle employer, 43.2 percent, with manufacturing making small gains. *Census of the Population: 1950,* Volume II, Part 40, (Washington, D.C.: Government Printing Office, 1952), 41.

[20]Interestingly, referring to a time more than 30 years later, L. S. James, a field representative for the South Carolina Council on Human Relations, made the very same observation in a weekly report detailing problems of black farmers and sharecroppers in Berkeley and Dorchester counties, who were prevented access to income from their crops through collusion of local institutions (e.g., banks, tobacco markets, county FHA) and the persons who directed these institutions: "Problems like these are keeping low-income farmers from handling their own income. It is making it very difficult for them to get any money to live on. It is almost like being in slavery." See L. S. James, "Weekly Report for August 15-19, 1966," (Atlanta, Ga.: Southern Regional Council, South Carolina Voter Education Project), Southern Regional Council Files, Atlanta University Center Special Collection.

[21]Mrs. Victoria Way DeLee 4 July 1988; Calvin Trillin, "U.S. Journal: Dorchester County, S.C. - Victoria DeLee - In Her Own Words," *New Yorker* 47 (27 March 1971): 86.

[22]Loc. cit. DeLee recalls two other specific lynchings during her childhood, Echard Ladson and Mose Wynn. "I remember I was a teenager when they kill Echard Ladson," she says. "They shot him down in Ridgeville because he was determined to walk the street. They wouldn't let blacks walk no street. They say blacks had to walk down in the road, and the streets was for the white people." Wynn, DeLee says, "was shot down in Summerville. Mose Wynn had these beautiful black daughters. . . . And one of the polices was going with Mose Wynn's daughter. She didn't want him, but he made her go with him. And when she told her daddy . . . Mose went and got at him about his daughter." Some days after altercation with the police officer about this matter, DeLee says, Wynn was shot and killed one evening as he stood on the steps of his home.

23DeLee, 4 July 1988; Mr. Thomas H. Ross, interview by author, Dorchester, S.C., 11 March 1994.

24DeLee, 4 July 1988.

25DeLee, 4 July 1988; Trillin, 86.

26Explicating lessons Zora Neale Hurston's grandmothers and father sought to teach her (how to maintain her zeal for life while recognizing the dangers of racism), Cannon names the content of the lessons "functional prudence." See Katie G. Cannon, "Moral Wisdom in the Black Women's Literary Tradition," in *The Annual of the Society of Christian Ethics* (1984), 176-7. It is noteworthy that Maya Angelou tells of a similar incident with her grandmother in one segment of her autobiography. At the time of the incident, Angelou, who spent a large portion of her childhood in Stamps, Arkansas, reared by her grandmother, recently had returned to Stamps from San Francisco, California where she lived for a time with her mother. Several days after her return to Stamps, Maya dressed "San Francisco style" and walked three miles into town to purchase a Simplicity pattern from the general store. Proud of her California exposure and manner, and refusing to be treated like a servant, Maya infuriated the two white women shopkeepers by "sassing" them. After the encounter she left the store without her pattern, but very proud of and satisfied by the fact that on principle she had not bowed to indignant treatment. By the time she reached home, Maya's grandmother ("Momma") had received a report of the incident. Momma censured Maya about such "showing out," and when Maya twice protested Momma hit her twice in the face, the second time knocking Maya to the porch floor. She warned Maya that her principle of justice would not protect the family from klansmen nor her from being raped. By afternoon, for safety, Maya boarded a train on her way back to California. See Maya Angelou, *Gather Together in My Name* (Toronto: Bantam, 1974), 78-9.

[27]DeLee, 4 July 1988

[28]Ibid.

[29]Ibid.

[30]DeLee, 8 August 1992.

[31]Ibid.

[32]Ibid.

[33]Ibid.

[34]Ibid.; Trillin, 86.

[35]DeLee, 8 August 1992.

[36]Trillin, 86.

[37]DeLee, 8 August 1992. DeLee says a dispute about the pastor between factions in the church effectively destroyed the congregation as a place where they felt comfortable to worship.

[38]The denomination was established circa. 1903, by itinerant preacher, now designated denominational founder, elder, and saint, Mary Magdalena Lewis Tate who, at the turn of the century "'felt moved by the Holy Spirit of God to go out into the world and preach the gospel, first at Steel Springs, Tennessee." Lewis traveled and preached to groups at towns in Tennessee, Alabama, Kentucky, Illinois, and Ohio. By 1908, she had set up a number of local bands. Later that year Tate called what must have been the denomination's first General Assembly in Greenville, Alabama. Today denomination's headquarters are in Nashville, Tennessee. See General Assembly of

the Church of the Living God, *The Constitution Government and General Decree Book* (Chattanooga: New and Living Way Publishers, 1923) and *75th Anniversary Yearbook: The Church of the Living God, the Pillar and Ground of the Truth, Inc., 1903-1978 (*Chattanooga: New Living Way Publishers, n.d).

[39]DeLee, 8 August 1992.

[40]Ibid.

[41]See discussion by Cheryl Townsend Gilkes regarding independence and fervor of community workers of the "sanctified" churches, in Gilkes, "The Role of Women in the Sanctified Church," *The Journal of Religious Thought* 43 (Spring-Summer 1986): 31, 36.

[42]Mrs. JohnEtta Grant Cauthen, interview by author, (telephone tape recording) ,Charleston, S.C., 8 April 1994; DeLee, 4 July 1988. DeLee identifies Josephine Banister as "the black white woman" who had some influence with local white officials. Banister's husband was the only African American on the school board that oversaw all county schools.

[43]DeLee, 4 July 1988.

[44]Ibid.

[45]Ibid.; Trillin, 86-87.

[46]Ibid.

[47]Ibid.

[48]"Question Is Posed on Halting NAACP Activity in State," *Charleston News and Courier*, 9 July 1956.

[49]Heidi Sinick, "Dealing for the Poor," *Washington Post* (8 February 1971): B1.

[50]Mike Daniel, "Hollings Says He'll Stop FBI Probe," *Charleston News and Courier* (29 September 1961): A1.

[51]"Report of the Secretary of State to the General Assembly of South Carolina," in *Reports and Resolutions of South Carolina for Fiscal Year Ending June 30, 1959* (Columbia, S.C.: State Budget and Control Board, 1959), 222.

[52]"South Carolina Voter Registration History: 1956 to 1979," in *Reports and Resolutions of South Carolina for Fiscal Year Ending 1979* (Columbia, S.C.: State Budget and Control Board, 1957), 447.

[53]South Carolina State Conference of the NAACP, Souvenir Program, "Testimonial Honoring Parent Plaintiffs and Their Children in the Clarendon County Case Against School Segregation," Liberty Hill A.M.E. Church, Summerton, South Carolina, June 17, 1951; quoted in Barbara Woods Aba-Mecha, "Black Woman Activist in Twentieth Century South Carolina," Ph.D. Diss., Emory University, 1978.

[54]"Governor Says S.C. 'To Resist Integration,'" *Richmond News Leader* (4 November 1955).

[55]W. D. Workman, Jr., "No Integrated Schools for S.C., Says Report to White House Meet," *Charlotte Observer* (17 November 1955).

[56]"Hollings Praises Assembly for Segregation Actions," *The State*, 28

May 1960. Also see "Two Attack S.C. Segregation Statute Change," *The State* (5 May 1960).

[57]"Negroes Are Turned Away at 2 Dorchester Schools," *Charleston News and Courier* (27 August 1965); Jack Bass, "44 School Districts Open; 41 Have Compliance Plans," *The State* (26 August 1964): D1.

[58]Office of Education, United States Department of Health, Education, and Welfare and United States Commission on Civil Rights, "Status of School Desegregation in Southern and Border States," an occasional report, March, 1966, Southern Regional Council Files, Atlanta University Center Special Collections.

[59]DeLee v. Dorchester County School District Three, CA#66-183 (USDC S. Carolina 1966).

[60]See, for example, "NAACP Asks Protection for Woman," in *The State* (25 July 1969): B4.

[61]DeLee, 4 July 1988. Also see United States Commission on Civil Rights, *Political Participation* (Washington, D.C.: Government Printing Office, 1968), 117.

[62]Roosevelt Geddis, Ridgeville, to Richard Detreville, Dorchester, 13 January 1969, South Carolina Council on Human Relations Files, The South Caroliniana Collection, University of South Carolina.

[63]Attendance List, Conference on Education Desegregation, Southern Regional Council Files, Atlanta University Center Special Collections.

[64]See DeLee v. Dorchester County School District Three, "Motion to Add Parties," 11 December 1967; DeLee, 4 July 1988.

[65]Mordecai Johnson, Florence, to Selected Persons with South Carolina. School Cases, 8 October 1969, South Carolina Council on Human Relations Files, The South Caroliniana Collection, University of South Carolina.

[66]Ibid.

[67]Ibid; Mordecai Johnson Interview; DeLee v. School District Three; Attorney Fred Moore, Charleston, to Paul Anthony, Atlanta, 3 March 1970, Southern Regional Council Files, Atlanta University Center Special Collections.

[68]"Hemphill Raps 'Political Rumors,'" *Charleston News and Courier* (18 July 1969): B6.

[69]McCollum, Matthew D./Paul Matthias/South Carolina Commission on Human Relations, Columbia, S. C., (telegram) to President Richard Nixon, Washington, D. C., 26 June 1969, South Carolina Council on Human Relations Files, The South Caroliniana Collection, University of South Carolina; "Hemphill Raps 'Political Rumors,'" *News and Courier.*

[70]Mr. Hayes Mizell, former Field Worker, American Friends Service Committee, interview by author, 18 June 1993, Tape recording, New York, New York.

[71]Mr. Hayes Mizell 10 June 1993; "Mitchell Reassures Protesters," *The State* (2 July 1969): A1; "30 'Occupy' Attorney General's Office," *The*

Washington Pos, (2 July 1969): A4; "The Administration: Tenuous Balance," *Time* (11 July 1969): 14-15; "Civil Rights: A Debt to Dixie," *Newsweek* (14 July 1969): 23.

[72]"NAACP Asks Protection for Woman," *The State* (25 November 1969): B4.

[73]County registration rolls date back only as far as 1968. Prior record books were destroyed "a few years after creation of the State Election Commission in 1967," according to Mrs. Jackie Knight who has been with the County Registration Board in St. George since 1965. These records were destroyed because "we didn't want any repercussions," Mrs. Knight said. Mrs. Jackie Knight, interview by author, Telephone, St. George, South Carolina, 24 September 1993.

[74]DeLee, 8 August 1992.

Chapter 6

Transformative Responsiblist Theory and Ethic of Justice: Martin, Malcolm, and Angela

William Anthony Thurston

We must remember as we boycott that a boycott is not an end within itself; it is merely a means to awaken a sense of shame within the oppressor and challenge his [or her] false sense of superiority. But the end is reconciliation; the end is redemption; the end is the creation of the beloved community.

Martin Luther King, Jr.
"Facing the Challenge of a New Age," 1957

We have formed an organization known as the Organization of Afro-American Unity which has the same aim and objective [as the Organization of African Unity]—to fight whoever gets in our way, to bring about the complete independence of people of African descent here in the Western Hemisphere, and first here in the United States, and bring about the freedom of these people by any means necessary.

Malcolm X, *By Any Means Necessary*, 1964

As Afro-American women, as women of color in general, as progressive women of all racial backgrounds, let us join our sisters—and brothers—across the globe who are attempting to forge a new socialist order—an order which will reestablish socioeconomic priorities so that the quest for monetary profit will never be permitted to take precedence over the real interests of human beings.

Angela Yvonne Davis
"Let Us All Rise Together: Radical Perspectives on Empowerment for Afro-American Women," 25 June 1987

Introduction

Relying upon several theorists along with the insights of Martin Luther King, Jr., Malcolm X, and Angela Yvonne Davis, my transformative responsiblist (TR) argument proposes a (tentative) social theory and political ethic to serve the emancipatory interests of African Americans.[1] After summarizing its principal assumptions, I wish to explain the relatively autonomous yet interrelated thought-praxis complexes arising from the national repression of African Americans. These complexes I label "reformationist," "nationalist," and "revolutionist," and I associate them, respectively, with Martin Luther King, Jr., Malcolm X, and Angela Davis. With these complexes as background, I then recommend ethical criteria for a conception and strategy of human fulfillment and social justice. These criteria include ideas of community, complex justice, individual and collective self-realization, transformative moral agency, and means to attain decentralized democratic pluralism. The end of pluralism thus would be to preserve values of democratic equality (King), republican liberty (Malcolm X), and social inclusiveness (Davis) by reformulating these values into a conception of shared democracy. Finally, my argument concludes with an indication that this reformulation of complex substantive *justice is born through struggle* as advocated by Martin, Malcolm, and Angela.

Principal Assumptions

Committed to a pluralism of cross-cultural discourse and praxis of justice, the TR theory of individual and social development contends, first of all, that our refusal to hear potentially opposing partial truths would be a confession of our own nonbelief in cooperative emancipatory activity. From different starting points, Christian, Islamic, and Humanist conceptions and strategies of liberation invite us to affirm human potentialities and to overcome human inclinations toward injustice in order to make complex justice possible within history. Hence, a TR ethic invokes our reconsideration of individual and collective efforts to build, through struggle, a pluralistic ethicopolitical community.[2]

Second, a TR theory of justice requires a critical method of understanding and changing repressive social structures, systems, and values. With H. Richard Niebuhr, I concur that concepts, processes, and movements of social change involve both individual and collective *transformation* and *responsibility*. The idea of transformation attempts to make *re-creative* use of the potentialities for making complex justice possible in the context of formally democratic institutions and civic virtues. The concept of responsibility invites *responsive* emancipatory thoughts and actions to overcome injustice in a manner consistent with principles of *accountability* and of *collaboration* among a *continuing community* of moral agents who seek a pluralistic, socially-democratic society and culture. Ultimately this concept leads to a multinational *community of complex re-creative justice born through struggle.*[3]

Third, the TR argument attempts to *preserve* the particular moral meanings of King's, Malcolm X's, and Davis's primary value commitments to co-equality, independence, and inclusive community, respectively. Moreover, it *elevates* and *transforms* these meanings into a broader conception of complex re-creative justice oriented to developing interdependent communities of pluralistic social democracy worldwide. Finally, as discussed below, this argument is a defense of freedom in covenant love for the ongoing determination of complex re-creative justice in history, society, and culture.[4] Hence, as a contribution to explanatory theory, I turn now to examine and correlate the ethical complexities in the responses to human repression and their ensuing movements for human freedom and social transformation.

Explanatory Social Theory and Praxis

The complex meanings of justice defended by King, Malcolm X, and Davis indicate that they are transformative responsiblists. They attempt to incorporate the prevailing conventional ways of understanding human repression and emancipation into their arguments for complex justice. Their respective primary value commitments serve to relate and explain the basis of their different conceptions and strategies of justice; however, their respective commitments to equality, independence, and inclusiveness also provide a framework to reconstruct a pluralistic moral meaning of re-creative justice. In this reconstructive task, pluralism means the voluntary (and often pragmatic) coexistence of complementary complex ideas and praxes of making justice. Hence, my developing social theory and political ethic intends not to suppress but rather to advocate pluralistic responsive thoughts and actions, as contributions toward the most inclusive possible community of complex re-creative justice.[5]

Ethical Complexities. That King, Malcolm X, and Davis each held commitments to all three of these social values—equality, independence, and inclusiveness—indicates ethical complexity in their giving primacy to one of these commitments and delimiting the other two. Their respective primary value orientations led each of them to interpret the mutuality of the other two commitments in a manner consistent with this orientation. For example, each claims that equality, liberty, and inclusive community emerge from the denial of substantive freedom (as disclosed in African Americans' resistance against domination). Hence, they argue that "freedom" is both *endemic* to human nature as well as *necessary* for individual and collective self-identity and determination in history, society, and culture.

Yet the shared meanings of freedom advocated by King, Malcolm X, and Davis, are informed by their primary value commitment to co-equality, liberty (as independence), and inclusive community, respectively. King asserted that freedom is the capacity to deliberate, choose, and act within the "limits" of the structures, systems, and values of society. Malcolm X contended that freedom is independent power to think, speak, and act by "any means necessary" without the imposition of restraint. Davis defends an understanding of freedom that transforms King's reformationist idea of co-equality and Malcolm X's internationalist notion of independence by reformulating freedom as *empowerment* for individual and collective self-realization (oriented to a pluralistic community of justice).

Here Warren R. Copeland is helpful in our attempt to reformulate the ethical complexities in a concept of freedom. He argues that the normative task should be to "create and preserve balance" between the relatively autonomous but interrelated meanings of empowerment as "equality, liberty and solidarity." He contends that all three of these "value commitments" have concrete "grounds" upon which to legitimate meanings and "claims of justice," because each is rooted in the *essential* and *existential* dimensions of our individual and collective experience.[6]

With Copeland, I contend that we defend *co-equality* because we often come to understand our true individual and collective identities and commitments through our different social relationships (see Figure 1, next page). These relationships are mediated by our (more or less) shared world views expressed through *language* and *activity* with other people (particularly those who are significant to our individual and social formation). We tend also to advocate *liberty* (individual and collective independence). For example, when we have a "sense" or experience of being "hemmed in by (so-called) outside forces," we often make the decision to act in pursuit of defending or attaining our interests or value commitments without outside interference. Furthermore, we have a tendency (more or less) to support *solidarity* or inclusiveness oriented to *equal justice* when it seeks to protect, support, or sustain individuals and collectivities, especially when these human beings are denied self-realization by unjustifiable force and coercion. Hence, our individual and social experiences orient us toward complex conceptions of the appropriate forms and the values of a pluralistic socially-democratic society and culture.[7]

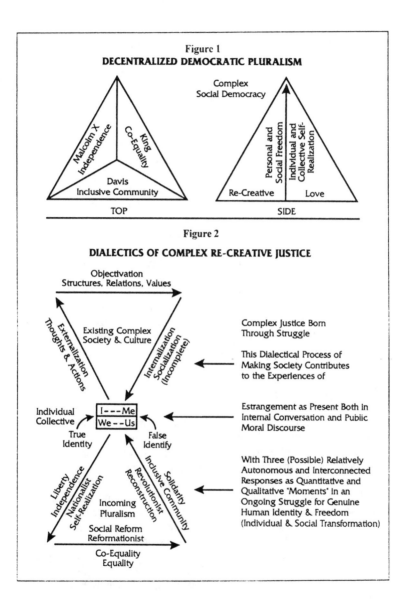

Figure 1
DECENTRALIZED DEMOCRATIC PLURALISM

Complex Social Democracy

Malcolm X Independence
King Co-Equality
Davis Inclusive Community

TOP

Personal and Social Freedom
Individual and Collective Self-Realization
Re-Creative
Love

SIDE

Figure 2

DIALECTICS OF COMPLEX RE-CREATIVE JUSTICE

Objectivation
Structures, Relations, Values

Externalization Thoughts & Actions

Existing Complex Society & Culture

Internalization Socialization (Incomplete)

Individual Collective
I---Me
We--Us
True Identity
False Identify

Liberty Independence Nationalist Self-Realization

Solidarity Inclusive Community Revolutionist Reconstruction

Incoming Pluralism

Social Reform Reformationist

Co-Equality Equality

Complex Justice Born Through Struggle

This Dialectical Process of Making Society Contributes to the Experiences of

Estrangement as Present Both in Internal Conversation and Public Moral Discourse

With Three (Possible) Relatively Autonomous and Interconnected Responses as Quantitative and Qualitative "Moments" in an Ongoing Struggle for Genuine Human Identity & Freedom (Individual & Social Transformation)

Plurality of Responses to Repression. The arguments of King, Malcolm X, and Davis express a plurality of radical responses to African-American repression. Peter L. Berger provides an interpretive sociological approach to explain the experiential basis for these responses. In appropriating his approach (see Figure 2, previous page), I assert that the three interrelated moments he identifies in the "dialectical process" of making society and culture parallel those of historical movements for true identity and freedom through struggle: (1) "externalization," or the continual outpouring of human thought and activity in the formation of society and culture; (2) "objectivation," or the consolidation of these formations in the normative structures, systems and values that shape the political, economic, and sociocultural life of a historically constituted community of people; and (3) "socialization," or the internalization of these norms in both individual and collective consciousness as expressed in patterns of personal behavior and social practices.[8]

Berger claims also that society (and culture) is a "social product" by externalization as well as an "objective reality" juxtaposed over and against individuals and groups by objectivation. He contends that individuals become a "product" of society and culture through the multiple processes of political, economic, and sociocultural socialization. He claims, however, that the process of socialization is never complete, because we are not (simply) human beings who internalize fully the values and practices of normative structures. Similar to King, Malcolm X, and Davis, Berger emphasizes the recurring problem of estrangement, as a "sense" or condition of separation (alienation) from institutional or social relations.[9]

In reformulating Berger's argument via the work of Jon Gunnemann, I contend that repression as alienation of the individual by means of institutionalized domination and dominance can never be complete. This is particularly true in a formally democratic society of procedural justice, like the United States, because (1) the *power* of those who are dominant in normative political, economic, and social structures is not absolute, and the normative cultural values are not inclusive of all members of society; and (2) the *process* of socialization through normative structures of domination and dominance does not include either all repressed human collectivities or all of their cultural meanings. Hence, there are potentialities for the existence of critical individual and social consciousness and forces that could resist domination and dominance.[10]

For example, the resistance by African Americans to the complex domination and dominance of Euro-American society may be expressed as internal and external conflict or estrangement. Internal conflict, in individual and social consciousness, arises between African Americans' understandings of their "true" individual and social identity and their "alienated" socialized identity imposed by multiple institutional roles, practices, and values. External conflict, in the context of multiple repression, centers on African-American struggles for substantive justice in the face of different forms of domination and dominance. As illustrated above in Figure 2, I suggest that there are three possible resolutions to the complex problem of African-American repression (or estrangement) in the context of movements to overcome and eliminate it. These movements are often struggles for *meaning* as well as for *power* to consolidate individual and collective identity and determination.[11]

Similar to Malcolm X's argument, the first resolution rejects Euro-American domination of normative institutions and their dominance of the normative "meanings" of sociocultural values. This resolution *recovers* "new images" of African Americans' identity and power to determine their individual and collective destiny. As expressed in narrow nationalist sects, this response may range from rebellion against, or withdrawal from, the white worlds of domination and dominance. Following King's position, the second strategy accepts the existing normative structures and their "ideal" democratic values. However, it seeks to *reform* the policies and practices of these structures, particularly those that contradict these values. This strategy may range from non-violent resistance to nonresistance in order to attain "equal participation" with Euro-Americans in determining the collective life of society (and its moral meanings), as articulated by the reformationist tradition. Similar to Davis's stance, the third approach attempts to make *re-creative* use of existing ("liberating") cultural values and social relations and transform these into new meanings and forms of pluralistic "social democracy." This approach, as defended by the revolutionist groups, varies from radical praxis to radical theoretical arguments for human liberation and social transformation.

These three possible resolutions of human repression suggest their dialectical relationship, as three interrelated moments or *movements* of negation, preservation, and transformation, *in a collective struggle* for racial and social justice. First, African-American nationalists negate white domination and dominance while affirming Africentric cultural identity and the power of individual and collective determination. Second, the reformationists support the nationalists in rejecting racially unjust institutional practices, policies, and values; however, they seek to preserve and extend notions of African-American identity and power to include ideas of coexistence and shared cultural meanings among all human collectivities. Third, the revolutionists claim that these two aims can be fulfilled only in transformed, socially-democratic structures undergirded by shared meanings and cultural values of justice.

For example, in the late 1960s and early 1970s, the polemic debate among progressive activists expressed an understanding of a dialectical relationship between the contemporary emancipating struggles in the interests of African Americans. These polemicists argued that Malcolm X prepared the way for the northern strategies of the Civil Rights Movement led by King. According to this argument, the social change experienced by this movement provided the basis for the rise of African-American revolutionary nationalism, in which the legacy of Malcolm X served as inspiration. The argument asserts also that Malcolm X, in the later part of his life, represented the vanguard of a social revolution by the oppressed classes. This assertion is supported further by those who viewed Davis's involvement in a political revolutionary party as a dialectical development of her activity in the movement of Africentric revolutionism.[12]

Hence, reëxplicating the interdependence of complex values in responses to individual and collective human repression, I conclude that there is a dialectical relationship among radical conceptions and strategies of justice as expressed in the thought and in the praxis of King, Malcolm X, and Davis. As illustrated above in Figures 1 and 2, this conclusion means that a TR argument for complex justice represents a synthesis (transforming yet preserving the essential elements) of the interconnected reformationist, nationalist, and revolutionist struggles for genuine human freedom and social transformation. It affirms theoretically and historically that a complex TR ethic could make re-creative use of shared values and social relations oriented to liberty, equality, and inclusiveness, by reformulating these into pluralistically-determined structures of procedural, distributive, and substantive justice. More specifically, this re-creative process could (1) critique and undermine existing values and social relations serving human domination and dominance; (2) preserve existing meanings and social relations that have liberating potentialities; and (3) transform these into a just political, economic, and sociocultural community of decentralized democratic pluralism for individual and collective self-realization. Therefore, we can now turn to a reconstruction of a possible conception and strategy toward this end of complex re-creative *justice born through struggle*.

Political Ethic of Justice

In summary, the elements for an empowering social philosophy are conceived as serving pluralistic and emancipatory theory, science, and praxis. This philosophy is informed by historical Africentric reëxplications of Western and Eastern *moral meanings* of equality, liberty, and inclusive community (as advocated by King, Malcolm X, and Davis). This complex of moral meanings is proposed as a differentiated hermeneutical principle upon which to make moral judgments about the jus-tice of interpersonal and communal structures, relations, and values, particularly within international contexts of the United States. With respect to a developing TR argument, these judgments would be limited to critical reëxplications of the claims concerning an adequate conception and strategy of justice oriented to the liberating interests of African Americans (as a differentiated national community). With an understanding of complex social philosophy and its context, this limitation would be restricted further to the remaining five subjects of this essay: politico-moral community, complex re-creative justice, self-realization, transformative agency, and an ethic of means to attain the most-inclusive-possible community of re-creative justice (within the framework of *decentralized democratic pluralism*).

Politicomoral Community. A TR ethic is oriented toward a decentralized, socially democratic, and pluralistic community of justice. This complex politico-moral community promotes individual and interest-group participatory democracy for the continuing determination of a substantively just political, economic, and social life. This community is conceived as a forum of cross-cultural moral discourse, where individual and collective value commitments intersect, in developing policies for procedural, distributive, and substantive justice. Viewed as an ethicopolitical community that promotes personal integrity and community in pursuit of progressive human freedom and social transformation, this multilevel forum reflects King's multiracial/ethnic "beloved community," Malcolm X's liberated collectivities in mutual coexistence, and Davis's pluralistic socially-democratic society and culture (See above epigraphs).

This conception of political-moral community relies also upon critical theories of social development in the thinking of Lucius T. Outlaw and Jürgen Habermas.[13] Their arguments indicate that the social organization principle has shifted from the economic to the political sphere, particularly in the United States. This indication represents a reformation of the market function of social organization by state regulation in the economic and the social spheres of American culture; however, the collective "isms" of human domination and sociocultural dominance represent a moral contradiction between the affirmation of shared or universal notions of human valuation, and the denial or limitation of certain rights or goods or needs to African Americans and other repressed racial/ethnic collectivities. This contradiction serves the claim that the normative structures of American society are unjust rationally with respect to consistent practices of human valuation. Hence, what might be considered as the meaning and form of a political-moral community?

A TR ethic contends that the idea of a politico-moral community as a covenant is more appropriate than the notion of social contract, particularly with respect to seeking the end of a just decentralized, socially democratic, and pluralistic society and culture. The notion of contract views the sovereign state as an instrument of preservation for free individuals to pursue their self-interest as the most efficient means of contributing to the common good. The idea of covenant (as expressed in the natural law, biblical, Quranic, and humanist traditions) understands individuals as social beings requiring genuine human fellowship for enduring personal and communal self-realization oriented penultimately to a pluralistic community of re-creative justice.

I concur with Milner S. Ball and Paul Louis Lehmann, who argue that the notion of covenant undergirded the constituting act of the American Republic.[14] This notion provides potentialities for a transcendent principle of human freedom grounded in TR love, which demands, evaluates, and fulfills relative values of complex justice. As indicated above in Figure 1, TR love serves individual and collective freedom (as a fundamental principle) oriented toward substantive liberty, equality, and inclusiveness (as multiple value commitments). Hence, informed by this principle, a TR ethic critiques, conserves, and elevates these value commitments as the framework for building a decentralized, socially-democratic, and pluralistic community of complex re-creative justice.

Complex Re-creative Justice. The conceptions and strategies of complex procedural, distributive, and substantive justice advocated by King, Malcolm X, and Davis include ideas of external values (equality, independence, and inclusive community) and internal values (sacrificial love, racial/ethnic pride, and human social essence). Along with Berkley B. and Essie A. Eddins and Outlaw, I assume a normative yet open-ended theory of rights and goods (based on objective human needs) which presumes that their conception precedes their formation and development. This theory attempts also to respond to the problems of human estrangement and alienation created by an arbitrary system of human valuation and devaluation. Along with Michael Walzer, I presuppose that the "use value" of goods as social resources delimits their "exchange value" within a mixed social and private market economy. Hence, a TR ethic seeks to delimit exchange value, which fuels the convertibility of normative goods or rights (needs) into social privileges beyond the "sphere" of their origination, and thus contributes to forms of human domination and sociocultural dominance.[15]

Justice, as interpreted from a TR ethical perspective, might thus take the form of a decentralized, socially democratic, and pluralistic community. This form of ethicopolitical community attempts to respond to three concerns: (1) the *decentralized* idea reflects the realist defense of a balance of power (reformationist); (2) the *socially democratic* notion suggests the pragmatic advocacy of coexistence with identity and power for each (historically-constituted) social collectivity (nationalist); and (3) the *pluralistic community of justice* concept indicates the transformationist demand of liberating political, economic, and sociocultural structures, relations, and values (revolutionist). A differentiated meaning and form of complex re-creative justice is subject to ongoing conception and determination in the cooperative movement for self-realization.

Self-realization. The quest for self-realization, in the context of the national repression of African Americans, raises the perennial question whether race or class is the primary determinant of this repression. A TR ethic argues against the claim of Cornel West that economic class position contributes more than racial status to the basic form of "powerlessness [of African Americans] in America." He asserts also that oppressed peoples within the structures of culture and religion (the sociocultural sphere) often provide the greatest resistance to racial/ethnic repression.[16] West's position represents a contradiction between economic and racial reductionist determinations of national repression. This contradiction may be resolved in a conception of the interrelatedness of racism, sexism, ageism, and classism as co-constitutive of African-American domination and dominance (as defended by Davis). I contend also that analyses of social classes are often narrowly defined in an economic sense. This view cannot account for the distribution of power in other normative structures where economic status is not the primary determinant of power arrangements. For example, in the political sphere, there may be antagonisms between political and economic interests with respect to questions of social repression or of social justice.

A derivative question here is the extent to which racism, sexism, ageism, classism, and other forms of repression contribute to the falsification of objective relationships in individual and social consciousness? I concur with James Boggs, Outlaw, Francis Beale, and Eugene V. Wolfenstein, who argue that exclusive focus of social movements on racism, sexism, ageism, or classism reflects the actual division of the subordinated classes along the lines of race, sex, age, and status across the spheres.[17] These movements also tend to obscure their participants' understanding of their objective repressed class interests. Thus, the particular struggles for substantive justice could serve the dominating classes in dividing and maintaining repression of the subordinated classes. These struggles, along with the class divisions within each particular human collectivity, also limit their cooperative unity. My hypothesis is that particular struggles against racism, sexism, ageism should be against classism. Conversely, this last "ism" is also conceived as a struggle against racism, sexism, and ageism. Hence, the intent here is to move from the battleground of interest-group politics to the broadest possible cooperative action by repressed peoples in their struggles against the dominating class and their movements for individual and collective self-identity and determination.

Transformative Agency. The question of inquiry here is: Which social forces provide potentialities for struggles against racism, sexism, ageism, and classism as part of a collective movement for self-realization oriented to complex re-creative justice? With respect to this question of moral agency, I will give particular attention descriptively to the issues of sexism and ageism on the African-American movement for racial and social justice. These forms of human domination and devaluation are interrelated to racism and classism within the context of national repression. The primary objection to this contention centers on the claim that the advocacy of struggles against sexism and ageism is counterproductive to a collective movement for African-American liberation. This objection assumes that such advocacy encourages African-American women or the elderly or the youth to join black or white sectarian struggles exclusively against sexism or ageism, respectively. As Jacquelyn Grant argues, however, this assumption glosses over the relationship of black male domination and black female subordination as well as the presumption of black male superiority in the "black church and community."[18]

King, Malcolm X, and Davis disclose the intraclass relations among African Americans. Not all African-American men are members of the power strata of those normative African-American institutions that promote or practice relations of male domination and female subordination. To a certain extent, racial and gender repression collectively falsify the consciousness of African-American women and men. Like other repressed people in the movements for self-identity and power, African Americans may align their particular interests with those of the dominating class of Eurocentric or Africentric normative institutions. This alignment represents derivatively a *re-creation* of the power and the identity of the dominating class in the relations and the consciousness of African-American men, women, elderly, youth, professionals, and workers, for example. Hence, it indicates the self-defeating nature of aligned struggles from the standpoint of their objective class interests. It limits also the potentialities for the African-American subordinated class in its primary objective struggle against the dominating political, economic, and sociocultural class.

Following Davis, Jacquelyn Grant, and Beale, in part, my hypothesis is that the repression of African-American women could serve as a paradigm for analyzing issues of sexism, racism, ageism, and classism. This paradigmatic form of multiple repression provides opportunities for insight into the interrelatedness of these issues with respect to the question of individual and collective self-identity and realization. This presumption resists reductionist views of African-American women's repression. The narrow feminist (reformist) emphasis on femaleness glosses over race. The nationalist stress on race de-emphasizes gender. The sectarian focus on age position neglects gender and race. The narrow revolutionist focus on (economic) class-position neglects the complexity of gender, race, and age (within interpersonal/communal life of society). These reductionist views of African-American women split their being along the lines of gender, race, age, and class, thereby contributing to the denial of true human identity and value.[19] The question of moral agency in the struggle for racial and social justice would be incomplete without an understanding of the interrelatedness of the issues involved in the complex empowerment of African-American women, men, elderly, and youth. Hence, I intend to pursue this question in its intranational and interregional/national contexts via progressive struggles against imperialism, neocolonialism, and militarism as potential movements for shared democracies.

Ethics of Means. The transformative responsiblist argument for a decentralized, socially democratic, and pluralistic community of justice is related to the problematic of an ethic of means to attain this end. This problem arises from the intention to provide a collective ethic that incorporates the essential elements within radical strategies of racial and social justice. It centers on the complex question of violence as an instrument of substantive justice. The African-American nationalists and revolutionists support nonviolent resistance yet claim that violence is justified if it represents a just intention for a just cause such as individual or communal self-defense. Conversely, the reformationists contend that both defensive and offensive violence are immoral because they destroy one's opponents; and, thus, they are counterproductive to coexistence or pluralistic community. This contention presupposes that nonviolent resistance is moral since it serves the end of an inclusive community of justice.

King, Malcolm X, and Davis advocated the politico-moral advantage of their respective strategies of social transformation. King's ethic restricted the moral use of political force and coercion to nonviolence, while the ethics of Malcolm X and Davis, though preferring nonviolence, both permitted and limited the use of defensive violence to achieve social justice. King's argument was grounded in the conception that the ends limit the means. The alternative perspective was shaped by the contention that the end justifies the means. King, Malcolm X, and Davis agreed that the use of force must work towards the end of a just intention to attain a complex community of substantive justice. They also related the morality of a particular strategy to its efficacy in achieving this end. However, Davis and Malcolm X insisted that the use of violence as a last resort for a just cause, like communal defense, must be conducted with proportionate means that will work towards just, attainable social goals of justice.

Reinhold Niebuhr might have asserted here that there is no inherent moral difference between violence used by the government and that used by broadly-based advancing groups to attain more tolerable justice, or to reform or create a political authority that is more responsible to the demands for freedom (as liberty) and equality. Niebuhr contended that the traditional theological theory of obedience to political authority (Romans 13:1-2) does contain a provision for civil disobedience (Acts 5:29), though illegal, in situations of evident unjust or immoral rule.[20] In advocating massive civil disobedience, King argued that it is moral to break an unjust law, particularly when a nonviolent resister willingly submits to imprisonment in order to awaken the consciousness both of the individual and of the community to injustice. He rejected the strategy of revolution through violence by African Americans to attain racial justice. However, violence was rejected more on pragmatic, rather than intrinsic, grounds.

TR criteria of defensible-force build upon the primary ethical concerns of King, Malcolm X, and Davis and a reformulated just-violence theory. As Theodore R. Weber argues, this reformulation provides a more adequate instrument for evaluating the morality of a strategy or tactic of injustice in the context of intrasocietal conflict.[21] These criteria are also intended to establish a viable alternative to the positions (1) of those who argue that any means are justified to attain a good end, thereby rejecting the necessity of moral limits to achieve justice; and (2) of those who maintain that nonviolence is the only ethical means to the end of social justice, thereby negating any moral necessity of violence to attain this end.

The four criteria for permitting and limiting defensive force (whether nonviolent or violent) are, first, the criterion of *just intention* for renewing or creating opportunities to attain an inclusive community of justice and order. As Weber contends, this criterion requires that the conflict be secularized by "dethroning ideology where it reigns over politics," humanized by prohibiting efforts to depersonalize an opponent, and institutionalized by transferring the conflict from violent to nonviolent modes of conflict resolution. Second, the criterion of *just cause*, like communal defense, with a just intention limits the use of defensible force as a last resort to the failure of nonviolent and legal efforts to eliminate aggressive violence.

The third criterion requires that the use of force be limited to a *competent and responsible authority* of broadly-based cooperating groups. This criterion assumes a situation where an unjust government fails to protect such groups form overt violent attack. It also presupposes the capacity of these groups to develop a refederated political authority that can legitimately create and maintain justice and order toward a more inclusive society. Fourth, the criterion of *just conduct* demands that force be used both with proportionate means that create more justice than injustice, and with discrimination which limits violent defensible force to an opponent's combatant forces, thereby excluding its noncombatant population. Finally, these four criteria presuppose that all belligerents posses a common humanity; therefore, the use of force must serve the *reformation* of noncombatant politico-moral relationships that seek to attain the most-inclusive-possible community of freedom with complex re-creative justice and peace.

Justice Born Through Struggle

My tentative proposals for a critical social theory and political ethic indicate my value commitment to cross-cultural discourse and praxis. These proposals promote social *responsibility*, which seeks ongoing personal and communal integrity with a commitment to pluralism in pursuit of just social *transformation*. This intention is open to the incoming indicative of freedom with power in TR (covenant) love, which is disclosed in the three moments toward the making and the remaking of complex re-creative justice. This indicative negates all pretentious claims of justice, preserves those meanings and relations that might serve complex justice, and fulfills these potentialities by reformulating and transforming them into a cooperative self-conscious struggle for their realization in history, society, and culture.

Although my proposed ethicopolitical criteria include moral limits for defensible force, I am committed to social transformation by nonviolent modes of conflict resolution in the making of complex justice. This conviction emerges from my thought and experience—of twenty-one years in a diversified range of African-American movements against multiple forms of human repression—before undertaking this study of King, Malcolm X, and Davis. Since their *actual praxes* expressed a preference for (radical) social transformation by mass, militant nonviolence, I think that they would support my position. In the context of formal democracy in the United States, this position is oriented to equality, independence, and inclusive community in the incoming possible future of decentralized democratic pluralism. Hence, in conclusion, I seek only to affirm the ancestral in the historical African-American witness that complex re-creative *Justice Is Born Through Struggle!*

Notes

[1] For the full text of this argument, see William Anthony Thurston, "Justice Born Through Struggle: Martin Luther King, Jr., Malcolm X (El-Hajj

Malik El-Shabazz), and Angela Yvonne Davis" (Ann Arbor, Mich.: UMI, 1994), 544-86.

[2]Unlike H. Richard Niebuhr, I am not implying a "primacy" of the "revealed" truth of Christianity or any world religion over that of Humanism. However, with Niebuhr, I am advocating pluralistic, politico-moral discourse and praxis oriented to a complex ethicopolitical community of complex re-creative justice. See H. R. Niebuhr, "Foreword" to *Essence of Christianity* by Ludwig Feuerbach, trans. George Eliot (Marian Evans) (New York: Harper Torchbooks, 1957), vii-ix.

[3]In a Niebuhrian sense, TR ethic also seeks to uncover, conserve, and elevate the teleological notion of "the good" and the deonotological idea of "the right" by reformulating these ethical claims into those of complex individual and social *human needs* for personal and communal self-realization as defended by King, Malcolm X, and Davis. See H. R. Niebuhr's *Christ and Culture* (New York: Harper Row, Harper Colophon Books, 1951, 1975), 43, cf. 1-44, and *The Responsible Self: An Essay in Christian Moral Philosophy*, with an introduction by James M. Gustafson (New York/ San Francisco: Harper & Row, 1963, 1978), 55-68; cf., James M. Gustafson's "Introduction" to *The Responsible Self*, 6-41; and Martin E. Marty's (General Editor) "Introduction" to *On Being Responsible: Issues in Personal Ethics*, edited by James M. Gustafson and James T. Laney (New York: Harper & Row, Harper Forum Books, 1968), 3-18.

[4]Here I concur with Reinhold Niebuhr, who argued that no political, economic, or sociocultural structure is absolute, and hence is subject to change. He also insisted upon human freedom to evaluate ultimately any claim to justice by the indicative of self-giving love or *agape* (as expressed penultimately with equal justice *in history*) in interpersonal/communal relations as advocated by King, Malcolm X, and Davis. See Reinhold Niebuhr, *Faith and Politics*, edited by Ronald H. Stone (New York: G. Braziller, 1968), 55; *Love and Justice: Selections from the Shorter Writings of Reinhold Niebuhr*, edited by D. B. Robertson (n.p.: W. L. Jenkins, 1957; Meridian, 1967; reprint Gloucester, Mass.: Peter Smith, 1976), 53-58, 257-62; and Robertson's "Introduction" to *Love and Justice*.

[5]Leonard Harris, ed., *Philosophy Born of Struggle: Anthology of Afro-American Philosophy from 1917* (Dubuque, Iowa: Kendall/Hunt, 1983), xv-xxi. My proposal to make a further study of explanatory social philosophies will rely primarily upon those presented in this anthology.

[6]Warren R. Copeland, *Economic Justice: The Social Ethics of U.S. Economic Policy* (Nashville, Tenn.: Abingdon, 1988), 94-101.

[7]Loc. cit.

[8]Peter L. Berger, *The Sacred Canopy: Elements of a Sociological Theory of Religion* (Garden City, N.Y.: Anchor, 1967, 1969), 81-87; cf. 3-22.

[9]Loc. cit. See also Jon P. Gunnemann, *The Moral Meaning of Revolution* (New Haven: Yale University, 1979), 129-32. The discussion below of three possible resolutions to the problems of alienation is based upon a reëxplication of estrangement resolution as interpreted by Gunnemann.

Following Marx and Peter L. Berger (in part), Gunnemann views "anomie" as the rejection of, and "alienation" as the acceptance of, the objective world of cultural meanings and identity in consciousness. This rejection and acceptance of meanings and identity is never universal, as Gunnemann con-tends, owing to the incompleteness of the socialization process in con-sciousness as discussed by Marx and Berger; and hence, "re-creative use of cultural meanings" is a third resolution.

[10]Loc. cit.

[11]Gunnemann, 129-32; cf. Bernard R. Boxhill, "Race-Class Questions"; Lucius T. Outlaw, "Race and Class in the Theory and Practice of Emancipatory Social Transformation"; Maulana Karenga, "Society, Culture and the Problem of Self-Consciousness: A Kawaida Analysis"; in *Philosophy*, ed. Harris, 107-116; 117-129, 212-227, respectively.

[12]*Ebony*, "The Black Revolution: Special Issue," August 1969, 29-166; "Which Way Black America?: Separation? Integration? Liberation?," Special Issue (August 1970): 83-173; and "Angela Davis and Struggle against Racism-Imperialism" in *World Marxist Review* 14 (February 1971): 143-45.

[13]Outlaw, "Philosophy, Hermeneutics, Social-Political Theory: Critical Thought in the Interest of African Americans," in *Philosophy*, ed. Harris, 80-83. This argument builds upon Jürgen Habermas, *Legitimation Crisis*, trans. Thomas McCarty (Boston: Beacon, 1979).

[14]Milner S. Ball, *The Promise of American Law: A Theological, Humanist View of Legal Process* (Athens: University of Georgia Press, 1981), 12-14, and Paul Louis Lehmann, "A Christian Alternative to Natural Law," in *Modern Constitutionalism and Democracy: Commemorative Volume for the 65th Birthday of Gerhard Liebholz*. Trans. by Karl Dietrich Bracher, et. al., with assistance by Han-Justus Rinck (Tübingen: J. C. B. Mohr [Paul Siebeck], 1966), 531.

[15]Cf. Berkley B. Eddins and Essie A. Eddins. "Liberalism and Liberation," in *Philosophy*, ed. Harris, 159-73; and Michael Walzer, *Spheres of Justice: A Defense of Pluralism and Equality* (New York: Basic Books, 1983), 17-30, 78-83, 106-108.

[16]Cornel West, *Prophecy Deliverance: An Afro-American Revolutionary Christianity* (Philadelphia: Westminster, 1982), 112-121.

[17]James Boggs, *Racism and the Class Struggle: Further Pages from a Black Worker's Notebook* (New York : Monthly Review Press, 1970), 146-160; Outlaw, "Race and Class," in *Philosophy*, ed. Harris, 117-129; Francis Beale, "Double Jeopardy: To Be Black and Female," in *Black Theology: A Documented History 1966-79*, ed. Gayraud S. Wilmore and James H. Cone (Maryknoll, N.Y.: Orbis, 1979), 368-376; Eugene Victor Wolfenstein, *The Victims of Democracy: Malcolm X and the Black Revolution* (Los Angeles: University of CA, 1981), 15-16, 31-32.

[18]Jacquelyn Grant, "Black Theology and the Black Woman," in *Black Theology*, eds. Wilmore and Cone, 423-26; c.f. Grant, *White Woman's Christ and Black Women's Jesus: Feminist Christology and Womanist*

Response, edited by Susan Thistlethwaite. American Academy of Religion Academy Series, 64 (Atlanta, Ga.: Scholars Press, 1989), 195-230.

[19]Ibid. Cf. Delores S. Williams, "Womanist Theology: Black Women's Voices;" and Cheryl J. Sanders, "Christian Ethics and Theology in Womanist Perspective;" in *Black Theology: A Documentary History, vol. II: 1980-1992,* ed. James H. Cone and Gayraud S. Wilmore, 265-72; and 336-44, respectively.

[20]Reinhold Niebuhr, *Moral Man and Immoral Society* (New York: Scribner, 1932, 1960), 240-56.

[21]Theodore R. Weber, *Modern War and the Pursuit of Peace* (New York: The Council on Religion and International Affairs, 1968), 28-39.

Chapter 7

Ecclesiology and Covenant: Christian Social Institutions in a Pluralistic Society[1]

James R. Thobaben

Christian social morality has traditionally been expressed in specialized institutions that reflect, formally or informally, the ecclesiology of the churches that established them. Through the service institutions, religious organizations declare their ecclesiological formulas, making theological assertions about the nature of God and the church's relation to the world. These institutions are the structured declaration of belief. In fact, Christian social ethics can be portrayed accurately only when institutional expressions of that morality are taken into account.

This study is an examination of Christian service institutions at the turn of the twenty-first century, specifically those institutions spawned by the mainline/old-line denominations in the United States. First, current organizational trends among these institutions and the denominations will be discussed. Second, a consideration of the theological and institutional transitions that occurred in the 1960s will be used to explain these organizational trends. Third, the organizations themselves will be matched with ecclesiologies, and the organizations' coherence with the Christian social values for which they were created will be examined. The study assumes that these core values remain unchanged, though how they are best served is altered by time and a changing cultural environment. Finally, the study will consider the dilemma faced by "Christian" institutions at the close of the twentieth century and the implications for Christian social ethics.

Changes to Be Taken into Account

Institutional expressions can be categorized or differentiated according to their predominant moral orientation. H. Richard Niebuhr's categorization in *Christ and Culture* is an effort to provide a typology for the Christology of social morality. The church/sect dichotomy offered by Troeltsch (and supplemented with Niebuhr's description of the denomination) is an analysis of ecclesiological patterns that suggests how and why certain institutional forms are generated.[2] While both of these models were ground-breaking and still remain useful, there have been at least three social changes that require further development of the typology. The first two of these social changes have to do with internal ecclesiological matters. The third has to do with the changing intersection of the church and the civil society.[3]

First, the denominational form of American Christianity (American Catholicism can be included in this description) has traditionally generated service institutions with ongoing religious affiliations. In other words, Christian service of specific kinds was separated from the church proper through a division of spiritual labor. While this had occurred earlier in church history, it reached its apex in nineteenth-century America when sectarian fervor combined with voluntarism. Typically, these institutions (hospitals, retirement homes, colleges, etc.) were begun to meet specific needs as an expression of Christian concern and ministry. Increasingly, however, these institutions have little (if any) religious accountability or sensibility. Time has changed the primary identity of many of these institutions that have drifted away organizationally from their parent denominations. Often the parent denominations see this as quite acceptable.[4]

Second, denominationalism as a mode of organization is going through a transition. Although the ultimate end of this change is not completely clear, it is likely that local churches will have increased autonomy, parachurch organizations will perform many of the national and international functions previously assumed by denominational organizations, and some denominations will split along an orthodox/liberal line.[5] In this environment, institutions will tend to grasp greater autonomy just as would most individuals in times of uncertainty. They will likely move to distinguish themselves organizationally. The principal criterion for institutional board membership will no longer be church affiliation. Mission statements will coincide with requirements of accrediting bodies, not denominations. In the event of schism, institutions will probably side with the least restrictive "camp" or will "stay out of the fray."[6]

Third, Christianity cannot be assumed to be the core or generally accepted world view in American society. It is not necessary to rehearse the various secularization arguments of the past five decades. Let it suffice to say that, whether persons are actually less religious at a personal level or less committed to particular forms of organized religion, there is clearly a dwindling assumption that Christianity is America's unifying world view. To some this is unfortunate, to others a blessing. Either way, as E. Clinton Gardner has observed, "the very possibility of a Christian social ethic in a pluralistic setting has been called into radical question."[7]

The "calling into question" is no more apparent than in the reidentifying of institutions. How many administrators at United Methodist or Presbyterian (USA) or Episcopalian institutions of higher learning would hesitate using—in fact, would reject—the moniker "Christian college?" How many would suggest there is an historical tie or, perhaps, a common "ethos," but not Christian doctrinal or moral specificity? How many healthcare institutions carry denominational or religious names, yet function in a manner not significantly different from any other provider?

For the institutions under consideration (hospitals, colleges, etc.), it may be that other priorities have necessarily displaced matters of religious obligation. For instance, the Joint Commission on the Accreditation of Healthcare Organizations (JCAHO) has the power, for all practical purposes, to determine whether or not insurers will pay a hospital. Satisfying the JCAHO naturally assumes greater importance than responding to ecclesiastical inquiries or discussing theological ethics. Similar, though somewhat weaker, assertions could be made for academic institutions submitting to the formal authority of regional accrediting bodies and the informal authority of professional and academic societies.

As any organization becomes bureaucratized and increasingly interacts with other bureaucracies, funding mechanisms and adherence to the rules of participation are routinized, as Max Weber showed. This is, apparently, inevitable for institutional ministries as the visionary figures that initiate a particular expression of Christian social outreach give way to those who can operate an institution according to societal requirements.[8] This identity drift is, to a great extent, organizationally necessary for the hospital or nursing home or college that wants to be legitimized (accredited) by the state (and, thus, eligible for funding through Medicare/Medicaid or student loans).

The shift from vision and strong doctrinal content to maintenance and weak doctrinal content reflects not only routinization but also the diminution of religious identity as a source of institutional legitimation in late twentieth century America. The institutional need to satisfy the demands of academia and the health-care industry can easily overwhelm weakened covenantal obligations with local congregations and irate "Christian" alumni.

The more important question, from a Christian point of view, is why the Church accepted this shift? What was the ecclesiological framework that tolerated organizational drift and institutional re-identification? Is there a way to respond? Is there even a reason to respond? If this shift in primary allegiance was only "natural" in organizational terms (which it seems to have been), then should there be or can there be a "supernatural" alternative? Ultimately, these are questions that can be answered only by considering the operational ecclesiology of American denominationalism, especially that functioning in the mainline/old-line churches.

A Brief Look Back for the Purpose of Looking Forward

It has already been suggested that some drift toward bureaucratization is inevitable. Further, it has been implied that this was all the more likely given the American tendency for greater and greater differentiation/specialization. This has been particularly manifest in health care and education, in so far as institutional bureaucracies found organizational legitimation within their fields of specialization, not with the church. Still, the question remains, what ecclesiology made this possible without significant conflict?

Since the Reformation, there have been numerous social reform movements. Frequently, these were associated with some segment of the church, especially in the United States. This was true of the response to poverty in the late eighteenth century (including prison reform), the abolitionist movement, the suffrage movement, child work and labor reform, Prohibition, and the antiwar movement during the Vietnam War. Sometimes these movements represented the strongest feelings of the majority of laypersons and denominational authorities; sometimes they were on the fringe of an otherwise socially reactionary organization. Sometimes participation was deemed prophetic, sometimes meddling, and sometimes arrogantly self-righteous. In each case, however, the response was conditioned, to a great extent, on the interpretation of the church's role in the world, the ecclesiology of Christian social participation. In turn, these movements themselves altered the operative ecclesiology.

Nowhere was this more evident than in the civil rights movement of the late 1950s and 1960s.[9] It is not that this movement alone caused a transformation in ecclesiology, but that the changes in ecclesiology were evident in the church's role in claiming civil rights for a disfranchised segment of the population.

The civil rights movement, by the midsixties, was marked by at least four specific theological-ethical assertions with associated ecclesiological assumptions. First, Christianity is intrinsically an inclusive religion. Second, the church has an obligation to speak and act prophetically. Third, Christianity has a shared spiritual heritage and *spirituality* with other religions. Fourth, spiritual progress is possible, and such progress includes both Christian and secular institutions working together to achieve a social *telos*.

Christians, white and black, willingly or grudgingly, joined in the movement against racial discrimination because, ultimately, such discrimination contradicted the vision of the church triumphant. The operative ecclesiology included a realizable eschatology. Clearly, the imagery of Martin Luther King, Jr., depended upon descriptions of the "lion and lamb" lying down together, the New Jerusalem where there will be trees for the healing of the nations, and the image from *Micah* 4:4 of each person having a vine under which to enter into peaceful repose.

Apparently for King, and certainly for many African-American church members, participating in civil rights activities expressed the priority of one's faithfulness to God. Such faithfulness was central in defining the social process. For many Euro-Americans from the mainline denominations during the sixties, on the other hand, the central concern was not faithfulness to God *per se*. For them, the covenant with God was subordinated to covenants with and among all persons. Moral obligations were reconstrued, so that the central concern was not the interaction of Christians with nonbelievers but rather the general covenantal obligations of all persons to all others. The peaceable kingdom was broadly construed as containing, (or potentially containing), all persons, regardless of race, gender, or even belief.[10]

Neither of these theological self-understandings could be organizationally sustained, and the ecclesiology that emerged after the sixties produced a superficially similar, but essentially altered, moral imperative. The demand was no longer one for mutual tolerance and certainly not one for peaceful evangelism. It went beyond calling for the civility necessary for a pluralistic society to a specific and obligatory social construct. In other words, the eschatological social ethic of the church was replaced by a deontological assertion about rights and entitlements. The "Kingdom of God" was discussed less in terms of heaven or even as a condition of the heart. It was presented, if at all, as a desired political configuration or, even worse, as submission to the sometimes arbitrary authority of those outside the church, but with political and bureaucratic power.[11] Unfortunately, in an effort to accomplish a worthy ethical goal, the Christian community (at least as represented by the mainline/old-line churches) allowed an ecclesiological change that ultimately diminished its theological integrity and its role in the broader society.

When the most fundamental claims for Christian social morality are made on the basis of a general covenant that looks a lot like a social contract, the church undermines its authority and social legitimation. Since it claims nothing special, it is perceived as having nothing to say. Of course, this impacts how seriously those outside the church will take its proclamations. If there is no claim to unique authority, then why listen to the church anymore than to talk radio, especially if the latter is more entertaining? To put this another way, the civil rights movement, though one of the most important social movements in American history, did not build the Kingdom on earth. Since its secular goal (civil rights) does not require a specifically Christian foundation, and its spiritual goal ("the brotherhood of man under the fatherhood of God") was never reached, the church now seems woefully impotent. In fact, it seems unnecessary for social movements and for social service institutions (including hospitals and universities).[12]

Now, twenty years later, those in the old Left who still maintain church affiliations push the organized church forward as a structure for change (a bit of an oxymoron). To most parishioners, however, the church is principally a site for individual comfort and acceptance, its leaders largely ignored on matters of social ethics. Further, this disregard is not limited to individual members of the church. The mainline/old-line ecclesiology lacks plausibility; it cannot legitimate the continuation of the current church structures.[13] This is evident to members and potential members, who feel little, if any, allegiance to denominational authorities. It is also evident to church service institutions—the universities, colleges, nursing homes, and hospitals—which recognize the diminution of the denominational authority, especially relative to that of accrediting bodies.

Why should institutions submit to the church, when the church has demonstrated itself to be unimportant, nearly superfluous, for Christian civic participation? If other bodies have real authority, then they are the powers to which institutions will respond. Further, why should Christian identity be claimed by these institutions, when Christianity is subsumed under a homogenized spirituality of relativism? If the specific truths of Christianity are relativized, then all that really matters are those points of commonality shared with other religions and life philosophies.

To answer a question raised earlier, institutions can pull away from denominations because few people care, and those who do care do not have the power to stop them. The lack of concern is a reflection of the belief that Christianity is not ultimately unique and preferable and, therefore, has nothing "peculiar" to contribute. The lack of power among those who do assert that the church has an important responsibility in spiritually, not just organizationally, guiding institutions is but a manifestation of their general disfranchisement, intentionally or unintentionally, by denominational leaders.

Even so, some religious organizations are forming or expanding institutions. These tend to be those with a more sectarian ecclesiology.

Models of Ecclesiology and Christian Social Service

The mainline/old-line denominations that have the largest number of historically affiliated healthcare and educational institutions seem to be less and less able to maintain a strong relationship with those institutions. Yet, these same denominations frequently assert that they have a role in the public arena, even if not through their institutional service. Some sectarian churches also assert that they have a place on the public square and have developed structures to facilitate participation—advocates in political forums, "think tanks," institutions of higher learning, etc. Still other sectarian groups remain unwilling to participate in such activity if it draws them too far onto the public square; they want to remain on the edge. The best way to understand the orientations toward institutional ministries of the different churches is by comparing the denomination/sect identity with the institutional willingness to participate in the public arena. This provides an "estimate" of the religious community's ecclesiology of social participation.

Contemporary denominational Christianity in America tends to be minimalistic and usually endorses one of two civic approaches: (1) a libertarianism that acknowledges the failures of the old-line denominations and associates those failures with the inevitable failure of communitarianism (this orientation is exemplified by the economic wing of the Republican Party); or (2) a paternalism that assumes that only the elite, be they political or ecclesiastical bureaucrats, know what is best (as manifest by the extreme left portion of the Democratic Party and most old-line denominational bureaucracies). The principal difference between religious advocates in these two groups is that members of the former believe there are no *teloi* but those of the individual. Members of the latter group argue for social *teloi* that are commonly held by all persons (certainly not unique to Christians). Both of these minimal forms of Christianity are the natural outgrowth of denominationalism.

Both groups ignore the priority given in orthodox Christianity to the church and to the fulfillment of the individual's life through the church.

Both deny or downplay the prophetic role of *living* the Gospel message. The libertarian group denigrates the prophetic task or transforms it into an individualistic "spiritual gift." The paternalistic group transforms the prophetic task into the making of pronouncements by denominational hierarchy. Affirmations of personal and social "holiness," once present in the social service institutions, were lost in many denominations when the specificity of Christianity was sacrificed to an inclusiveness so broad that it made identity with the faith nearly impossible.

Sectarian responses also take two forms. One is that expressed by the Religious Right, typified by organizations that express themselves in the public square by insisting on the particulars of Christian personal morality as social policy. The other sectarian form is more separatist; if it makes any comment on the public square, it is by example rather than active participation in the political arena.

Both of these sectarian approaches, to use the familiar typology, emphasize the covenant of the church with its members and of the members with one another, rather than emphasizing a general covenant. The church is the site of the highest covenant. The individual as individual acknowledges Christ, and the individual as a part finds direction through the Body of Christ. The Body of Christ is not the civil society, the state, all humans, or all creation. Although believers may have covenantal obligations to these, such covenants are relativized by the absolute covenant with Christ.

Different ecclesiologies can be described, as in the figure on page 141, by crossing the sect/denomination dichotomy with a private/public dichotomy (the latter based on participation in the public square as central *vs.* peripheral).

The Civil Church ecclesiology legitimates institutions, such as Emory University, that attempt to provide a Christian identity without any fundamental claim for preferring Christianity.[14] The Purifying Church ecclesiology produces institutions like Liberty University, which attempts to meet the core requirements of and, ultimately, supplant other institutions in the civil community; the operating assumption is that a superior set of values directs such public participation. The Marginal Church ecclesiology does not spawn institutions, nor can it long continue to legitimate those that already exist. Rather, the Marginal Church ecclesiology generates occasional donations from individuals, with institutions living off the religious capital of the past. This describes many of the hospitals that continue to use names that are religious, but which do not guide care practices with reliance (explicit or implicit) on Christian values. The Distinct Church ecclesiology promotes the maintenance of the spiritual community, which then serves as the basis for institutional decisions. "Witness" in the public square comes from the way the community functions. An example is the recent purchase by the Chicago-based organization, Jesus People, U.S.A., of a building that contained elderly residents with daily care requirements; JPUSA chose to allow the people to remain, providing shelter and meals, and to include those who so desired as community members.

THE CHURCH ON THE PUBLIC SQUARE [15]

	DENOMINATION	SECT
CENTRAL	*Civil Church* (Old Left)	*Purifying Church* (Religious Right) [in the future, should the Right obtain political control, the Religious Left will occupy this space]
PERIPHERAL	*Marginal Church* (Economic Right & Libertarians)	*Distinct Church* (Separatists & those disengaged from politics, but socially active)

Another way to understand these social structures is to understand their relationship to other religious groups. The state church denies all others. The Purifying Church disregards all others in favor of itself. The Marginal Church disregards the social in favor of the individual's beliefs. The Civil Church relativizes all religious communities, counting itself as one among all others. The Distinct Church relativizes all other community identities on the basis of its theological claim.

These types and the institutions they develop and/or maintain can be considered theologically using a model suggested by Gardner. Appropriating and modifying H. Richard Niebuhr's work, Gardner notes that human social morality is a response to "the three-fold pattern of divine action" as Creator, Orderer, and Redeemer.[16]

Applying this functional, tripartite description of God to the service institutions that are supposed to express love for God, one can roughly categorize three of the four types developed above. The Civil Church emphasizes a theology of creation and an inclusive covenant in which all persons are in a satisfactory relationship with God (or could be even without those orthodox affirmations traditional in the Christian faith). The Purifying Church emphasizes God as Orderer.[17] This is, of course, a manifestation of Calvinist theology and the belief that theocracy is, or can be, legitimate—or, at the very least, that religious values are superior in ordering a functionally efficient state. A closed covenant is viewed as an effective model for the state. The Distinct Church emphasizes the role of Savior, both in its assertions of an historically unique redeemer and in the continuing redemptive power of God manifest in the church. The Christian covenant holds principally within the church and with God. Manifestations of service are, then, manifestations of internal character for the church. If they succeed, that is well and good; if they do not, then the church still has been obedient. The Marginal Church does not correspond to these "modalities" of God; its lack of some theological continuity is part of the reason (along with organizational factors) that its demise through attrition and drifting of its institutions is almost inevitable.

Disagreement over these "assertions" about covenant and the nature of the church (frequently unspoken, so perhaps better called "assumptions") are a fundamental reason for the realignment of American Protestantism. It has been and will be a factor in the continuing trivialization of denominational designations and structures. Likewise, it has been and will be a factor in the changing role of Christian service institutions.

The Dilemma of Being a "Christian" Institution

E. Clinton Gardner writes:

> In its empirical quest, social ethics is a search for the structures, or forms, of human existence in community. In itself such empirical investigation is not social ethics; yet the former is prerequisite to the latter. In addition to a description of the fundamental structures of the human sociality, social ethics includes a critique of the concrete forms in which the latter appear based upon a normative conception of human nature. Such a normative concept is grounded ultimately in faith. Empirical form and normative criteria are united in moral experience. The one cannot be reduced to the other; yet the two are inseparable. Methodologically speaking, the most fundamental problem of ethics is how the relationship between descriptive and normative dimensions of morality can be most adequately understood. [18]

Ecclesiology provides the justification for social structure within the Christian community and, consequently, its institutions. The institutions verify or challenge the normative claims of the ecclesiology. The problem being faced by many so-called Christian service institutions is that they are now challenging or have challenged the very values upon which they were created. More importantly, they are doubting the identity that gave them birth.[19]

The hospitals and colleges were started: (1) as an expression of gratitude to God for saving grace; (2) out of obedience to God as the ultimate authority over the activities of the Church; (3) as sites for educating and strengthening the faithful; a means of evangelism; and (4) as an expression of Christian love and compassion. These became imperatives that found structural expression in service institutions. When the church allows these imperatives to be discarded by service institutions or compels them to discard these imperatives in order to maintain the institution, it has, implicitly or explicitly, encouraged the institutions to modify or terminate their Christian self-identification.

There seem to be four options or possible responses to this process of "modification." The first, and the easiest, is simply to allow the drifting away to continue, unabated. This is the logical response of those holding a Marginal Church ecclesiology. It is also a reasonable choice for those having a Civil Church ecclesiology. With its libertarian commitments, the Marginal Church would not want to limit institutional liberty (especially if it promotes individual liberty). The Civil Church will tolerate the drifting out of fear of sectarian control. After all, a principal value of the Civil Church is the relativity of all values except those governing civility. But this first response will not lead to new institutions.

It is also true, however, that the Civil Church is paternalistic about tolerance and views equality of ends as a key imperative of the covenant of creation. Consequently, a second response to institutional drift is the "Public Church Institution." This institution is somehow Christian, but not exclusively so. Ultimately, since little of what is distinctively Christian can be used for institutional formation, the institutions of the Civil Church begin to look a great deal like the civil religion upon which they are ultimately based—that is, a lowest common denominator "faith" that is theistic (but not Christocentric), that has some notion of intrinsic human goodness, and that holds a belief in the redemptive power of the political process. This ecclesiology will not spawn many new institutions, but will push existing institutions toward higher levels of professional excellence.

The Purifying Church will attempt to completely take over existing institutions when possible, as in the case of Southern Baptist seminaries. Complete control will not always be possible, however, especially when outside accrediting bodies (such as the JCAHO with hospitals) wield considerable authority. Alternatively, the Purifying Church ecclesiology will generate new institutions. These will attempt to compete on the public square (and in the marketplace). They seek to become as big, as rich, and, ultimately, as powerful as those against which they compete.

The Distinct Church will spawn institutions, too. These institutions, however, are far more likely to be small and to spring up spontaneously. Almost inevitably they will be closely linked with particular and *peculiar* Christian communities. These institutions, likely, will not be highly visible nor highly vocal. In fact, these institutions probably would not be competitive in the public square nor in the marketplace even if the churches involved wanted them there. They will rely on significant volunteer participation or high financial commitment from devotees. Often, they will serve persons who cannot pay for services.

Conclusion

Ultimately, the question for Christians is not whether something can "succeed" in a worldly sense. Rather, the question is one of continuity with Gospel.

Marginal Church ecclesiology is nothing but an ecclesiology of decline. SAince the Margianl Church is essentially a gathering of individuals with no long-term commitments nor shared spirituality, the continuation of organizations with a common religious base is unlikely. The Civil Church ecclesiology is one of maintenance through acquiescing to the world; it is too inclusive to be truly covenantal in the Christian sense. It has a covenant based on a theocentric, not Christocentric, theology. It is, then, not essentially Christian, though it is essentially theistic and followers may assume that there is room under the tent for Christians as well as other theists.[20] The effort to reinvigorate institutions spiritually through the Civil Church ecclesiology will almost inevitably fail. The institutions may well get "stronger," but not as Christian institutions. This ecclesiology denies the very authority that gave rise to those institutions in the first place. The Purifying Church erroneously seeks to reclaim lost sociopolitical power, while not recognizing that such power was the primary source of spiritual contamination for the mainline/old-line congregations. The Purifying Church too readily becomes oppressive; Christian ecclesiology, after all, should reflect the servanthood of Christ as well as His sovereignty in its Christology.

One is left with the Distinct Church ecclesiology. The Distinct Church is a communitarian church with strong doctrinal self-identification and moderate to strong commitment mechanisms. There is a strongly exclusive and voluntary character to the communitarian groups who choose to remain in the society but distinct from it. On one extreme, using commitment mechanisms such as attire and titles, are groups like the Salvation Army. At the other extreme are parachurch organizations, such as those that arose out of the Jesus People Movement of the sixties and seventies.

The Distinct Church, though peripheral on the Public Square, must accept that some participation in social dialogue needs to occur. Minimally, the Distinct Church must endorse and advocate for the civility and tolerance that allow it to maintain its distinctiveness without persecution. That does not mean all is "up for grabs," nor does it mean that others are or ought to be invited to participate in the internal moral discussions of the Church.

Christian institutions with a Distinct Church ecclesiology can seek areas of coincidence with society. Christian virtue does correspond to natural virtue, on occasion.[21] Such is the case with civility. Such is the case when Christian institutions submit to the state or regulatory bodies on matters of hygiene and practice standards. But the Distinct Church cannot compromise on the ultimate "truth" of Christianity, including on fundamental matters of bioethics (for healthcare institutions) and on the moral education of young adults in colleges (for institutions of higher learning).

Unfortunately, the state fails to be truly tolerant when it demands the abandonment of Christian claims of distinction and the right to exclusivity. Compromise will be demanded. Both those with Civil Church and those with Purifying Church ecclesiologies are extremely vulnerable to such compromise as they attempt to maintain their central position in the dialogue on the public square. The Christian institution that abandons its claim to exclusivity has ceased to be Christian; of this the Civil Church should be wary. The Christian institution that accepts the sometimes vicious political practices of the state abandons its claim to purity; of this the Purifying Church should be wary.

As Niebuhr asserts, there is a "fitting" response to particular circumstances, and the circumstances of postmodern Protestantism in the West require the Christian institution to be tolerant of sinners, and even of sin—when it is not to the opint of fundamental compromise—when it is not an immediate threat to the community of faith. If this assertion is taken to its logical end, then it has specific implications for Christian social structures. Those with a Civil Church ecclesiology should assume some of the characteristics of a Distinct Church institution. Those with a Purifying Church ecclesiology should maintain their particularity while adopting some of the civility of the Civil Church. Institutionally, a Christian college ought to accept students of different backgrounds while expecting adherence to the moral order of the church. Christian hospitals should accept all patients possible, but also should set standards for practitioners that would forbid activities such as euthanizing the distraught or deeming the quality of life for disabled persons to be lower than that of the "healthy."

Christian denominational bureaucracies should recognize that in the seventies and eighties they "over-corrected" for the institutional failures of the past and should resume a commitment to proclaiming Jesus as Savior while maintaining a commitment to social justice and order. Christian institutional missions and ministries should declare unashamedly that salvation comes uniquely through Jesus Christ, but should do so in recognition of the particularities of the societies and sub-cultures in which the church finds institutional expression. These requirements can be met only when denominational and institutional leaders recognize that the church is, indeed, to be "in the world, but not of it." Denominations must become a bit more sectarian. If the denominational leaders do not reclaim this portion of the heritage, even while being aware of the changing cultural and regulatory environment, then only the sectarian groups will have institutions that are both vital and distinctly Christian.

Notes

[1] With pleasure and great respect, this paper is offered in honor of E. Clinton Gardner. As a scholar, he is knowledgeable. As an instructor, he accepts disagreement while demanding clarity. As a mentor, he helps both with practical matters of employment and spiritual concerns of "calling." As a friend, he is simply that—a friend. It is a mark of his stature as a teacher that Dr. Gardner would likely disagree with the conclusions of this paper, but would nonetheless willingly engage in dialogue on its content and its claims.

[2] Troeltsch outlined the typology that serves as the basis for much of the sociology of institutional religion in the West. Ernst Troeltsch, *The Social Teaching of the Christian Church,* trans. by Olive Wyon, (Chicago: The University of Chicago Press, 1931), II: 691-693. His arguments may not extend to non-Western communities but do continue to have some applicability in the modern West. In the United States, and now in Europe, too, one must add to Troeltsch's categories of state church and sect a third category, denomination, as suggested by H. Richard Niebuhr. Troeltsch included another category of religious understanding, the mystic. This term, essentially, refers to organizationally individualistic religion.

In this study, Troeltsch's church is referred to as state church. It is a highly inclusive organization for which membership is conferred by citizenship. Baptism, the usual initiation rite, is as much a matter of state function as church function. This inclusiveness means that the church does not have strong commitment mechanisms because there is such a strong correspondence between church membership and citizenship. The state church is highly involved in sociopolitical matters and participates intimately in state functions.

The sect, on the other hand, requires of members a much stronger self-identification with the religious organization. The commitment mechanisms are much stronger because the sect operates over and against the state or culture. It has an exclusive membership that, under most circumstances, is voluntary, and it quite often involves withdrawal from the state. A covenantal relationship with the state is unlikely.

H. Richard Niebuhr recognized that neither of these two categories fully described the American situation and so added a third in his *Social Sources of Denominationalism.* H. Richard Niebuhr, *Social Sources of Denominationalism* (New York: New American Library, 1929, 1857). The denomination, like the state church, has a weak identification and does not have strong commitment mechanisms. Like the state church, it is highly involved in the sociopolitical arena. It also can be extremely inclusive, if not through formal membership, then through the willingness to assign spiritual equivalency to nonmembers. The principal differences between the denomination and the state church are that there is no state endorsement of a denomination and that membership in the denomination is voluntary. The denomination often endorses the state or the activities of particular political parties. Another distinction between it and the state church is a slightly greater emphasis on the desire for societal transformation. In some ways, the Marginal Church may be an expression of the "mystification" (in Troeltsch's sense) or individualization of spirituality. At some point, such individualization negates the need for formal ecclesiastic structures.

3 For another approach to the impact of social changes on the Troeltsch/Niebuhr typology, see Anthony Battaglia, "'Sect' or 'Denomination?': The Place of Religious Ethics in a Post-Churchly Culture," *The Journal of Religious Ethics* (Spring 1988):

4 This acceptance on the part of the denominational leaders may reflect a fear of litigation or a recognition that the differentiated institutional responsibility is simply more than the denomination can continue to assume. Certainly, there is a great deal of self-examination. For instance, "[m]embers of United Methodism's University Senate, charged with reviewing and approving church-related schools, pondered the reciprocal roles of the nine-million member church and its schools."(*East Ohio Today* 12:3:7, February 5, 1995).

5 See R. Stephen Warner, *New Wine in Old Wineskins: Evangelicals and Liberals in a Small-Town Church* (Berkeley: University of California Press, 1988). See also Robert Wuthnow, *The Restructuring of American Religion: Society and Faith Since World War II* (Princeton, N.J.: Princeton University Press, 1988).

6 An exception may be the free-standing denominational seminaries. For instance, some Southern Baptist Convention seminaries (voluntarily or through institutional force) have sided with the Fundamentalists (this term is used in its technical sense); they have faced the negative response of accrediting agencies. Other .SBC institutions (hospitals and universities) have followed the trend of 'drifting' away. In the midst of this, some SBC members have attempted to resist both trends by asserting a Christian

distinctive while arguing for continued positive interaction with persons not sharing the Fundamentalist world view.

[7]Gardner, *Christocentrism and Christian Social Ethics*, 2.

[8]To extend Weber's terms a bit further than he probably intended, the visionary has the authority of a prophet while the organizational leader has the authority of office. The former tends toward creating new expressions (often based on old values), while the latter maintains the organization once created. Arguably, both are necessary. The questions are: What ought the mix of office and prophet be?; and, Who or what legitimates the authority of office? The former question is an old one, especially among Protestants, and is probably irresolvable. The latter is a different form of the question that may be underlying much of the reorganization of American Protestantism.

[9]One small indication of how important this social issue was to the church and its institutions is that E. Clinton Gardner chose to conclude his book *Biblical Faith and Social Ethics* not with a summary chapter but with one on race relations. This concluding analysis of race relations, inside and outside of the institutional church, is suggestive. Gardner correctly anticipates much of what will happen in race relations during the sixties. In retrospect, however, he seems a bit optimistic about the role of the mainline (now old-line) denominations and super-denominations.

It is important, in this connection, to make certain that emphasis upon the obligation of the churches to become inclusive in their membership shall not be allowed to hide the fact that the realization of this goal is ultimately a means of grace and spiritual enrichment. Those who have participated in the life and activities of the World Council of Churches and National Council of Churches of Christ in the U.S.A., as well as in other genuinely interracial organizations *which are no longer self-conscious about their inclusiveness*, are aware of the freedom and the enrichment which such fellowship brings. [E. Clinton Gardner, *Biblical Faith and Social Ethics* (New York: Harper & Row, 1960), 372-373. *italics added*].

Gardner's error, I would suggest, lay not in theological ethics but in his underestimation of how much church institutions can be co-opted by the society in which they function and in his underdeveloped ecclesiology. The latter point he addresses in his later work on covenant.

[10]Included among the various social positions was a new interpretation of what it meant to be a Christian pacifist (though some tendencies had existed among the intellectual and ecclesiastical elite at least as early as the 1930s. Previously, Christian pacifism usually had been based on the assumption that nonviolence would often result in persecution or, at best, benign neglect. Pacifism was an expression of Christian character, and nonparticipation was the usual political orientation of pacifists. Under King's influence, pacifism was generally accepted as a characteristic of certain political tools, like the sit-in and the economic boycott, by which particular

political ends could be achieved. For some, it was also an expression of Christian character, as in traditional pacifism, but not for all.

[11]Those with power on the left were the powers in the left-wing of the Democratic Party; on the right, the power was lodged, eventually, in the Religious Right.

This tendency remains among both the left and the right. Both "sides" assume that the correct way of interpreting the role of the church in social activity lies somewhere on a continuum between the far-left wing of the Democratic Party and the so-called Religious Right. Both sides assume that Christian participation in the political process must be overt and aggressive ("prophetic" becomes a cliché). Both sides assume that nonparticipation indicates a lack of understanding (thus, requiring appropriate indoctrination) or lack of obedience (thus, requiring disciplinary action) or a lack of commitment (thus, requiring attendance at a seminar, participation in a "retreat," or membership in some voluntary advocacy organization). See *From Max Weber: Essays in Sociology*, trans. and ed. by H.H. Gerth and C. Wright Mills (New York: Oxford University Press, 1946), 262, 297 (selections from *Wirthshaft and Gelleschaft*).

[12]The breakdown of politically liberal humanism within the civil rights movement was not due solely to internal factors. The Nation of Islam and the Black Power movement raised questions of social identification that challenged the legitimacy of the "one, big, happy family" motif. Without a strong Christian moral foundation to justify integration (by the late sixties it had been abandoned), the movement could not survive in its once-vibrant form.

[13]Berger describes the role of those churches woven into the social fiber in this manner:

Religious developments originating in the Biblical tradition may be seen as causal factors in the formation of the modern secularized world. Once formed, however, this world precisely precludes the continuing efficacy of religion as a normative force. We would contend that here lies the great historical irony in the relation between religion and secularization, an irony that can be graphically put by saying that, historically speaking, Christianity has been its own grave digger. (Peter Berger, *The Sacred Canopy*, 128-129)

[14]This category corresponds, generally, with the "Public Church" model suggested by James W. Fowler III and others. See James W. Fowler, *Faith Development and Pastoral Care* (Philadelphia: Fortress Press, 1987), 113-120.

[15]The terms do not include Troeltsch's "state church," since that is not functional in the United States and, indeed, may not be applicable in Europe any longer either.

[16]Gardner, *Christocentrism in Christian Social Ethics*, 210.

[17]Gardner writes:

Order and justice are grounded primarily in the governing action of God. The former are not, however, related to creation primarily in a negative way. On the contrary, both are related directly to creation as the structure or form in which the fulfillment of creaturely human life becomes possible in community. But order and justice also have a negative or preserving function, viz., the restraint of evil which results from human sinfulness. While the preserving work of justice has a certain priority over its positive task of human fulfillment, the former cannot be separated from the latter; nor can it be defined in terms of a different set of moral criteria. In both its negative and its positive forms justice is a condition of order in community. Order rests upon the promise of justice in both its restraining and its creative forms. Since sin is universal, covenant means the acceptance of shared responsibility and mutual accountability for the restraint of evil as well as the pursuit of common goals such as freedom, justice, and peace. (Gardner, *Christocentrism in Christian Social Ethics*, 215)

It is apparent, however, that Gardner does not see the ordering function of the Church in the same light as a Calvinist reconstructionist. Still, Gardner's reference does make clear that these categories are "ideal" and that each ecclesiology will likely include reference to creation, order, and redemption, but will do so with differing emphases.

[18]Gardner, 1983, p.176.

[19]A notable example is Oberlin College. The institution was created by Christian utopians. It was raised under the parental authority of Charles Finney, who emphasized both evangelicalism and social responsibilityand demanded the admission of African-Americans and women. It has now reached a point of being so intolerant of Christian uniqueness that significant student *and faculty* protests were lodged against a professor who held an interpretation on a controversial social issue that was clearly within the dominant stream of Christian thought and clearly held by him for religious reasons.

[20]The Public Church is an effort to describe a church that is simultaneously strong in identification, highly inclusive, and a legitimate participant in the public arena. It seems, in fact, that many of those who advocate for such a model are Christians concerned about intolerance within the church. Indeed, the church should avoid intolerance. It should tolerate other religions and moral systems, but not accept them as equal to Christianity. Christianity is an exclusive religion. The capacity of Christianity to include persons of all races, nationalities, genders, etc., is due to its exclusive nature that relativizes all other values/characteristics that claim exclusivity. This includes loyalty to a democratic, pluralistic state. Conversely, when Christians fail to accept others who are Christian, regardless or race, nationality, gender, etc., they are erroneously asserting that other loyalties take precedence.

[21]Gardner says this of Paul:

Paul has much less to say about the relationships of Christians to non-Christians than about their relationships to each other. He recognizes that complete separation from pagan society is impossible (I Cor. 5:10).

The moral standards of non-Christian neighbors are to be respected (Rom. 12:17; I Thess. 4:12; I Cor. 10:32; Col. 4:5). Moreover, there are certain moral standards common to both Christians and pagans(Rom. 2:14-15), and *agape* demands that the Christian make the most of such common convictions as a basis for harmonious relations. The Christian will strive to live peaceably with all men (Rom. 12:18). Not only will he refrain from offending his pagan neighbors, but will seek to do them positive good. Beyond this, if one suffers injury, he is not to seek reprisal against his enemy. Rather, he is to bless those who persecute him. "If your enemy is hungry, feed him; if he is thirsty, give him drink" (Rom. 12:20). In short, Paul says, "Do not be overcome by evil, but overcome evil with good" (Rom. 12:21). (Gardner, *Biblical Faith and Social Ethics,* 90)

Gardner thus asserts a duty of Christian beneficence from Christians toward non-Christians. This is not the simple and ultimate duty of presenting the Gospel through word and deed. It is, according to Gardner, the positive duty to do good of a penultimate nature (Bonhoeffer). Gardner maintains this argument in a much later work, though makes an apparent shift from a responsiblist ethic based on the salvific experience of the community to one which is more explicitly a response to God's creative act (Brunner, Gustafson). In both cases, though, Gardner's social ethics rely on the Niebuhrian dynamic of "fitting response" (*Biblical Faith and Social Ethics,* .209).

Section II

Responsiblist/Covenantal Ethics and Social Policy

Chapter 8

Virtue Ethics and Political Responsibility

Peter Gathje

What are the political assumptions inherent to contemporary expressions of virtue ethics and to the criticisms of these expressions? Is there a way to understand virtue ethics as politically responsible apart from those assumptions? One way to begin answering those questions is to shift the debate about political responsibility and virtue ethics from a focus on theological issues, such as doctrines of creation or ecclesiology, to an analysis of the assumptions about political responsibility implicit both in the criticisms of virtue ethics, and in the thought of the two virtue ethicists most frequently criticized for being politically irresponsible, Stanley Hauerwas and Alasdair MacIntyre.

Such an analysis reveals that those who criticize the sectarian temptation in virtue ethics tend to presume a type of liberal political theory that emphasizes the state as the primary actor in social transformation, to the neglect of other social and institutional actors within civil society. At the same time, Hauerwas and MacIntyre leave themselves open to the sectarian charge because, in rejecting this liberal political theory, they have not developed cogent arguments concerning how a community of virtue might function to nurture social transformation apart from the liberal state and its form of justice within a modern, pluralistic society. In making this analysis, I will draw upon recent work on the role of "civil society." This work describes a type of political responsibility not narrowly focused upon state power and the formation of governmental policies through interest-group politics. Instead, it proposes a politics in which groups or movements with substantive conceptions of the good creatively seek the transformation of the whole of society through an ongoing debate about what kind of life we might share together.

One place to begin examining these issues is with Clinton Gardner's analysis of virtue ethics. Gardner develops his criticisms in an article on the conception of justice in the thought of three "virtue ethicists," James Gustafson, Alasdair MacIntyre, and Stanley Hauerwas.[1]

Political Assumptions in Critiques of Virtue Ethics

Stanley Hauerwas's thought on virtue ethics is representative of positions within contemporary Christian virtue ethics that are criticized for being sectarian and politically irresponsible. His dialogue partner in secular moral philosophy, Alasdair MacIntyre, has deeply influenced Hauerwas, and also has been criticized for his sectarian visions of how a life of virtue ought to be practiced within a society structured by liberal political and economic institutions. It is entirely appropriate that Gardner, in posing the question of the relation between virtue ethics and the pursuit of justice within a liberal polity, reserved his most stringent criticisms for Hauerwas and MacIntyre. Though he found Gustafson equally guilty with Hauerwas and MacIntyre for failing "to give adequate attention to the relation of justice conceived as a virtue to law," he rightly saw Gustafson moving toward a more "responsible" social ethics.[2] Gustafson's recent work and (as I will detail below) his own critique of Hauerwas confirm Gardner's original analysis.

What are the political assumptions evident in Gardner's criticisms of Hauerwas and MacIntyre? Gardner's critique of MacIntyre focuses on the famous ending of *After Virtue*[3] as indicative of MacIntyre's social ethics. There, MacIntyre called "for the construction of . . . local forms of community in which morality and virtue can be sustained and nurtured during the new age of barbarism which is upon us." MacIntyre concluded, "we are waiting for another—but doubtless a very different—St. Benedict."[4] Gardner understands MacIntyre as giving us a "double morality based upon our relationships to two different communities, one ruled by law and one by virtue."[5] As Gardner sees it, MacIntyre's argument is that since justice in the virtue tradition is incompatible with the liberal state and its justice, people seeking to practice a more substantive justice grounded in a shared vision of the good (and thus hoping to become just persons) have no choice other than to form local communities apart from liberal political and economic institutions. Gardner believes MacIntyre's proposal is important, but flawed. Although the West might need the sort of community and virtuous persons that MacIntyre suggests "as an answer to the problem of justice . . . [such a community] is finally inadequate, for it makes the latter [justice] basically irrelevant in modern pluralistic societies."[6] This is the case, Gardner argues, because we live in a pluralistic society in which politics is structured by a liberal state, and "the questions of justice and community necessarily include questions of responsibility and accountability in the midst of our given pluralism."[7] For Gardner, the communities MacIntyre suggests need to attend to how they would interact with a liberal politics in which a procedural justice provides the shared public language necessary in a pluralistic society. Since MacIntyre's communities will not speak that language, they will be sectarian and politically irresponsible.

Gardner's charge of political irresponsibility reveals his assumption of a liberal political theory. In such a theory, political responsibility is defined as direct engagement with the liberal state in order to form policies consistent with a procedural justice that places the right prior to the good. Given the pluralism of modern society, liberal justice champions a procedural approach that claims a neutrality in terms of substantive visions of the good, and instead seeks impartially to adjudicate rival claims and interests.

Gardner's assumption of this political theory is even more evident when he criticizes Hauerwas. Hauerwas, Gardner writes, sees a fundamental opposition between liberal justice and the church's practice of the virtue of justice. As Gardner summarizes, "Hauerwas's emphasis . . . is upon the essential moral opposition between the church and the world based upon the different narratives in terms of which the two understand themselves."[8] Gardner finds that Hauerwas's attempts to define a political role for the church lacks both theological and political clarity. Though Hauerwas clearly wants the church to be socially transformative, he provides neither a theological base for this work of the church nor a political theory for transformation within the existing liberal institutional order and its justice attuned to a pluralistic society. Gardner writes, "Hauerwas is unable to integrate the resources of natural justice and the common good into his social ethics because he does not have an adequate doctrine of creation."[9] Without a doctrine of creation that gives some theological legitimacy to the existing liberal state (or any state) and its form of "natural" justice, "the church has little to offer in terms of political strategy."[10] Gardner concludes that Hauerwas is left with the sectarian and politically irresponsible position that "the church's main contribution to justice lies in the formation of a people informed by the virtues."[11] Again, Gardner's theological critique reveals his assumption that political responsibility is largely confined to the formation of policies within the liberal state and its procedural form of "natural" justice. Since Hauerwas lacks a doctrine of creation that underwrites the procedural justice of this state, his church is rendered politically irrelevant.

Gardner's critique of MacIntyre and Hauerwas is supported and sharpened by other critics who share Gardner's assumptions about political responsibility within a liberal polity and pluralistic society, and how virtue ethics fails to be responsible in this context. For the sake of brevity I will restrict my examples of this to critics of Hauerwas, though what they criticize could more or less directly apply to MacIntyre also.

Wilson D. Miscamble judges Hauerwas's ecclesiology to be "quite sectarian," because it "effectively removes the church from the life and death policy issues of the human community."[12] He finds Hauerwas dismissive of the value of dialogue and the possibilities for "cooperation with those outside of the church who work in pursuit of justice."[13] He contrasts Hauerwas's approach with the process of the United States Catholic Bishops in their writing of their pastoral letter on nuclear arms. Unlike the Bishops, "Hauerwas, effectively, runs from responsibility."[14] Miscamble goes on to define political responsibility as "working within the system."[15] In contrast to this type of political responsibility, he finds that Hauerwas "self-righteously dismisses efforts to deal with the 'problems of the world,'" which involve "acquiring power at the top, which I take to mean influencing public policy."[16] Miscamble, in language stronger than Gardner's, thus tends to narrow responsible political activity to attaining and participating in state power. Still, at the end of his critique, Miscamble offers a tantalizing clue that Hauerwas might not be so easily dismissed as politically irresponsible. Miscamble writes that Hauerwas does not claim to reject political involvement, even though "he never elucidates what form such involvement should take."[17] Miscamble offers an example of this when he suggests that Hauerwas argues for nonviolence but does not address how Christians should actively participate in nonviolent resistance. I will return to this point later.

Michael J. Quirk also finds Hauerwas open to the charge of "sectarianism of some sort."[18] Quirk defines sectarianism as taking the position that outside of the sect there is no possibility of rational dialogue, and therefore no possibility of forging a consensus beyond the truth of the sect. Quirk notes that Hauerwas does not have a foundationalist inflexible epistemology, so he is not like other sectarians. If Hauerwas had that type of epistemology he would recognize no truth apart from that defined by the church. Instead, Hauerwas has a narrative epistemology that stresses that how we know the truth is shaped by the community we participate in and its story. Truth is not limited to that community, but our knowledge of truth is always filtered through a particular narrative; we know what is true because our character has been shaped in such a way to recognize what is true.[19] Hauerwas thus is critical of the universalism in liberalism, which does not so much respect different visions of the truth as seek to find under pluralism a common denominator grounded in an abstract rationality. It is that type of rationality that he finds undergirding liberal procedural justice, which asserts that public argument must take the form of reasons that can and must be made from anyone's point of view.[20] Given Hauerwas's antipathy toward liberal justice, Quirk concludes, "Hauerwas's nod toward secular political involvement seems to be at best an example of 'gestural' politics."[21] Quirk does not pursue what he means by "gestural politics." Instead, he proceeds to state his own assumption that a politically responsible church must speak to the state in the language of the state—the language of liberal justice. He asks, "How effective can the church's 'worldly' political presence be if its first commitment is to speak a language that the world does not presently share?"[22] For Quirk, too, responsible political engagement means participation in politics as defined by the state.

Thomas Ogletree takes a slightly different approach in his critique. Instead of focusing on language, he finds Hauerwas unrealistic and therefore irresponsible because of the institutional and practical difficulties in Hauerwas's virtue ethics. Ogletree's chief criticism is that Hauerwas advocates a "sectarian witness" without attending to the social conditions necessary for that witness actually to be practiced. This failure opens the door to political irresponsibility.

As long as Christian people are heavily involved in the major institutions of a society and are dependent in fundamental ways for their well-being on those institutions, they are not likely to have the personal and social resources necessary for sustaining a radical witness to society. A call for sectarian witness which does not from the beginning address those problems is itself apt to be a temptation to self-deception, i.e., a justification for noninvolvement with persons and groups struggling for justice and for their own liberation as human beings.[23]

Ogletree presents the options facing those who would attempt to practice Hauerwas's ethics and engage in social transformation.

> If Christians are to occupy the offices of society, then they must attend to "compromises"—indeed, to the involvement in evil—those offices entail. If they would stand over against society in radical criticism, then they must to the highest degree possible become materially independent of its institutions and be prepared to bear the additional burdens such independence imposes.[24]

Thus, while Ogletree recognizes that radical criticism might have some role in social transformation, it is practically impossible (or nearly so) to sustain such a politics. In particular, Hauerwas's advocacy of such a politics of witness is unrealistic given his inattention to how it might be structured and practiced. If Hauerwas urges the rejection of goods secured by state power (and violence), then he must give some sense of how a community might be organized around an alternative way of life. Since he fails to do that, he promotes an irresponsible attempt to avoid getting one's hands dirty while continuing to share in the goods secured by the state's dirty hands.

Gustafson's critique of Hauerwas shares with other critics the assumption that political responsibility involves political engagement on the terms of the existing liberal political institutions. He shares Gardner's theological argument that Hauerwas lacks a doctrine of creation that would legitimate Christian participation in "natural" human institutions such as the liberal state. Gustafson finds Hauerwas succumbing to the "sectarian temptation" because he ignores the doctrine of creation and instead attempts "to isolate Christian theology and ethics from external points of view in order to maintain the uniqueness or historic identity of Christianity."[25] This theological mistake, Gustafson contends, results in Hauerwas's political irresponsibility because it "isolates Christianity from taking seriously the wider world of science and culture and limits the participation of Christians in the ambiguities of moral and social life in the pattern of interdependence in the world."[26] Gustafson's critique, like Gardner's and the others, emphasizes that "to take seriously" the cultural and institutional setting means acting responsibility within existing liberal institutions. To attempt to stand apart is irresponsible; it is a "tribalism" that makes no contribution to the "critical ambiguous choices" of public life.[27]

Together, these criticisms of Hauerwas and MacIntyre assume that political responsibility requires participation in state-centered politics and thus in the formation of policies that conform to the cultural and institutional requirements of such politics. Within a modern society with institutional and cultural pluralism this means participating in a liberal politics organized around a liberal state. Political responsibility thus comes to be defined by two qualities. First, one must recognize that state power is the engine of the political system. Other institutional actors or social movements must use the language and practices of the state when interacting with the state. Second, responsible political engagement must focus on effectively interacting with and participating in state power. In the context of the liberal state this means using a public language shaped by the demands of a procedural approach to justice.

Yet within these criticisms of Hauerwas and MacIntyre there are hints that the formation of communities of virtue that do not focus on the state, and that act publicly without using the language of the state, might have some political importance. As Gardner recognized, the formation of people in virtue does have political consequences, even if they are insufficient. Likewise, Quirk noted a form of "gestural politics" that might have some limited role in politics. Finally, Miscamble, Ogletree, and Gustafson see that Hauerwas wants some degree of political involvement, but he inadequately describes what that might require within the existing institutional and cultural order. These critics recognize the possible political import of what Hauerwas proposes, but their own expectations of political responsibility lead them to dismiss his propositions as inadequate and irresponsible. Still, in admitting some political thrust in Hauerwas and MacIntyre, the critics raise an important question for such forms of virtue ethics: Is it possible to develop an alternative view of political engagement that defines responsibility within a pluralistic, institutionally-differentiated, modern society, and yet is not restricted to the procedural justice of the liberal state?

Promise and Problems With Political Responsibility in Hauerwas and MacIntyre

This is not the place, nor is it necessary, to reconstruct MacIntyre's and Hauerwas's critiques of the modern institutional and ethical order. Suffice it to say, that both are critical of this order (in particular the state and the economy) for its inability to be just, owing to its rejection of a teleological view of human life, in which human good would be defined by a substantive account of what it means to be human, and in which institutional life would be unified around that account and its end. In Hauerwas, that account or narrative is distinctly Christian. In MacIntyre, it appears at first to be an Aristotelianism and then later a Thomistic Aristotelianism.[28] Both Hauerwas and MacIntyre recognize that the creation of a unified institutional and cultural order that would sustain such an account of what it means to be human is not currently possible. Absent that, how are persons to live with moral integrity and be politically responsible (concerned to foster a just and therefore good society) in an institutionally and culturally pluralistic society?

As we have seen, MacIntyre's initial suggestion at the end of *After Virtue*, that we wait for a new St. Benedict, hints at the creation of distinctive resistance communities that might eventually transform the larger society and its institutions. If a previous chaotic "dark age" could be redeemed in this way, why not our own? In a later article, MacIntyre develops that suggestion further, even as he takes it in a slightly different direction. Instead of St. Benedict, MacIntyre turns to community as envisioned by Aristotle and Aquinas, stating that "the strengths of an Aristotelian and Thomistic position will only become clear insofar as it . . . is seen to be embodied in particularized forms of practice in a variety of local modes of communal activity."[29] He suggests that in terms of farming, at least, Andrew Lytle and Wendell Berry "provide as good example of what I am saying as any available."[30] MacIntyre underscores his commitment to some form of political responsibility when he writes that such morally exemplary communities that institutionalize the practice of virtue are "a necessary first step in the transformation of public debate, let alone of public moral practice."[31]

MacIntyre's insistence upon politically transformative communities of virtue is further elaborated in *Three Rival Versions of Moral Inquiry*. There he chastises modern moral philosophers for their failure to attend "to the complementary character of narrative and theory both in moral enquiry and in the moral life itself."[32] One important test of a moral theory, MacIntyre argues, is how it is actually enacted and embodied in peoples' lives. An embodiment of a moral theory (and thus of conceptions of justice as part of such a theory) is an important test of both the morality and the validity of the theory. In this context, MacIntyre urges the creation of a "postliberal university of constrained disagreements" that would provide "a place of systematic encounter for rival standpoints concerned with moral and theological justification."[33] This university would "initiate students into conflict" so that they could analyze and argue rival moral and theological systems. MacIntyre's hope is that out of such analysis and argument the current structures of society (including the liberal state and economy) that "have exempted themselves from and protected themselves against being put in question by such systematic intellectual and moral enquiry" would in fact be put into question and thus transformed.[34]

MacIntyre's deeper hope appears to be that out of such substantive moral enquiry the best approximations of truth and justice would start to emerge, and our lives together would begin to be organized around shared conceptions of the good. In making such an argument, MacIntyre is holding out for a substantive politics in contrast to the liberal politics that admits of no shared conceptions of the good, only procedures to produce a neutral adjudication of different interests. It appears that MacIntyre is attempting to propose ways in which social transformation might take place within a culturally pluralistic and institutionally diverse society. Yet, in responding to critics who find his proposals utopian, MacIntyre is less than convincing. He simply charges that such critics see only what contemporary social reality allows them to see and learn only what it allows them to learn, with the result that the very problems that need attention and may be redressed by "utopian solutions" are ignored.[35] Be that as it may, in raising the possibility that an alternative vision might well bring forth what modern society most desperately needs, MacIntyre's failure to give more specific examples of the communities or universities that he is talking about makes the alternative he proposes seem irresponsible—even on his own terms of testing a moral theory by seeing how it is enacted and embodied.

Like MacIntyre, Hauerwas does not call for a withdrawal from public life but looks rather for social transformation grounded in the transformation of persons who participate in and thus embody an exemplary community of virtue. For Hauerwas, the church should be such a community and should provide such a witness to the society as a whole. He writes, "It is the duty of the church to be a society which through the way its members deal with one another demonstrates to the world what love means in social relations. So understood the church fulfills its social responsibility by being an example, a witness, a creative minority formed by obedience to nonresistant love."[36] The church's first social task "is to be the church which entails being a community capable of being a critic to every human pretension."[37] Christians "serve the cause of justice best by exemplifying in their lives" what justice means.[38] Hauerwas envisions a community of virtue in which there are virtuous "disciplined persons capable of challenging the state."[39]

Yet, contrary to his critics who think Hauerwas allows for no cooperation between Christians and non-Christians within the political realm, he insists that Christians should cooperate with others to help secure justice in the world through nonviolent means, since "God's kingdom is wide indeed."[40] Still, it remains accurate given his overall approach to see Hauerwas as primarily conceiving of the church as an institution set in opposition to the existing political and economic order. This stance is, of course, what compels his critics to label him "sectarian."

Hauerwas recognizes the difficulty of creating an oppositional church as a community of virtue, and he seems at a loss to give concrete examples of such a church. Noting Ogletree's criticism, Hauerwas concedes that creating and sustaining a church as an exemplary community of virtue is difficult because of the church's social position in developed economies; people tend to join churches because church communities are "friendly" or provide certain personal services.[41] Hauerwas has also admitted that, despite his conviction about the importance of the church as an alternative community of resistance, he was for a certain length of time "not disciplined by, nor . . . feel[ing] the ambiguity of, any concrete church."[42] Further, though he described himself as a "High-Church Mennonite," he stated that "I find I must think and write not only for the church that does exist but for the church that should exist if we were more courageous and faithful."[43] Finally, in actually proposing practices consistent with what he identifies as a central virtue in Christian life, namely nonviolence, Hauerwas (as noted by Miscamble) has been hesitant and cautious. In particular, he bows to economic considerations, saying he would not en-gage in a serious resistance action because "I want to continue to be paid to teach."[44]

Hauerwas thus appears to be searching for a way to speak of the church's role as politically responsible and transformative, without having the church deny or restrict its own distinctive practices or moral language. He defines political responsibility as engaging in efforts to create and embody in community and in witness an alternative moral vision that remains in public resistance to the state. But, like MacIntyre, Hauerwas has not adequately developed examples of such communities, nor has he given a compelling account of just how these communities of virtue might be socially transformative and politically important within the existing cultural and institutional order. The position of both Hauerwas and MacIntyre may be summarized by the words of John Coleman, who writes, "Political problems are best solved not by technology and instrumental means, but by education to virtue, communal self-sacrifice and restraint and a love for the substantively good society."[45] Still left unanswered, however, is how political problems are to be solved this way within a culturally pluralistic society institutionally dominated by a large, centralized, bureaucratic state and corporate capitalism.

Civil Society and Political Responsibility

One way to begin answering this question is to link MacIntyre's and Hauerwas's visions of exemplary moral communities as transformative with the work of a number of contemporary political theorists who find a role for resistance communities within civil society. By looking at Hauerwas and MacIntyre through the analytical lens of civil society and its role in modern politics, it is possible to start sketching how their emphasis upon alternative communities as the locale for substantive moral and theological discussion, and as embodiments of visions of the good, might put forward a type of political responsibility often overlooked or disparaged by their critics, who assume (as we have seen) a type of liberal political theory as determinative of what is responsible.

Briefly, there is a large and growing literature in contemporary political theory that focuses attention on civil society and its role in political and social transformation in modern societies.[46] Civil society is variously described by such theorists, but they share a number of insights. Without reviewing the differences, I will focus here on some common themes that are especially consonant with MacIntyre's and Hauerwas's vision of communities of resistance.[47]

Generally, civil society may be defined as a cultural and institutional sphere made up of voluntary associations distinct from the state and economy. As such, civil society is a diverse collection of people, organizations, and institutions including but not limited to the church, education, family, fraternal organizations, political organizations, and so on.[48] Civil society is a modern and classically liberal creation. It emerges and exists through the differentiation and limitation of political and economic institutions. It is a public space, secured in part by negative political rights, in which persons may associate, assemble, and communicate in ways free from state or economic control.

Even though the groups within civil society are protected by institutional differentiation and liberal political rights, many of them existed prior to the rise of liberal society, and so do not see themselves as creations of the liberal polity. Thus they engage in activities that "create spaces of opposition to remote, disempowering, bureaucratic and corporate structures."[49] In this way they remain distinct from mere interest groups oriented toward the state and its policies. Instead, they seek to practice a "politics of moral suasion" that includes social and cultural concerns outside the state.[50] Though transformative, such groups resist utopianism based upon either the state (communism, socialism, and at least some forms of liberalism) or the economy (capitalism). Instead they seek to provide for a "self-limiting revolution" in which there is always present a "highly articulated, organized, autonomous, and mobilizable civil society."[51] In this view, both the state and the economy are continuously resisted but not abolished or taken over by a revolutionary group. The dream of a single model of the good society that breaks completely with the present and is beyond conflict and division is rejected.[52] At the same time, oppositional activities are engaged in with the intent of continual transformation of the state and economy.[53]

Hauerwas's vision of the church as a witness community, and MacIntyre's vision of the university as a place of enquiry into substantive conceptions and practices of the good can be seen as having some important affinities with the understanding of civil society engaged in a self-limiting revolution. Both Hauerwas's church and MacIntyre's university are institutions committed to substantive moral languages and practices that provide moral alternatives to contemporary political and economic liberalism and its institutions. Neither Hauerwas nor MacIntyre describes what he is proposing as a "new Christendom" in which the church or university assumes the role of the state. Neither Hauerwas nor MacIntyre advances a single model of the good society that is to dominate all others through force. Hauerwas in particular is careful to emphasize that the central Christian virtue of nonviolence rejects a universalism predicated on force. At the same time, we have seen that both Hauerwas and MacIntyre urge the transformation of society through the witness and activities of their respective communities.

By placing Hauerwas and MacIntyre within a political theory that recognizes the importance of civil society, we may begin to see how both of them are politically responsible, insofar as they stake out a sphere within the modern institutional setting of state and economy that seeks both to resist and to transform those institutions. MacIntyre's longing for a new St. Benedict, for local forms of community structured by the practice of virtues teleologically organized, and for a postliberal university, along with Hauerwas's portrayal of the church as a community of virtue, can be understood as attempts to define a place in which persons can resist the morally corrosive culture and practices of both the liberal state and the capitalist economy. Their efforts may be seen as both requiring and playing a role within civil society that "presuppose[s] the development of autonomous social and political spaces within civil and political society that are guaranteed by rights and supported by the democratic political culture underlying 'formal' representative political institutions."[54]

At the same time, MacIntyre's and Hauerwas's stress on opposition to the liberal polity is consistent with the "rebellious politics" and "politics of moral suasion" practiced within civil society as outlined by Jeffrey Isaac.[55] Within this civil society, Hauerwas's and MacIntyre's "resistance communities" may be understood as practicing what Cohen and Amato identify as "a dualistic politics of identity and influence, aimed at both civil society and the polity (or political society)."[56] The politics of influence seeks to use public speech not to gain power or money but to limit their influence within human life by proposing a moral alternative to their dominance.[57] Political success and responsibility are not, in this case, narrowly defined by or limited to changing public policy, so that the state will give more power or money to a particular group. Rather, political responsibility is the defense and transformation of society on the basis of moral and religious visions of the good.[58] Further, this type of political responsibility recognizes that immediate policy changes may not be as important as changes that evolve over time owing to the continual existence of a resistance movement.[59]

In the United States, the civil rights movement is a case in point. Grounded in the black churches (communities of resistance), this movement sought more than civil rights that could be granted by the state. It also sought by means of a religious vision to transform the cultural attitudes (religious and moral) and institutions supporting racism into what Martin Luther King, Jr., called the "beloved community." Through meetings, marches, civil disobedience, songs, speeches, and writings, this movement reached out to the American people and appealed to their religious and political traditions in order to effect a more profound change than simply the change of law, important as that was. Its aim was higher and broader than a politics consistent with liberal political theory focused on the state and on acquiring rights and social benefits from the state. Instead, the civil rights movement represented a substantive politics concerned with deliberation about what kind of life we share together and with movement toward a vision of the good society, namely, the beloved community. Although it did seek to change particular laws and thus influence the state, it also practiced a politics of identity in which it sought to "undo traditional structures of domination, exclusion, and inequality rooted in social institutions, norms, collective identities, and cultural values based on racial and class prejudice."[60] It is this latter type of transformation that appears similar to but stronger than the "gestural politics" referred to by Quick. This politics of identity does not aim exclusively at the state, but seeks to influence "the norms, social relations, institutional arrangements, and practices" in society as a whole.[61]

Other "case histories" within the United States could be easily given.[62] The antebellum abolitionist movement and elements of the peace movement that have coalesced into communities such as Jonah House or Catholic worker communities are examples of ongoing resistance that is publicly active and uses language and symbols drawn from biblical narratives to shape witness actions that seek to influence public discourse. Jonah House, for example, founded by Philip Berrigan and Elizabeth McAlister and other anti-Vietnam war activists, has for nearly twenty-five years been a community shaped by the virtues of nonviolence, resistance, and community. The formation of the community came as its founders realized that, if they were to continue resisting militarism, war, and an economy premised upon violence, they would need an alternative space of mutual support. McAlister wrote, "There have been no roots in our so-called 'movements' in this country. That is why we sprang up so quick, so energetically, and were burned out so quickly. We've got to dig deeper for them these days. The choices we move among are clear: roots or rockets, tradition or progress, tragedy or arrogance, weakness or power, the gospel or Caesar."[63] In the Jonah House resistance community, members "learn nonviolence as it applies to their personal lives and to the public arena."[64] community they attempt "to create a style of life that would enflesh (however seminally) our vision of the kingdom, that would somehow sustain people, that would somehow resist this society where it is most destructive of life."[65]

In addition to their shared work and simple lifestyle in an inner city neighborhood, community members "study together the sources of nonviolence and resistance, current events and their responses to them, their resources—personal and collective—to confront or diminish those sources of violence." In this way community members come to "assume personal responsibility to become more human, to relearn their cultural heritage, to find ways of reducing complicity in institutionalized violence."[66] The plowshares actions that have emerged from this community symbolically and nonviolently use hammers and blood to "beat swords into plowshares." The community members also engage in other symbolic witness actions at such sites as the White House, the Pentagon, and military research labs. Such actions witness to their faith and thus to their opposition to the bloodshed covered up by "clean" military planning and technology. Daniel Berrigan, also a plowshares activist following his anti-Vietnam war work, writes, "The symbols are an effort to make death concrete.... It is horrifying to see human blood in the immaculate corridors of the Pentagon. Nothing is more dismaying to the people responsible for that enormous Greek temple. Suddenly the truth of the situation is in the air, and under your feet, and it is terrifying."[67]

The point of these actions is to break one imaginative order with another; to present an alternative moral vision. Such public witness thus transcends narrow procedural definitions of justice within the liberal state, and asserts a religiously informed vision of the good society. Daniel Berrigan writes,

> We do not go to the Pentagon and White House to offer an "alternative policy," . . . whatever that might mean. Our task is simply to proclaim the sin of mass destruction, the blasphemy against the God of life implied in weapons of mass killing. Only indirectly could this be called political activity. We see such symbolic events as a

proclamation, an announcement of gospel truth. . . . Our acts are simply extensions of the sacraments . . . celebrations of the liturgical year.[68]

The Berrigans, McAlister, and other participants in such communities of resistance structure their lives and their witness actions in such a way that they embody a virtue ethics that publicly challenges the state and the economy. They undertake in concrete and sustainable ways a kind of resistance that seems to express what Hauerwas urges for the church, and what MacIntyre hoped for the communities that would be inspired by a new St. Benedict.

It is certainly consistent with these communities and with both Hauerwas and MacIntyre to see them as attempting to focus "primarily on issues of social norms and collective identity."[69] MacIntyre, for example, urges that the university be a place of "systematic encounter for rival standpoints concerned with moral and theological justification."[70] Hauerwas, for his part, urges that the first social task of the church is to be the church, whose witness can be transformative.[71] These and other statements made by MacIntyre and Hauerwas advance a view of political action as transformative witness within the diverse collection of social movements that act through a politics of identity and influence involving "social conflict around the reinterpretation of norms, the creation of new meanings, and a challenge to the social construction of the very boundaries between public, private, and political domains of action."[72]

We have seen how both the civil rights movement and the lesser known example of Jonah House might be understood in the same way. Likewise, if seen from within this approach to politics, MacIntyre and Hauerwas are far from politically irresponsible or sectarian. Rather, they share with theorists of civil society a concern to define a crucial role for the church, the university, and other institutions and organizations that stand in resistance against the state and the economy as dominant cultural and institutional powers in modernity.

The political responsibility of Hauerwas's and MacIntyre's positions, and their political success or failure, thus might be better evaluated within a political theory that recognizes the important role of resistance groups active in civil society through practices of "disruptive mischief"[73] or "rebellious politics."[74] In contrast, if one takes the perspective of a liberal political theory that narrowly focuses on easily measurable influence on the state and specific policies, Hauerwas's and MacIntyre's advocacy of such groups would clearly be seen as irresponsible. Seen, however, from the perspective of a political theory that emphasizes a vital civil society, it is clear that both Hauerwas and MacIntyre are urging a form of substantive politics concerned to broaden political discourse beyond the procedural language of the liberal state and to include visions of the good.

In this politics, Hauerwas and MacIntyre challenge liberal (whether Christian or secular) types of political theory that urge leaving political action to professionals who know how to speak and act in the political sphere so as to steer the state effectively. Instead, the communities of resistance Hauerwas and MacIntyre recommend would practice a more direct form of political action through the witness of their lives, which would challenge the moral presuppositions of existing cultural and institutional norms. This substantive politics would push beyond specific policies and aim to expand public discourse and debate into areas left undiscussed and not critically challenged because restricted by liberal definitions of what is "political." This is a politics consistent with Cohen and Amato's discussion of civil society, in which movements and groups insist

> there is more to the political process than the representation of interests, more to legislation than interest compromise, more to the common good or common interest than aggregated preferences, and more to the moral principles underlying constitutionalism and majority rule than the protection of individual rights.[75]

The activities of the resistance communities urged by Hauerwas and MacIntyre are, in this light, political in the sense that they are concerned to challenge and thus influence the moral and political culture or collective identity of society. Communities of resistance provide space in which persons may practice, be shaped by, and give witness to moral lives more profound and soulful than is possible within the state or economy alone. In doing so they carry on a patient but continual revolution against the dehumanizing features of our institutional and cultural order.

Conclusion

Because they do not draw upon this literature about civil society, both MacIntyre and Hauerwas leave themselves open to charges of sectarianism. Although both might wish to modify certain claims made by some (or all) theorists working on the notion of civil society, they nevertheless could respond more forcefully to their critics who make liberal assumptions about political responsibility, if they drew upon such theorists. Further, by enriching their own political theory by attending to the notion of civil society and the groups within it that are engaged in a "politics of moral suasion" or "rebellious politics," Hauerwas and MacIntyre might also become less reticent in giving concrete examples of existing resistance communities that at least approximate the powerful visions of the good they have offered. In this way we could gain a clearer understanding of how, in fact, the virtue ethics they propose, in terms of the church and the university, might actually be embodied in our institutionally diverse and culturally pluralistic society. This would further their own claim to political responsibility since, as MacIntyre himself argued, the test of an ethics is in how it is lived.

Notes

[1]Gardner, E. Clinton, "Justice, Virtue, and Law." *Journal of Law and Religion.* 1984 (No. 2): 393-412. The danger of over-generalizing the charge that virtue ethics is politically irresponsible is evident in that only a few years after Gardner's article appeared, Gustafson himself warned of the "sectarian temptation" in Hauerwas's form of virtue ethics. James Gustafson, "The Sectarian Temptation: Reflections on Theology, the Church, and the University," *Proceedings of the Catholic Theological Society* 40:83-94.

[2]Ibid. p. 393.

[3]MacIntyre, Alasdair, *After Virtue* (2nd Edition) (Notre Dame, Ind.: University of Notre Dame Press, 1984.)

[4]Ibid., 263.

[5]Gardner, *op. cit.*, 395.

[6]Ibid. p. 396.

[7]Ibid.

[8]Ibid., 398.

[9]Ibid., 393. Gardner's theological critique anticipates James Gustafson's, which raised a similar point against Hauerwas. See Gustafson, "The Sectarian Temptation."

[10]Gardner, *op.cit.*, 393

[11]Ibid..

[12]Miscamble, Wilson D., "Sectarian Passivism?" *Theology Today* 44 (April 1987): 69-77.

[13]Ibid., 73.

[14]Ibid., 74.

[15]*Loc. cit.*

[16]*Loc cit.*

[17]Ibid., 75.

[18]Michael J. Quirk, "Beyond Sectarianism?" *Theology Today* 44 (April 1987): 78-86.

[19]For an extended discussion of this see Hauerwas and David Burrell, "From System to Story: An Alternative Pattern for Rationality in Ethics," in Hauerwas and L. Gregory Jones, eds., *Why Narrative? Readings in Narrative Theology* (Grand Rapids: Eerdmans, 1989), 158-190.

[20]Ibid., 162.

[21]Quirk, 85.

[22]*Loc. cit.*

[23]Thomas W. Ogletree, "Character and Narrative: Stanley Hauerwas' Studies of the Christian Life," *Religious Studies Review* 25 (January 1980): 30.

[24]Loc. cit.

[25]James Gustafson, "The Sectarian Temptation."

[26]Ibid., 84.

[27]Ibid., 87, 90-91.

[28]In *After Virtue*, MacIntyre favors Aristotle, but in *Whose Justice, Which Rationality* and *Three Rival Versions of Moral Inquiry*, Thomism comes to the fore.

[29]Alasdair MacIntyre, "The Privatization of Good: An Inaugural Lecture." *The Review of Politics* 52 (Summer 1990): 344-361.

[30]Ibid., 360.

[31]Ibid.

[32]Alasdair MacIntyre, *Three Rival Versions of Moral Enquiry* (Notre Dame, Ind.: University of Notre Dame Press, 1990).

[33]Ibid., 234.

[34]Ibid., 235.

[35]Loc. cit.

[36]Stanley Hauerwas, *Truthfulness and Tragedy: Further Investigations in Christian Ethics* (with Richard Bondi and David B. Burrell) (Notre Dame, Ind.: University of Notre Dame Press, 1977), 211-212.

[37]Stanley Hauerwas, *The Peaceable Kingdom* (Notre Dame, Ind.: University of Notre Dame Press, 1983), xviii, 99-100.

[38]Ibid., 114.

[39]Stanley Hauerwas, *After Christendom?* (Nashville: Abingdon Press, 1991), 88, 98-99.

[40]Ibid., 90-91.

[41]Ibid., 94-96.

[42]Stanley Hauerwas, *A Community of Character: Toward a Constructive Christian Social Ethic.* (Notre Dame, Ind.: University of Notre Dame Press, 1981), 6.

[43]Loc. cit.

[44]Stanley Hauerwas, "On Learning Simplicity in an Ambiguous Age," *Katallagete* (Fall 1987): 43-46.

[45]John D. Coleman, *An American Strategic Theology*, (New York: Paulist Press, 1982).

[46]There are numerous works concerned with civil society. One that provides an excellent overview is Jean L. Cohen and Andrew Amato, *Civil Society and Political Theory* (London: The MIT Press, 1994). I will rely primarily on their treatment of civil society, but also draw from several other sources.

[47]In developing my argument here I will not draw upon theorists who are linked with conservative politics, such as Peter L. Berger and Richard J. Neuhaus. Nevertheless, their arguments about mediating institutions in their book *To Empower People: The Role of Mediating Structures in Public Policy* (Washington, D.C.: American Enterprise Institute, 1977) urge that mediating structures can serve as places to resist and reform the state. They want to expand the notion of the public beyond the state to include structures such as the family, church, and neighborhood as helping to shape public discourse and policy. Unfortunately within conservative circles such arguments are often used to justify policies which weaken the state's ability to address economic injustice created by corporate capitalism. Neither Hauerwas nor MacIntyre appears sympathetic to such conservative aims in their discussions of resistance communities.

[48]See Cohen and Amato, 38, 48; Jeffrey C. Isaac, "Civil Society and the Spirit of Revolt," *Dissent*, 40 (Summer 1993): 356; and Michael Walzer, "The Idea of Civil Society: A Path to Reconstruction," *Dissent*, 38 (Spring 1991): 293-304.

[49]Isaac, 356-361.

[50]Ibid., p. 357; Iris Marion Young, "Social Groups in Associative Democracy" *Politics and Society*, 20 (December 1992): 529-534.

[51]Cohen and Amato, *passim*.

[52]Isaac, 357.

[53]Andrew Szasz, "Progress Through Mischief: The Social Movement Alternative to Secondary Associations," *Politics and Society*, 20 (December 1992): 521-528. Isaac, 357.

[54]Cohen and Amato, 503.

[55]Isaac.

[56]Cohen and Amato, 504

[57]Loc. cit.

[58]Ibid. 510-523.

[59]Szasz, 525; Isaac, 359-360.

[60]Cohen and Amato, 508.

[61]Ibid., 552-553.

[62]For an analysis of such groups from the perspective of their role within civil society, see Szasz, 521-528.

[63]Elizabeth McAlister, "Soil for Social Change," *Theology Today*, 30 (October 1973): 239-342.

[64]Philip Berrigan and Elizabeth McAlister, *The Time's Discipline: The Beatitudes and Nuclear Resistance* (Baltimore, Md.: Fortkamp Publishing, 1989).

[65]Philip Berrigan, "An Interview with Liz McAllister (sic), Phil Berrigan, Dan Berrigan," *Sojourners*, 6 (February 1977): 22-26.

[66]P. Berrigan and McAlister, 11, 125.

[67]D. Berrigan in James Forest, "Do This in Memory of Me: Activist Daniel Berrigan Answers Questions About His Priorities, Perspectives, and Christian Lifestyle," *The Other Side*, 15 (October 1979): 34-38.

[68]Daniel Berrigan, *Ten Commandments for the Long Haul*, (Nashville: Abingdon Press, 1981), 129.

[69]Cohen and Amato, 511.

[70]MacIntyre, *Three Rival Versions of Moral Enquiry*, 234.

[71]Hauerwas, Stanley. *The Peaceable Kingdom*. (Notre Dame, Ind.: University of Notre Dame Press, 1983), xviii.

[72]Cohen and Amato, 511.

[73]Szasz, 527.

[74]Isaac, 357.

[75]Cohen and Amato, 589.

Chapter 9

Renewing the Welfare Covenant: Covenant and Responsible Poverty Policy

Frederick E. Glennon

Welfare reform is back on the national agenda. What makes the recent welfare debate so intriguing is that the debate centers around two competing but related visions of community: contract and covenant. As a result of the recent election, the Republican leadership in the Congress has articulated a vision of community in its "Contract with America." In this endeavor, they hope "to restore the bonds of trust between the people and their elected representatives." This contractual vision seeks to limit government while expanding personal liberty and, with it, personal responsibility. With regard to welfare reform, they propose the "Personal Responsibility Act" which has the following aims:

> Discourage illegitimacy and teen pregnancy by prohibiting welfare to minor mothers and denying increased AFDC for additional children while on welfare, cut spending for welfare programs and enact a tough two-years-and-out provision with work requirements to promote individual responsibility.[1]

Clearly the emphasis is on making the poor more personally responsible for their own livelihood, a common refrain in contract notions of community which stress autonomy and self-sufficiency.

In his acceptance speech at the Democratic National Convention and in his recent State of the Union address, President Bill Clinton also articulated a vision of community: new covenant. Clinton's vision stresses the intricate connection between the themes of opportunity, responsibility, and community. With regard to welfare reform, Clinton states:

> We will say to those on welfare: you will have and you deserve the opportunity through training and education, through child care and medical coverage, to liberate yourself. But then, when you can, you must work, because welfare should be a second chance, not a way of life. That's what the New Covenant is all about.[2]

Clinton's vision of covenant community seeks to balance the importance of individual responsibility with social obligation. The nation has the obligation to provide opportunity for all Americans to get off of welfare roles. Poor people have the responsibility to take advantage of the opportunities afforded them. Both aspects are part of our covenant with one another.

The visions of contract and covenant have both influenced American public life over the years. Most Americans are more familiar with the contract vision being articulated by the Republican leadership. However, the language of covenant and mutual obligation in American public life has a long history as well. In his sermon, *A Model of Christian Charity*, John Winthrop uses the language of covenant to speak about the new venture the early settlers were about to undertake.

> Beloved, there is now set before us life and good, death and evil, in that we are commanded this day to love the Lord our God, and to love one another, to walk in his ways and to keep his commandments and his ordinance and his laws, and the articles of our covenant with him, that we may live and be multiplied, and that the Lord our God may bless us in the land whither we go to possess it.[3]

H. Richard Niebuhr reminds us that the pattern of the covenant or federal society reflected in Puritan thought was one of the guiding frameworks for the founders of our American democracy and constitution.[4] Milner Ball refers to this covenantal influence on the foundations of American society as our "biblical beginning." Although the framers of the Constitution used the language of the social contract tradition, "covenant realities were prominent in their acts, and covenantal ideas were prominent in their minds."[5] Similarly, Daniel Elazar contends that covenant is the root idea behind all federal systems of government.[6]

So it makes sense for a President to speak of covenant community as a basis for public policy. However, what does covenant community as the norm for American public life really involve? More specifically, what would a serious application of covenant community, which is rooted in the Judeo-Christian tradition, mean for poverty policy and welfare reform in the United States?

In this essay I articulate six aspects of the Judeo-Christian covenantal tradition of community and discuss their implications for poverty policy and welfare reform. I do not look at the specific details of one program over another but suggest the broad directions poverty policy should follow under the rubric of covenant community. What I demonstrate is that the covenantal tradition of community provides more substantive directions for poverty policy because it incorporates the values of freedom, responsibility, equality, and community better than contract views.

Covenantal Theological Framework

Covenant is one of the central concepts in the biblical tradition. The primary covenant stressed in that tradition is the covenant made between God and God's chosen people at Sinai. Yet many biblical interpreters suggest that the theme of covenant permeates the entire biblical record. Instead of looking at each place where covenantal ideas are present, I would like to look at six characteristics that the covenantal tradition affirms.

First, covenants are inclusive of all members of the community. The Christian tradition of covenant contends that the primary covenant is the covenant between God and all of humanity. All human beings are intended for membership in it whether they affirm it or not. Thus everyone comes under its promise and protection. This inclusive covenant implies two things. On the one hand, it points to the essentially social nature of human life. Contract conceptions of society affirm the autonomous, self-sufficient individual who enters into contracts with others, but whose relationships are not essential to his/her selfhood. In contrast, a covenantal view suggests that we are dependent upon others not only for life, but also for true human meaning and fulfillment. The Genesis 2:18-25 account of humanity's creation points to the incompleteness of the individual. We only become selves, persons, in community. Thus, the essential image of God (Gen. 1:26-28) is that we are relational beings. God created us capable of entering into relationship (covenant); in this way we mirror God.[7]

On the other hand, God's inclusive covenant bestows worth on each person as God's creation and as members of the same moral community. As a result, members must recognize the worth of each member for his/her own sake and not for her/his value as an instrument to one's own self-interest. It is true that in society we find more brokenness and irresponsibility in communities than wholeness and mutual love. This inclusive covenant is, therefore, always an eschatological hope. However, its existence is still present, and it acts as a judgment upon all societies that fail to live up to its standards. Members of the covenant must see one another as belonging to the same moral community (Gal. 3:28). They must respect the intrinsic worth of each member equally. They must be faithful in the fulfillment of their responsibilities to each other.

This same inclusivity characterizes other covenants made in the biblical account as well. God's covenant with the Hebrews at Sinai includes all the members of the community, from the powerful to the most marginal members of the community, such as widows, orphans, and the poor (Ex. 22:22-27; Deut. 24: 17-22). The covenant even extends to the strangers and resident aliens who come into the community (Ex. 22: 21; 23:9; Deut. 24:17-22). The members of the covenant are to respect each person and to show them the same regard that they would for the most powerful and important members. Thus, the laws of the covenant reflect an increased sensitivity to the value of all persons, even if they were only sporadically implemented.

Second, the covenant stresses mutual obligation and responsibility. The covenantal affirmation of humanity's social nature has another dimension. Our experiences of interdependence lead to a sense of obligation. Not only are we dependent upon others, cared for by others, others are also in our care. There is a reciprocity that is entailed in the patterns of relationship and interdependence central to human experience that evokes an awareness of our responsibility and obligation to others. Our participation and cooperation in this process are required. Similarly, the biblical account of covenant also suggests that as we are dependent upon others, others are dependent upon us which means that we have responsibilities to and for others, whether we live up to them or not.[8]

This sense of covenant as mutual obligation is clear in the biblical accounts of covenant-making. The key idea of covenant is the stress on the pledge to another, "to undertake an obligation towards another."[9] This assumption of an obligation can be unilateral (YHWH's first covenant with Abraham) or mutual (the Sinai covenant). In either case, it becomes an "agreement to give someone a special privilege, advantage, benefit."[10] It did not involve imposing an obligation upon another. Rather, both parties to the covenant take on the responsibility and obligation. Thus, the relationship is one of moral response and commitment, not a natural bond.

These covenants are not simply contracts between self-interested individuals or associations in which members further the values they share. Contracts and associations depend merely on the ends people are trying to achieve; covenant community, on the other hand, is concerned not simply with the ends but with the nature of the interaction itself.

The essential virtue here is faithfulness or loyalty.[11] Daniel J. Elazar contrasts covenant with contract:

> A covenant is much more than a contract . . . because it involves a pledge of loyalty and morally grounded obligation beyond that demanded for mutual advantage, often involving the development of community among the partners.[12]

The biblical account of the covenant at Sinai demonstrates that the people were agreeing to something far beyond any contract. They were connecting their lives together with one another and with their God. The obligations and responsibilities that they pledged to one another covered all aspects of life together.

One can see the same type of covenantal commitment in America's Pilgrim founders. John Winthrop's sermon, *A Model of Christian Charity*, captures clearly the covenantal framework characteristic of the early settlers.

> Thus stands the cause between God and us. We are entered into covenant with him for this work. . . . For this end, we must be knit together in this work as one man. We must entertain each other in brotherly affection, we must be willing to abridge ourselves of our superfluities, for the supply of others' necessities. We must uphold a familiar commerce together in all meekness, gentleness, patience, and liberality. We must delight in each other, make others' conditions our own, rejoice together, mourn together, labor and suffer together, always having before our eyes our commission and community in the work, our community as members of the same body.[13]

As one can see, the commitment expressed here goes far beyond any contractual sense of community and obligation.

Moreover, the obligations are societal and communal. There is a collective sense of responsibility affirmed in the covenantal tradition. The prophetic literature illustrates this point. Amos condemns the leadership of Israel for its failure to fulfill covenantal obligations to those citizens marginalized by the political and economic establishment, namely, the poor and needy. He speaks harsh judgments against those who actively engage in behavior that undermines the covenant. However, his judgment extends also to those members in the community who profit from such behavior.

> Alas for those who lie on beds of ivory, and lounge on their couches, and eat lambs from the flock, and calves from the stall; who sing idle songs to the sound of the harp, and like David improvise on instruments of music; who drink wine from bowls, and anoint themselves with the finest oils, but are not grieved over the ruin of Joseph!

Therefore they shall now be the first to go into exile, and the revelry of the loungers shall pass away (Amos 6:4-7, NRSV).

The entire community, not merely individual members, shares the moral responsibility for providing justice to all. Injustice on the part of some in the community can have consequences for all.[14]

Third, the covenant has a vision of community designed to produce a society that encourages the meaningful participation and well-being of all. Bruce Birch characterizes the biblical conception of covenant as "a community living toward a vision that fully values all persons."[15] This is most clearly seen in those aspects of the biblical covenant that stress the need to protect the marginalized and the vulnerable members of society. Undoubtedly, the biblical Israelites never fully realized this vision of community. At every point of its development, Israel tolerated class distinctions, patriarchal and hierarchical social and familial structures, and limited participation in rights. However, like most ideals, this vision of community provided a goal toward which the community should strive and against which the community could judge itself.

One implication of a vision of community that values all persons is the affirmation of a common good toward which everyone in the community must contribute in order to make this vision a reality. This is the vocation of all members of the community. Recognizing our interdependence and fostering the growth of that relationship through solidarity means that we are always interested not only in our own good but also in the good of others. In addition, exercising one's rights responsibly means that one does so in ways that promote one's own good and the good of others in the community. One must use one's rights in ways that create the conditions for the flourishing of all.

The primacy of the public good over private interests can be seen in the Puritans' conception of vocation. Clinton Gardner suggests that, according to the Puritans, each person's calling or vocation was directed by God toward the common good. Using one's vocation purely for private interests was an abuse of one's calling. The priority of the public good is also embodied in the Puritans' idea of "a holy commonwealth." Society was characterized in terms of commonwealth, that the purpose of government and ruling authorities was to promote the well-being of all.[16]

A covenantal conception of the common good is neither individualistic, as in contract views, nor collectivistic. The vision of the common good provides the transcendent referent toward which a just community aims. Yet a covenantal conception also affirms that society achieves the common good best when people can pursue a plurality of goods. The social nature of the human person means that each person's good is bound up with the good of the community. Therefore justice in society (the conditions for human flourishing) can only be achieved when each person contributes to the common good in some way. The common good is the vision of social community in which all members share through their participation. All people share in the benefits that come from social advance. If this is not the case, then the interdependence we share easily becomes a source of domination and exploitation.

Fourth, covenant community is egalitarian. Covenantal thought clearly affirms the inherent equality of all persons in the eyes of God. Moreover, this has socioeconomic as well as religious implications. Norman Gottwald contends that early Israelite society was a radical, egalitarian departure from the hierarchical systems of surrounding nations and city-states. Their organization into an intertribal federation guaranteed roughly equal access to resources for the entire population.[17] This egalitarianism may never have been realized; it may simply have been a theological construct. However, some of Israel's theologians envisioned the covenantal society as egalitarian.

Egalitarianism recognizes that having resources is critical to membership in the community. Extreme inequality in the distribution of resources can undermine the basis of community by excluding the poor from meaningful participation in society and by making them susceptible to exploitation by the wealthy. No conception of meritocracy can ever justify such a state of affairs.

Such exploitation happened with land as Israel moved toward monarchy. In the earlier covenant community, there was wide, fairly equitable distribution of land ownership to every family through the institution of inheritance or sacred patrimony. God was the true owner of the land, and each family had some inheritance to manage as God's steward. Structurally there were benefits to ownership of land at this time. Land was the basis of freedom, providing for a family's physical needs and reducing the chance that the family could be enslaved by other members of the community. Land was also a sign of God's salvation and the basis of participation in assemblies, religious festivals, and mutual defense. That is why the sacred patrimony was neither to be sold nor to be bought.[18] Maintaining the sacred patrimony helped to maintain the Israelites' identity and free participation in the community.

But monarchy introduced a new social system and the notion of continual "inheritance" was not a part of it. Land was used to reward royal service, and was accumulated as the basis of new, wealthy classes. To those deprived of the land, through foreclosures and oppressive sharecropping arrangements, the loss of "inheritance" meant a loss of material welfare and reduced many to poverty. It also meant lost economic and social position, making them susceptible to oppression by the wealthy classes.[19]

This is clearly the situation the prophet Amos addresses. Because many of the poor in Israel during the reign of Jeroboam II had lost their inheritance, they were subject to whims of the large landholders for whom they farmed. As a result, their value in the community was greatly reduced. They could be sold for a few shekels or "bought for a pair of sandals" (Amos 2:6-7a). Economic inequality led to social and political inequality. A critical dimension to assuring that the vulnerable members of the covenant community had some voice was by insuring the fairness and impartiality of the judicial system (Ex. 23:6-8). It provided a check against the potential abuse of the poor by the wealthy and powerful. However, during the time of Amos, Israel's judicial system had become corrupt. The corrupt landowners were trying their own cases and other judges were taking bribes (Amos 5:10-12). As a result, the poor had no way to have their concerns met. They became second class citizens who could be cheated and abused by the wealthy without possibility for redress (Amos 8:4-6).

As a means of restoring equality within the covenant community, the biblical covenant includes various provisions, including the notion of Jubilee. The year of Jubilee required that every fiftieth year the land would return to the original owners and served to redistribute resources so that people would find some relative equality (Lev. 25). Although never fully implemented, it recognized the inherent duty upon all members of the covenant community to insure that justice is available to all.

Fifth, the covenant community has a special concern for the poor and marginalized. The vision of covenant community is a society that enables all members to participate meaningfully in the community. The covenant ideal is a community in which there is no want or need. "There will...be no one in need among you" (Deut. 15:4, NRSV). Although this is the ideal, the biblical account recognizes the sinfulness of humanity and the potential for developing social and economic structures that exclude and oppress some members of the community. Therefore, the covenant includes specific protections for vulnerable members of the community, including the poor, the widow, the orphan, and the stranger. These were persons who had little protection in society and toward whom the biblical account reflects a divine bias or orientation. God measures the justice of a community by its treatment of the most vulnerable of its members.

Stephen Mott shows us that God is more than concerned for the weak and vulnerable; God works to redress the inequities when their needs are unmet or denied (Ps. 146:7-8). "The goal of redress is to return people to a normal level of advantage and satisfaction in the community, particularly with respect to the capacity to earn a living and to have a reasonably happy life."[20] Of course, in a world of scarcity redressing inequities has implications for the interests of others. Some people, especially the advantaged who have profited from those inequities, must be willing to give something up (Psalm 107:39-41). But this is one of the obligations that faithfulness to covenant community requires of the advantaged, obligations that societies organized by contract can pursue only as philanthropy or charity. Ideally, this obligation is taken on willingly out of a sense of commitment or loyalty to all members of the community, the powerless as well as others. As God seeks justice and mercy, so too will those who "walk humbly" with their God.[21]

Sixth, the covenant deals with internal disposition as well as external actions. What is most important in the covenantal tradition is that we become covenantal people. It underlies both the old and new covenants. The demands of the covenant go beyond external acts of obedience. To reduce covenant demands simply to external acts would create a legalism that does not fully capture the essence of the covenantal tradition. Undoubtedly the 613 commandments in the Deuteronomic code resemble a very legalistic framework. Israel did sometimes reduce covenant to legalism. More significant, however, is the intention of these laws to create a sense of community and to build ties of affection between the members of the community. That is why both Hillel and Jesus could easily summarize the entire law in two commandments: love God and love your neighbor. If we truly care for one another, we will seek to strengthen the relationships that bind us. Loyalty and faithfulness, not simply personal responsibility, become the key virtues in this context.[22]

At every act of covenant-making in the Hebrew Bible, one sees the connection with the spiritual or inward dimension because a solemn ceremony and pledge seal the covenants. Even the external sign of covenant membership, circumcision, is given an inward dimension when Moses tells the people of Israel, "Circumcise the foreskin of your heart" (Deut. 10:16). This metaphor foreshadows Jeremiah's hope, "I will put my law within them, and I will write it on their hearts" (Jer. 31-33).[23]

The same is true in the New Testament account. Jesus speaks about being the firstborn of a new covenant, a covenant in which the spirit of God works within each believer; a covenant that is characterized by the story of the Good Samaritan. The person who comes to Jesus speaks in terms of the covenant requirements that are summarized in the command to love God and love your neighbor. When asked, "Who is my neighbor?", an external attempt to fulfill the letter of the law, Jesus replies with a story that puts less stress on fulfilling the commandment than on the character of the hero. The Samaritan is a neighbor, it flows from his being. He has the covenant written on his heart. A covenant person is one who cares for the well-being of the others in his/her community and who is as interested in their well-being as he/she is in his/her own. He/she sees the connection between his/her well-being and that of the community.

The same type of inward dimension of covenant characterized the Puritans and the founding of this country. John Winthrop argues that for the settlers to fulfill their covenant with one another and with God they must be "knit together" as one body in this work and they must follow the counsel of the prophet Micah: to do justly, to love mercy, and to walk humbly with their God.[24] Members of the covenant must see one another as belonging to the same moral community. They must respect the intrinsic worth of each member equally. They must be faithful in the fulfillment of their responsibilities to each other.

To summarize, the covenantal tradition emphasizes that the mutual obligation and responsibility of all members of the community is to contribute to the well-being of all, especially the poor and the power-less. Moreover, this is done out of a spirit of willingness and coopera-tion because of our interdependence and loyalty to one another, not simply our self-interest. What would the implications be for welfare re-form if we took this conception of the covenantal tradition seriously?

Implications for Responsible Poverty Policy

What is Poverty? Before considering what welfare policies are neces-sary to address adequately the problem of poverty, we must look seri-ously at what the problem of poverty is. A major concern for welfare reform is the issue of dependency, the creation of a permanent welfare underclass. Some argue that the welfare state has created a situation of dependency, thereby undermining personal responsibility and leading many welfare recipients to forsake the common obligations of citizen-ship (such as work). Dependency on government can have debilitating effects on individual freedom and responsibility. An overbearing, pater-nalistic state can contribute to the problem it is attempting to solve by undermining the self-respect of the poor.[25] Thus, poverty is primarily a behavioral problem.

However, in spite of some evidence that suggests dependency is a problem for the poor, the fundamental problem of poverty in American society is not dependency but exclusion: the poor are excluded from meaningful participation in society. Poverty represents an undeserved exile which is fairly complete. The poor are excluded from meaningful participation in every sphere of life in society: political, economic, and social. If American society wants to end poverty as exclusion and promote justice, then a covenantal perspective contends that its efforts must transcend insuring a minimum income level to securing the ability of the poor to participate in the common activities of society.

Surely because work is a primary means to participation, then work should be a central focus of welfare reform. However, the issue of work for the poor is primarily structural, not simply behavioral. The poor are exiles because of inequities and changes in the economic and social structures. The labor markets available to the poor are low-wage and cyclical; adequate daycare facilities for their children are lacking; the educational systems that tutor the poor do not prepare them for productive contribution. This does not mean that dependency in not a problem. From a covenantal perspective, excessive dependence is every bit as much a problem to mutual respect and responsibility as excessive independence. Behavioral dependence can have debilitating effects on the ability of the poor to act creatively and responsibly in the community.

My point is that much of the dependent behavior of the poor is an adaptive response on their part to counter their marginality. It is so easy to blame the poor for their problems because they lack the appropriate motivation and sense of responsibility for fuller participation in our societal and economic institutions. However, dependency and poverty are interrelated. Some poor may be behaviorally dependent, but many have not always been so. They passed over that line, that psychological chasm, that separates poverty from dependency, as a result of chronic deprivation and want. Society should change the structures that shut the poor out before it asks the poor to change their adaptive behavior.

Yet it is safe to say that a behaviorally dependent group, an underclass, will continue to exist.[26] Dealing with this group of persons requires more than changed structures to get them to participate fully in society. That is why an adequate approach to the problem of poverty from a covenantal perspective means addressing both its structural and behavioral components. Dependence, inequality, and exclusion all contribute to the problems of the able-bodied poor in the United States. Social welfare policies should promote the autonomy of the poor as well as their solidarity with the nonpoor; they should promote freedom as well as equality; they should promote personal responsibility as well as society's obligation toward the poor. Opening the door to opportunity and meaningful participation alone will not eliminate the need for self-help programs in which the behaviorally-dependent poor learn to participate more meaningfully.

Welfare Society or Welfare State? In the face of the problem of dependency associated with welfare statism, many people stress the importance of the smaller, voluntary and involuntary, communities and organizations in which people participate to provide for people's welfare needs. In particular, they stress the importance of those communities and institutions that provide the opportunities for personal interaction and involvement, including families, neighborhoods, and civic organizations. They are the "vital sector" in welfare policy.[27] Theorists of all stripes have affirmed the normative significance of these "mediating structures" recently.[28] They do so for several reasons.

First, mediating structures give individuals greater social power over/against the large governmental and economic bureaucracies they face. James Luther Adams defines social power as "the process of influencing and being influenced."[29] In relationship to large scale bureaucracies of the state and the economy, individuals generally experience only the latter power. This is especially true for the poor. Our disappointment with the welfare state is that, although welfare state programs were meant to make us more independent and not dependent on charity, the opposite has been the case: "the poorest citizens, the unemployed and the helpless, are not significantly more independent, more responsible, more capable of shaping their own lives and joining in the common work of citizenship."[30]

Participation in mediating structures empowers poor people in society. On the one hand, the participation of the poor in various mediating structures, many of which are networks and institutions for mutual aid, enables them to play an active role, to exercise some influence, in the decisions that affect their lives and communities. By finding ways to help themselves, the poor enhance their freedom and independence. Community improvement and development organizations are good examples.

On the other hand, participation in voluntary and civic associations provide important links for the poor to influence the wider communities that affect them. Adams argues that voluntary associations "bring about the dispersion of power and responsibility."[31] His point is that voluntary associations are able to impact large-scale political and economic institutions in ways that individuals are unable to do alone. Individuals in community united around a cause can influence economic and political centers of power.[32] Participation in these associations gives poor individuals greater social power. The successes of welfare rights organizations and labor unions are good examples.[33]

Second, mediating structures provide the context for promoting important societal values. Cultural understandings of poverty suggest that, in the past, the institutions in poor communities, such as the family, the church, the school, and the neighborhood organization, functioned much the same as in nonpoor communities. They promoted functional and moral behavior and sanctioned dysfunctional and immoral behavior. With the demise of those institutions, poor communities no longer have that countervailing force to hold the negative tendencies in check.[34] Welfare state programs only make these problems worse. To promote societal values in poor communities requires the restoration of these mediating structures or the creation of new ones.[35] Participation in voluntary and civic associations can help the poor to acknowledge their responsibilities and empower the poor to meet them. The "habits of the heart" these voluntary institutions generate can assist in creating a moral social order.

Third, mediating structures promote the development of a spirit of mutual concern and mutual obligation necessary for a democratic, welfare society. Welfare society advocates affirm the role that mediating structures play in enabling people to place restrictions on their self-interest to promote the common good. Alexis de Tocqueville saw this clearly.

> The free institutions . . . remind every citizen . . . that he lives in society. They every instant impress upon his mind the notion that it is the duty as well as the interest of men to make themselves useful to their fellow creatures; . . . Men attend to the interests of the public, first by necessity, afterwards by choice; what was intentional becomes an instinct, and by dint of working for the good of one's fellow citizens, the habits and the taste for servicing them are at length acquired.[36]

Repeated interaction with others leads one to value one's relations with others and to set one's own desires and interests in the context of a wider moral community and interest. This is as true for the poor as it is for the nonpoor. Part of the problem in poor communities is that residents make choices on narrowly self-interested grounds without thought for the interests of the community.

Some welfare state advocates suggest that the push for equality can enable people to recognize their similarity and work together.[37] However, equality does not breed mutuality. As Tocqueville noted, the opposite is true. Equality keeps people apart, placing them "side by side, unconnected to any common tie."[38] On the contrary, one's experience of mutuality opens the door for a more egalitarian society. When people live and struggle together, they learn to see other people as equals and to take the latter's interests into consideration. It may even enable people to see beyond the barriers of race and class. However, the end is not equality, but community.

In summary, mediating structures are important for generating a welfare society that resists any attempt by a centralized state to usurp all welfare functions. Not only is there the danger of tyranny, but there is the danger that the philanthropic spirit will die. Mediating structures between the individual and the state not only preserve freedom but also contribute to the development of the spirit of mutual concern and mutual obligation necessary for a participatory community that includes the poor. This socialization provides a variety of new ways—"a multitude of networks and institutions for mutual aid"—to enable people to find ways to help themselves.[39]

Clearly, the covenantal tradition would affirm efforts to socialize welfare, especially where the results include recognition by all of the ties that bind us together and the empowerment of the poor to participate meaningfully in society. However, for all of its merits, the welfare society as developed through mediating structures is insufficient to attend adequately to the cumulative inequalities of race, class, and power which the poor experience. Justice from a covenantal perspective calls for the development of a welfare state that provides enough resources to make the goal of equal opportunity a realistic possibility for the disadvantaged.[40] These resources include money, education, health care, and access to good paying jobs. This is the only way to "recognize and uphold the underlying equality of membership."[41] Social conditions and the accidents of birth do not justify unequal treatment in the distribution of these essential social goods.

Conservatives who link advocacy for the expansion of the welfare society through mediating structures with calls for a minimalist state are wrong.[42] As James Luther Adams argues, this view makes "too great claims for the competency of voluntary associations."[43] Historically, when confronted with serious economic depression or other structural social needs, voluntary associations have been unable to respond to the challenge and their response has been motivated by class or group interest and ideology. Moreover, voluntary associations can be as tyrannical as large-scale organizations, restricting freedom for the sake of conformity and repressing minority opinion. "Associations," Adams argues, "are prone to all of the evils to which the flesh is heir."[44]

More importantly, however, such a view misunderstands the inclusive nature of the national covenant and the role of the state in securing its aims. The underlying conception of political community of those who seek limited government is too negative. Membership in the national covenant entails certain (human as well as civil) rights and responsibilities that are owed to one another; it is part of our social responsibility to one another. Individuals do not have to be a part of these other communities for the means to their individual well-being (and in the case of the poor, it is unlikely that they will be). It is their right by virtue of their membership in the more inclusive covenant. The state, therefore, has a positive welfare role to play that cannot simply be transferred to other, less inclusive, communities.

Responsible Poverty Policies The covenantal affirmation of the welfare role of the state is implicit in President Clinton's emphasis on opportunity. Society has the obligation to provide the opportunities for the poor to participate actively in society. This includes, first and foremost, work opportunity. It is unfortunate that in our society we have limited our understanding of work to paid employment. This loses sight of the many contributions that people, including the poor, make to society that are unpaid. But given the fact that paid employment has become more significant, the covenantal tradition argues strongly that work ought to be guaranteed to all who want to work.

This guarantee is important because work provides more than income. The unemployment and marginal employment of the poor devalues their citizenship. Friedrich Hegel observed this moral dilemma in modern society. When civil society organizes its economic life through the unfettered market, it inevitably inflicts undeserved suffering on those at the bottom. Membership in civil society depends upon having the resources to participate in the activities society deems meaningful. For workers, gaining these resources depends upon the opportunity to sell their labor in the market. Where the normal operation of the market prevents some from selling their labor, or forces them to do so at poverty wages, markets undermine their membership in society.[45]

Lee Rainwater makes a similar argument. Studying the social meanings of income in our society, he contends that, in our materialistic, consumption-oriented society, money buys membership. The reason is that membership depends upon an opportunity to engage in the "validating activities" of society, which Rainwater defines as "activities that confirm a person's sense of himself as a full and recognized member of his society."[46] This activity requires having and using goods and services not simply to meet one's basic needs, but also to engage in recreational and cultural events.

The work available to the poor seldom generates enough income to provide adequately for themselves and their families without public support. Millions need food stamps and other social programs to buy the basic necessities. As a result, these persons suffer more than poverty; they become exiles in their own communities.

Most Americans believe that any job that is worth doing should pay an income that insures that the worker does not have to live in poverty.[47] This is reflected in President Clinton's own agenda.[48] If society expects the poor to work in paid employment as the primary means of gaining the resources needed to participate in those activities that affirm membership, then wages ought to be sufficient to do so. If they are not, then society will have to implement some form of social wage or public subsidy, but without the stigma attached to welfare.

Full-employment, defined as more jobs than people looking for them, is also essential from a covenantal perspective. This commitment would guarantee a right to work for those who want to work. The focus of the job creation needed to fulfill this commitment must not be on low-paid, menial, service work. Rather, the focus must be on employment at a living wage. What I envision is similar to what Lester Thurow advocates: "to change the structure of the economy so that the entire economy generates the kinds of jobs that are now open to white males and ensures that there are enough of these job opportunities to go around."[49]

A full employment employment policy that guarantees work at a living wage can enhance the self-respect and responsibility of the poor by allowing them to live up to the norm of working for their support, but until we achieve full employment, we must implement some form of social wage or public subsidy. Provision for a social wage until full-employment measures are in place will enable people to make appropriate choices about work, to seek work that is intrinsically interesting or socially beneficial, and to avoid desperate exchanges. To promote the importance of work and to minimize the stigma associated with welfare, this social wage could take the form of more communal provision for important goods and services, such as health care, high-quality child care, and quality public education. Or it could take the form of a mix of income and services. In either form, this communal provision would promote the underlying equality and membership of the poor in ways that current poverty and welfare policies do not.

In addition, we should fund training and placement programs that develop the skills our changing, knowledge-intensive economy requires. Current human capital programs for the poor make few connections with trends in economic development. Many of them train participants for dead-end jobs, a major reason why targeted groups are unwilling to participate. (This situation will only get worse if Congress implements fully the Personal Responsibility Act.) On-the-job training, skills upgrading, and apprenticeship programs that provide income support during the training period would provide new incentives for workers to learn new skills and seek better jobs. Increased and prudent public investment in human capital that focuses on the poor, when combined with a full-employment policy, would secure justice for the poor and would enable them to become responsible citizens.

These welfare state policies should not lead us to abandon our efforts to socialize the welfare state. As we have seen, vital mediating structures can enable individuals to participate more fully and more meaningfully in society than state institutions. Therefore, they are significant agents in empowering the poor. What is needed is a society in which each individual and social group works together to insure the basic welfare of all, and a state that works with and empowers others to realize this end.

Conclusion

Undoubtedly, the implications of the Judeo-Christian tradition of covenant community for responsible poverty policy described above are broad and incomplete. The way these implications translate into more specific public policy recommendations needs to be spelled out in detail. However, enough has been said to suggest that a covenantal perspective is a viable contender for public policy attention, not only because it has deep roots in American culture, but also because it pulls our cultural values of freedom, responsibility (personal and social), equality, and community together better than the contract tradition.

Yet the real promise of the Judeo-Christian tradition of covenant community in our pluralistic society lies in its recognition that we are social beings who have a boundedness that transcends our individual self-interest. By stressing the need for mutual respect and mutual responsibility, and the need for common, disinterested deliberation about the directions and goals of our society, a covenantal perspective opens the door for more substantive solutions to the problem of poverty than we have had in the past.

Notes

[1] *Contract with America*, ed. Ed Gillespie and Bob Shellhas (New York: Times Books, a division of Random House, 1994), 18.

[2] Governor Bill Clinton, *A Vision for America: A New Covenant*, Democratic National Convention, New York City, July 16, 1992.

[3] John Winthrop, "A Model of Christian Charity," in *The Puritans in America: A Narrative Anthology*, ed. Alan Heimert and Andrew Delbanco (Cambridge: Harvard University Press, 1985), 81-92, 90-91.

[4] H. Richard Niebuhr, "The Idea of Covenant in American Democracy," *Church History* 23 (1954): 126-135.

[5] Milner S. Ball, *The Promise of American Law* (Athens: University of Georgia Press, 1981), 14.

[6] Daniel J. Elazar, *Exploring Federalism* (Tuscaloosa, Ala.: University of Alabama Press, 1987).

[7] See Joseph L. Allen, *Love & Conflict: A Covenantal Model of Christian Ethics* (Nashville: Abingdon Press, 1984), chap. 2.

[8] Ibid., 37. See also H. Richard Niebuhr, "The Idea of Covenant and American Democracy."

[9] Ernest W. Nicholson, *God and His People: Covenant and Theology in the Old Testament* (Oxford: Clarendon Press, 1986), 89.

[10]Ibid., 96.

[11]H. Richard Niebuhr, *Radical Monotheism and Western Civilization* (New York: Harper & Row, 1960), 41.

[12]Daniel J. Elazar, "Introduction," in *Kinship and Consent: The Jewish Political Tradition and Its Contemporary Uses*, ed. Daniel J. Elazar (Washington: University Press of America, 1983), 9.

[13]Winthrop, "A Model of Christian Charity," 82.

[14]See Bruce Birch, *Let Justice Roll Down* (Louisville: Westminster/John Knox Press, 1991), 259.

[15]Ibid., 179.

[16]E. Clinton Gardner, "Justice in Puritan Covenantal Tradition," *The Annual of the Society of Christian Ethics* 1988:99. See also his, *Justice in Christian Ethics* (Cambridge: Cambridge University Press, 1995).

[17]Norman K. Gottwald, *The Hebrew Bible: A Socio-Literary Introduction* (Philadelphia: Fortress Press, 1985), 285.

[18]Paul D. Hanson, *The People Called: The Growth of Community in the Bible* (San Francisco: Harper & Row, 1986), 64.

[19]See Birch, *Let Justice Roll Down*, 262-267.

[20]Stephen S. Mott, *Biblical Ethics and Social Change* (New York: Oxford University Press, 1982), 68.

[21] "Loyalty involves active concern for the well-being of all the people of God, but particularly for the weak and underprivileged among them--the poor or any whose status offers no ready advocate in the society." Katherine Doob Sakenfeld, *Faithfulness in Action: Loyalty in Biblical Perspective* (Philadelphia: Fortress Press, 1985), 102.

[22]See Margaret Farley, *Personal Commitments* (San Francisco: Harper & Row, 1990) chap. 8.

[23]Birch, *Let Justice Roll Down*, 171.

[24]Winthrop, "A Model of Christian Charity," 90-91.

[25]Recent studies of the University of Michigan's Panel Study on Income Dynamics suggest that there is empirical support for the argument that an underclass has emerged, especially in our inner cities, which exhibits the traits of long-term poverty and welfare dependency. See Greg J. Duncan, et. al., *Years of Poverty, Years of Plenty: The Changing Economic Fortunes of American Workers and Their Families* (Ann Arbor: University of Michigan, 1984).

[26]David T. Ellwood, *Poor Support: Poverty in the American Family* (New York: Basic Books, 1988), chap. 6.

[27]*A Community of Self-Reliance: The New Consensus on Family and Welfare*, ed. Michael Novak (Washington: American Enterprise Institute, 1987), 107.

[28]Peter L. Berger and Richard John Neuhaus, *To Empower People: The Role of Mediating Structures in Public Policy* (Washington: American Enterprise Institute, 1977).

[29]James Luther Adams, "Mediating Structures and the Separation of Powers," in *Voluntary Associations*, ed. J. Ronald Engel (Chicago: Exploration Press, 1986), 221.

[30]Michael Walzer, "Socializing the Welfare State," in *Democracy and the Welfare State*, ed. Amy Gutmann (Princeton: Princeton University Press, 1988), 16.

[31]Adams, "The Political Responsibility of the Man of Culture," in *Voluntary Associations*, 148.

[32]Philip Wogaman, "The Church as Mediating Institution: Theological and Philosophical Perspective," in *Democracy and Mediating Structures: A Theological Inquiry*, ed. Michael Novak (Washington: American Enterprise Institute, 1980), 71-73.

[33]See Frances Fox Piven and Richard A. Cloward, *Poor People's Movements* (New York: Pantheon Books, a Division of Random House, 1977).

[34]A recent study points to the correlation between the socioeconomic composition of poor neighborhoods and rises in the dysfunctional behavior of nonwork, dropping out of school, and teenage childbearing. See Jonathan Crane, "Effects of Neighborhoods on Dropping Out of School and Teenage Childbearing," in *The Urban Underclass*, ed. Christopher Jencks and Paul E. Peterson (Washington: The Brookings Institution, 1991), 299-320. However, it is important to realize that although many of the traditional structures are dysfunctional, many poor communities have generated other forms of family and kinship networks that function quite well. See Carol Stack, *All Our Kin* (New York: Harper & Row, 1974).

[35]The Atlanta Project, initiated by former President Jimmy Carter, is one example of how communities are attempting to address the problems associated with poverty by creating new institutions.

[36]Alexis de Tocqueville, *Democracy in America*, 2 vols. (New York: Vintage Books, a Division of Random House, 1945), 2:112.

[37]See William Ryan, *Equality* (New York: Pantheon Books, A Division of Random House, 1981).

[38]Tocqueville, *Democracy in America*, 2:109.

[39]Walzer, "Socializing the Welfare State,"24.

[40]I am following Jennifer Hochschild's definition of the right of equal opportunity: "All citizens must have enough resources (such as education, access to desirable positions and money) so that they have a realistic possibility of overcoming the obstacles posed by cumulative inequalities of race, class, and power." "Race, Class, Power, and the Welfare State," in *Democracy and the Welfare State*, ed. Amy Gutmann, 170.

[41]Walzer, *Spheres of Justice* (New York: Basic Books, 1983), 84.

[42]See the Lay Commission on Catholic Social Teaching and the U.S. Economy, *Toward the Future: Catholic Social Thought and the U.S. Economy, A Lay Letter* (New York: American Catholic Committee, 1984), 5-6.

[43]Adams, "The Political Responsibility of the Man of Culture," 150.

[44]Ibid.

[45]G. W. F. Hegel, *The Philosophy of Right*, trans. T. M. Knox (New York: Oxford University Press, 1981), par. 241, 193.

[46]Lee Rainwater, *What Money Buys: Inequality and the Social Meanings of Income* (New York: Basic Books, Inc. 1974), 17.

[47]In my social ethics course, I always ask students what they think is the minimum income people who work full-time, year-round ought to make, regardless of the job they do. Invariably, they suggest incomes in excess of $20,000 per year, well above the poverty line.

[48]In his State of the Union Address (January 1995), President Clinton argued for a raise in the minimum wage as an effort to insure that the poor have a "living wage."

[49]Lester Thurow, *The Zero-Sum Society* (New York: Basic Books, 1980), 205.

Chapter 10

The Ethics of Leaving Ms. Smith Alone: A Responsiblist Corrective to Autonomy in Medicine

Adele Stiles Resmer

In a meeting of the pediatric ethics committee, a case was presented of a little girl born with cardiac abnormalities incompatible with life beyond a few years. The pediatric cardiac specialist gave a thorough review of the medical history and the alternative medical interventions that had been examined. She told of the intricacies of the surgery that had finally been completed. The committee discussed the probability that the surgery would correct the heart abnormalities so that the little girl not only would survive short-term but also would have a chance for a long life. The committee discussed issues of economics, because the surgery had been costly, and the little girl's mother had few financial resources. The committee, in fact, spent the bulk of its time on two questions: Were the expected chances of success with the surgery worth the considerable risks involved? And should the hospital have spent its resources on this surgery rather than on some other area of medical care?

While both of those questions warrant a good deal of attention, the comments made by the specialist toward the end of the conversation caught my attention. Someone asked, "When Ms. Smith was deciding which alternative to choose, what was your recommendation?" The specialist responded, "I didn't give her my recommendation. I didn't want to influence her thinking. I simply laid out all of the alternatives with the pros and cons and told her to let me know what she wanted to do."

Heads nodded around the table in affirmation. Yes, this seemed the right answer. The patient (or in this case the patient's parent) was the undisputed decision-maker. It would not do for a physician to push that decision in one direction or another. Her role was to list the medically-appropriate options and then be prepared to follow through on the one chosen.

Yet this attitude was troubling on a couple of levels. Here was a knowledgeable, experienced, and caring physician unwilling to give her best recommendation to a young woman overwhelmed with a situation that called for a life and death decision. How could the mother make that decision wisely without the best recommendation of her physician? Not all alternatives were equal. They did not carry equal benefits and burdens. They did not have equal risks and chances of success. A simple listing of the pros and cons somehow seemed inadequate to the weighty decision that needed to be made.

Further, why were we bothering to discuss this situation in the first place? Why waste time asking whether the surgery was warranted given the risks, or whether the hospital should have used its resources here rather than on another area of care? These were really moot points, if indeed no one beyond the patient (or parent) had any authority to influence or shape the decision. Other than to receive basic information, we did not need to hear about Ms. Smith and her daughter.

Not so long ago such a situation would not have existed. When paternalism was the hallmark of the physician-patient relationship, physicians decided what patients ought to know or not know about their condition. Physicians stated which treatment ought to be followed, and not infrequently overrode patient wishes if they thought it was in the patient's best interests.

Placing such knowledge and authority in the hands of the physician was considered appropriate. Physicians were the ones with the specialized education and experience. Patients were thought to be compromised in their ability to make decisions because of illness. Patient and family were often glad enough to have the responsibility for decision-making about medical treatment in the hands of a physician. Conversely, if patients balked at such interference, they were labeled "difficult."

There are still those who support paternalism in medicine.[1] More typically, however, paternalism has a bad name in medical care. Physicians occasionally have misused their authority. Medical research has sometimes been conducted without patients' knowledge. The emphasis in clinical medicine shifted to the knowledgeable patient expected to be centrally involved in decision-making. Mobility and specialization broke the connection required for a physician to know patient and family. The role of the physician shifted to that of the medical expert who supplies highly technical information. Physicians now are expected to provide the fullest possible amount of information without bias for the patient who will choose or refuse a particular course of treatment. Paternalism has been replaced rather soundly by autonomy.

It is not difficult to see how, in this changed environment, our specialist felt it was her task to provide a range of options, but not to include her own opinion about which of those options was best. After she had laid out the pros and cons for each medically indicated course of action, she had fulfilled her responsibilities to Ms. Smith. Likewise, the committee's lack of interest in Ms. Smith beyond her identity as decision-maker for her daughter was completely consistent with an environment that heralds the absolute right of the patient to decide.

My intent in this essay is not to argue for a return to paternalism, as though all things could be corrected by going back to "the good ol' days." The passing into history of the physician who automatically knows best and acts solely at her own initiative—and the consequent rise of the informed, decision-making patient—is all for the good. But, as is often the case, in an attempt to correct the abuses of the past, the correction has gone too far in the opposite direction.

In an attempt to limit properly the undue influence of the physician, we have limited, if not eliminated, the physician's ability to be an active partner with patients in care and treatment. Physicians have become sources of information and technicians who carry out treatment decided by another, the patient. Yet at its heart, good medical care is fundamentally relational. It is about people working together to preserve or renew health. Physicians, other health care professionals, patients, and their families are in their circumstances together. What I will argue is decision-making within medicine ought to reflect this basic relational reality.

Autonomy

The contemporary situation, in which Ms. Smith is left alone to make her decision on the basis of physician-supplied information, is grounded in an extreme form of autonomy that has become ingrained in the very life and practice of medicine. Its philosophical foundations can be traced to the work of Immanuel Kant and his successors. Kant's central concerns for human freedom, human dignity, and human obligation grounded in reason can be found in his concept of the "end in itself."

This concept requires that we treat ourselves and others "always as an end and never as a means only."[2] Treating people as ends and not means requires only that we not interfere in another's freedom to make reasoned choices and act upon them. Interference might include physical constraints, such as literally restraining someone from acting. Equally important, interference might include rational constraints, such as deception or corruption, conditions that would preclude someone from truly making a reasoned decision.

The heart of the matter is the autonomous person, who "determines his or her course of action in accordance with a plan chosen by himself or herself."[3] Several conditions must be met for people to express their autonomy: they must be capable of reasoned thought; honest and open exchange of necessary information must occur; and freedom must exist for them to act consistently with their reasoned decisions.

A commitment to the autonomous person and to the conditions required to support such a person can readily be found in several defining aspects of medical care today. Grounded in early-twentieth-century court cases,[4] strengthened by the Nuremberg Code, and integral to the identity of good medical practice today, the concept of informed consent is a hallmark of autonomy. It has several conditions that coincide with the conditions of autonomy itself. First, patients must be capable of understanding the medical information being given them; they must be able to comprehend what is being said and be competent to make a decision about which course of action to follow. Second, physicians must provide full disclosure of the medical situation, including which treatment options exist; the benefits and risks of each option must be discussed. Finally, patients must be free to make decisions in an environment free of coercion.

Another expression of autonomy in medical care can be found in the development of advance directives. Many patients and families found that when it came to making decisions about treatment at the end of life, they were more often than not left to the whims of the medical establishment, which saw as its primary task the extending of life. The rights of patients to determine and then to act freely on their own wishes were often denied. As a result, the United States Congress passed the Patient Self-Determination Act (PSDA), signed into law in December 1990. This act requires hospitals, nursing homes, and other health-care providers who receive Medicare or Medicaid monies to give patients information about their legal options to accept or refuse medical treatment.

In an attempt to "ensure that a patient's right to self-determination in health-care decisions be communicated and protected," the PSDA requires that health-care providers provide written information to patients, at the time of admission, about their right to "accept or refuse medical or surgical treatment and the right to formulate advance directives."[5] Most institutions provide a brochure that explains the availability of the two leading forms of advance directives, the living will and a durable power of attorney for health care.

The question appropriately arises about those who are unable to speak for themselves. How do children, teenagers, and adults who have lost decision-making capacity because of illness or accident express their autonomy? How are their "rights" concerning medical treatment protected?

Those who have decision-making capacity are encouraged to designate a surrogate by naming a durable power of attorney for health care. For those who do not have decision-making capacity, legal steps can be taken to name a guardian or surrogate. States such as New York have convened task forces to recommend processes for identifying surrogates when a patient lacks decision-making capacity.[6]

Two standards guide the decision-making of a surrogate: substituted judgment and best interests. "Substituted judgment" requires that a surrogate make decisions just as the person herself would. In order for this to occur, the patient's beliefs, values, and goals must be known and taken into account. When such information is not available, then best interest is the guide. "Best interest" requires that the surrogate decide with the well-being of the patient in mind. Calculations of benefits and burdens are central to establishing what well-being might entail in these situations. Thus the concepts of informed consent and advance directives provide two central means by which the voice of the rational individual is protected in decision-making about treatment. When the individual does not have decision-making capacity, legal supports exist to make sure her wishes or well-being are protected.

There is much about these concepts to applaud. As a result of the commitment to recognizing patient autonomy, medical treatment decisions are made by those most centrally affected. Individuals are now central in determining their own medical destinies. Respect for an individual's dignity rests not on deciding for her but on providing her or her surrogates with the information needed to make decisions.[7]

At the same time, when autonomy is *the* principle for guiding care, the physician-patient relationship is reduced to a contract. Physicians provide necessary medical information; patients make their wishes known; physicians follow through on those wishes or recommend the patient to another physician who will. The traditional physician-patient relationship has been reduced to a series of transactions. In the midst of such transactions, the patient is treated as an isolated individual. The intention of autonomy is to give voice to the individual, to empower individual decision-making. Any decision made by a well-informed, free, and autonomous person is, therefore, assumed to be the right one.

While few would argue with the importance of respecting an individual's autonomy, in and of itself it is not enough. Individual autonomy is not unlimited, primarily because people do not exist as isolated units unencumbered by the give-and-take of significant relationships. The complex of important relationships within which most of us live out our days give and enhance, take and set limits. These relationships affect an individual's ability to make decisions, just as they influence the kind of decisions that she makes. It only makes sense that decision-making in general, and medical decision-making more specifically, reflect this relational context within in which people live and make sense of their lives.

What is needed, then, is an approach that recognizes the relational nature of human existence and takes into account the central relationships that inform, influence, and shape the decisions the patient eventually must make. These relationships include not only family, friends, and significant others, such as clergy, but also medical professionals, including physicians. These relationships also provide some context for evaluating the "fittingness" of decisions. Such an approach may be found by examining the foundations of responsibility. Responsibility as an ethical perspective recognizes that decision-making and action are shaped and informed by relationships between self and others.[8]

Responsibility

Central elements in the work of H. Richard Niebuhr provide a correction to the overemphasis on autonomy in medicine today. Niebuhr understood that at its root, human life is fundamentally relational. Built into his very understanding of the person as "answerer"[9] is the acknowledgment that the moral person is one who is engaged in a lifelong dialogue with others. In comparison with Kant, who viewed rational capacity as the basis for moral action, Niebuhr suggested that it is this capacity for and necessity of dialogue that defines and shapes us as moral beings.

What does this dialogue look like and what makes it responsible? For Niebuhr, responsible dialogue has four components. First, dialogue is responsible when a person recognizes that her actions are in response to other actions upon her.[10] She does not simply act in a vacuum. She is not uninfluenced. Her actions take place within a larger context, preceded by a history of actions that have an effect on her responses.

Second, dialogue is responsible when a person recognizes that her response to an action is affected by her interpretation of what is going on.[11] When something happens, it is not simply an isolated event, or part of a series of isolated events. Rather, it is part of a larger pattern, a larger history. The responder's interpretation of this pattern or history within which an event occurs affects the significance or meaning of the response.

Third, dialogue is responsible when a person expects that others will in turn respond to her action.[12] She anticipates how her action will affect others. She thinks ahead of the possible positive and negative responses that could occur. She considers the short- and long-term consequences of her action for herself and others.

Finally, dialogue is responsible when a person acknowledges that her action is part of an ongoing dialogue among people who are part of an ongoing community.[13] She is contributing to the history and future of a broader community when she responds. Hers is not an isolated event. She is not the only one affected. She influences the lives of others by contributing to the history of events and interpretation of events in the larger community.

As a result of this understanding of the responsible self in ongoing dialogue within a larger community of people, Niebuhr shifts the traditional question "what ought I do?" to "to whom or what am I responsible and in what community of interaction am I myself?"[14] Again, this restatement shifts the focus away from an isolated individual, placing individuals firmly in a rich context of dialogue in community.

What shapes the content of this dialogue over time? Niebuhr believed that individuals are engaged in a triadic dialogue; that is, not only with those around them in community but also with a third entity. That entity is best expressed as a transcendent value, something to which individuals are committed beyond themselves.[15] For some, this transcendent value is God; for others, it is a cause.[16] Commitment to God or to cause shapes the content of human dialogue over time; individuals want to engage each other in ways that reflect their higher commitments. Beliefs about God or cause, shaped over time by the human community, influence how individuals understand themselves, how they interpret their dialogue with others, and how they understand their responsibilities to the world around them.

For Niebuhr the responsible self is actively involved in this ongoing engagement with transcendent value and with others. This self recognizes its fundamental link with others; therefore, it knows that there is no such thing as an isolated action that affects only oneself. The responsible self knows that in all interactions, it is engaging others in a dialogue that reflects the transcendent value by which the self and others live.

Implications for Medicine

If we accept the premise that moral decision-making is grounded not in autonomy but in responsibility, as outlined above, what difference might this make in how we understand the patient and her physician? How does responsibility speak to the concern suggested at the outset, that patients (and their surrogates) are being left inappropriately to their own devices when making decisions about treatment?

Patients come encumbered with a history of interactions that give shape to beliefs, values, and patterns of decisions. This history of interactions with family, friends, clergy, and medical personnel affects what patients expect of themselves, what they want for their lives, and what they expect from others. This complex reality accompanies the patient when she engages the medical system about a particular medical condition. Even if this reality is not explicitly acknowledged by medical personnel in their dealings with her, it is nonetheless at work throughout the interaction. That history and the current dialogue elicited by illness will shape which options seem most fitting. Good decision-making illumines these patterns and articulates established beliefs and values, so that they are of use to the patient and her physician as they attempt to make a decision that is most "fitting."

It is not the patient alone but the patient in conjunction with the physician (and other appropriate persons) who make the treatment decision. If it is true that humans are fundamentally relational in nature and are engaged in an ongoing dialogue with significant others, then supporting a process that seeks to isolate the patient as decision-maker is no longer an option. The relationality and dialogue of patients and medical personnel must be taken into account. The *condition* for good medical decision-making is not isolation but dialogue. The best decision-making is not freed from all interferences and influences but makes constructive use of those very interferences and influences. Good decision-making brings together the principal actors in any particular situation. It requires their input into the dialogue about what defines appropriate treatment in this particular situation.

It is important to acknowledge that this shift, from protecting the patient from undue influence to encouraging dialogue that highlights unavoidable and appropriate influence, has its dangers. Part of the reason autonomy is emphasized the way it is today is because of the previous undue influence of physicians and others in the decision-making process. What is being advocated here is not a return to the days when physician knew best and decided on the behalf of the patient. The patient remains a central participant in the decision-making process. No treatment option is chosen without her approval. But the integrity of her voice is protected in such a way that others are engaged in the decision-making process, and the patient is not overwhelmed and, for all practical purposes, left voiceless.

While informed consent and advance directives are designed to protect the autonomy of the patient, it is worth asking whether anything exists within the medical setting that fulfills the intention of dialogue among patient, medical personnel, and significant others. I believe that a much underused and often undervalued process called the family conference, if modified and utilized, could be quite helpful.

Family conferences were designed to provide a place for the family and the physician to meet and discuss the care and treatment of a patient, particularly if there were concern or disagreement about what was being proposed. Often called once a disagreement arises, the intent is to clarify miscommunication among family and medical personnel, to correct misconceptions about different treatment options, and to develop agreement about the direction of care.

A family conference-like process, where patient, family, medical personnel, and significant others are brought together earlier rather than later in the decision-making about treatment, could support the new possibilities for decision-making that have been suggested. It is a place where participants are intentionally engaged in a dialogue about the situation of the patient and potential treatment options. It includes discussion about medical appropriateness. Economics will come into the discussion, brought in by the patient and family or by medical personnel. While it is inevitable in this society that economics enter into the deliberation, economics alone ought not be the single determinant for or against any particular treatment option. The goal of such a process is to reach a decision that all can live with—that is, to reach consensus.

What brings all of these people together in such a dialogue? What unites them, in the face of differing opinions and strongly held ideas? Here Niebuhr's notion of commitment to a cause is most helpful. While patients, medical personnel, and others come with varying backgrounds and experiences, they do share a commitment to the cause of health and well-being. All participants in the process are committed to the cause of preserving or renewing health. The key, of course, is coming to common ground on what that means in a particular situation. Some patients or medical personnel will come with quite different or unrealistic expectations of what it means to preserve or renew health. Some will come with misinformation. All will bring a history of interactions that will influence how they hear each other. The importance of dialogue can not be overestimated in working through these challenges to arriving at common ground on basic issues like which treatment option to follow.

Because of the differences that are more often than not brought to the dialogue about treatment options, it is usually helpful to have a facilitator guide the discussion. This facilitator as much as possible ought to be viewed as a neutral person and be knowledgeable about medicine in general and the issues that come to bear in this situation particularly. The facilitator ought to illuminate the ethical issues at stake in different options, but as facilitator ought not be wed to any particular treatment option itself. The goal of the facilitator is to see that consensus is reached.

This is not to suggest that any decision is the right one as long as consensus is reached. If dialogue is the condition for decision-making, then "fittingness" is the *criterion* for evaluating decisions. What determines the fittingness of a decision? "Fitting" decisions are made by responsible people. Responsible people are those who know that they are not the beginning and end of things. They know they are linked with other people and understand that their decisions affect other people. They strive to make decisions that are consistent with transcendent value—in this case the cause of good medicine, the preservation or renewal of health.

All who are involved in this process recognize that their pattern of dialogue and decision-making contributes to a larger historical pattern, both within medicine and within the broader society. The final decision contributes to what will be determined to be good medicine and good decision-making in the future. Participants in the dialogue understand this contribution while not allowing it to stymie them in deliberation and decision-making.

What About Ms. Smith?

What would all of this mean for Ms. Smith, whose physician gave her medical options and left her to decide on her own? Frankly, it would mean a complete turning around of the situation. First, Ms. Smith would not be left alone to decide. She would be engaged in a dialogue that respected her position as the mother of this child but did not isolate her as the lone decision-maker. It would mean bringing her into dialogue with her physicians and other medical personnel. Family or significant others identified by Ms. Smith would be included. If she were a woman of faith, her clergyperson could be included. Members of the ethics committee might well be involved. Indeed, one of them could facilitate the process.

Second, Ms. Smith would be engaged in a dialogue that saw as its goal not the making of a decision for her daughter, in and of itself, but rather the making of a decision for her daughter that was consistent with the transcendent value of good medicine. This might be difficult for Ms. Smith or any other patient to accept at first. The pattern of deciding only in one's own best interest is part of the legacy of autonomy. The decision-making that Ms. Smith will participate in is not driven by the goal of serving one's own best interest in isolation. It is driven by the goal of serving the interests of the patient that are consistent with preserving or renewing health within the parameters of good medicine.

In the end, the consensus of the group might match the decision made by Ms. Smith on her own. What she and we would gain, however, from emphasizing responsibility in decision-making, is a firm sense that the decision "fit"; that is, that it evolved from a dialogue that took her concerns seriously, it took the input of other participants into account, and it was consistent with the value of good medicine.

Those of us on the ethics committee would likely have been involved in the dialogue about Ms. Smith's daughter. The committee would have learned something about decision-making that furthers health and contributes to good medicine. As a result, we could more adequately engage the ethical issues involved in the provision of medical care to Ms. Smith's daughter and to others.

Notes

[1] See both *Priorities in Biomedical Ethics* (Philadelphia: Westminster Press, 1981); and *Who Should Decide? Paternalism in Health Care* (New York: Oxford University Press, 1982).

[2] Immanuel Kant, *Foundations of the Metaphysics of Morals* (New York: The Library of Liberal Arts, 1959), 47.

[3] Tom L Beauchamp and James F. Childress, *Principles of Biomedical Ethics*, 2nd. ed. (New York: Oxford University Press, 1983), 59.

[4] Judge Cardozo, writing for the New York Court of Appeals in the case of Mrs. Schloendorf (1914), lays the legal foundation for informed consent. Susan M. Wolf, an audiotape lecture, "The Termination of Life-Sustaining Treatment and the Care of the Dying," The Hastings Center, Briarcliff Manor, NY, 1993.

[5] Patient Self-Determination Act, December, 1990.

[6] The New York State Task Force on Life and the Law, *When Others Must Choose: Deciding for Patients Without Capacity* (March, 1992).

[7] It ought to be noted that these realities still exist only in theory in many places. Some physicians still decide for patients.

[8] For a different take on responsibility and its role in influencing medical care, see John F. Tuohey, "Moving From Autonomy to Responsibility in HIV-Related Healthcare," *Cambridge Quarterly of Healthcare Ethics* 4/1 (Winter 1995): 64-70.

[9]H. Richard Niebuhr, *The Responsible Self* (New York: Harper & Row, 1963), 56.

[10]Ibid., 61.

[11]Ibid., 63.

[12]Ibid., 64.

[13]Ibid., 65.

[14]Ibid., 68.

[15]Ibid., 84.

[16]Ibid., 83.

Chapter 11

Casting One Stone After Another: The Failure of Moral Responsibility in the American System of Capital Punishment

Darryl M. Trimiew

Introduction

Let him who is without sin cast the first stone"[1] So said Jesus of Nazareth. Fortunately for the woman caught in adultery, and for us all, Jesus escaped having to agree with the scribes that stoning was the appropriate punishment for her offense. Adultery is the quintessential act of covenant-breaking. In this passage of scripture, Jesus does not assure the woman that she will not be punished in any way for her sins. Instead he reminds the religious authorities that the taking of a human life calls into question the moral adequacy of all, including the government. The missing figure in this scenario is, of course, the other adulterer; adultery takes two. The absent adulterer's punishment, if any, remains unspoken in this story, as the fate of the more convenient scapegoat figure in the patriarchal society, the woman, is the only one addressed.

Metaphorically transposing this story to modern America, it is possible to imagine that the woman caught in adultery is personified by the African-American criminal element, while the missing adulterer is personified by the European American criminal element. Today's scribes and Pharisees are the American criminal justice system. Jesus, alas, is nowhere to be found. Currently the caution against casting the first stone has been ignored, as a hailstorm of rocks, stone after stone, pummels African-American criminals mercilessly. In short, capital punishment is a cruel tool wielded to control and punish the Black community with very little reflection on the moral responsibility of its use.

This essay will scrutinize the state of moral relations in the United States of America with regard to the issue of capital punishment and racism by reviewing briefly the passage of the 1994 "Crime Bill" and the formal abandonment of the Racial Justice Act. The rejection of the Racial Justice Act is construed here as the European-American community's rejection of the equality of persons vis-a-vis the African-American community. This essay will analyze the conditions that produced this policy result and the conditions that allow the widespread acceptance of its tragic outcome. Finally, this essay will describe the moral meaning of the failure of the Racial Justice Act to change radically the ongoing relationship between American covenant partners. That the European- and African-American communities are indeed covenant partners makes this conflict between them so difficult and painful.

Gardner's Approach to Law, Covenant, and Morality

This essay, along with the others in this *festschrift*, is intended to honor our teacher E. Clinton Gardner. Never content to limit his ethical inquiries to the realm of private morality or ecclesiastical practices, E. Clinton Gardner has always known and demonstrated that the private virtues and vices of a society are irrevocably tied to its public practices and policies. Like Plato, he has also understood the important dynamic inherent between the practices of a society and the laws that regulate it. Accordingly, he has launched several specific investigations into Anglo-American systems of law in relation to the workings of the moral community.[2] For Gardner, American morality has always been more than simply the interaction between laws and social arrangements: it has also had the character of a biblical covenant. From his perspective, the covenant has been the source and author of the community's understanding of morality in a dialectical process: changing notions of covenant have caused different understandings of morality and led round about again to different notions of covenant. This dialectic is ongoing and deserves scrutiny.

Dr. Gardner is, of course, a recognized practitioner of ethical responsiblism, an approach best articulated by his most influential teacher, H. Richard Niebuhr. Though this essay does not represent Dr. Gardner's' views, my approach is indebted to the ethical tradition that he has helped to carry.

Covenant is an ongoing relationship. It is distinguished from common understandings of contract by its permanence. When covenant partners fail each other the covenant does not automatically collapse, but, generally speaking, continues to limp on in a broken and wounded fashion. Biblical covenant involves God, the people of God, and others—foreigners and sojourners in the land. The biblical covenant was one that was grounded in an acceptance of God's law for the people of ancient Israel. It constituted both the moral and political law of the land in their theocracy. In such a state the relationship among law, covenant, and morality was quite obvious. If one were executed, presumably God was clearly as angry at the executed as were the protectors of society. This ancient notion of covenant and of punishment and law was instituted in a different form on these shores by the Puritans.

Law is, of course, one social apparatus for regulating a society's practices and relationships as well as a mechanism for upholding its covenants and attendant mores. If individuals act irresponsibly, the law can make them accountable and punish irresponsible behavior, provided the offense falls under the purview of the law. It was this steady, regulating function of the law that initially drew my attention to it as a social instrument and as an outlet for my own career path.[3] Several years of practicing law revealed to me its impersonal, relentless regulation, which was both admirable and abhorrent. As an African American, deeply impressed by both the successes and failures of the proverbial "Civil Rights Movement," I, like Dr. Gardner, am also clearly appreciative of the dynamic interplay between law and morality. Yet what has most deeply perplexed me with regard to this interplay is the maddeningly exclusive and truncated notions of covenant that Dr. Gardner has correctly identified as being predominant in Puritan thought and practice, the narrowness of which he clearly acknowledges.[4]

The Tragedy of the American Covenant

The tragic present outcomes in the system of capital punishment may be traced directly to the tragic origins of America. The notion of a full-fledged covenant with native American or African-American slaves was, generally speaking, anathema to the Puritan colony and other European settlements. What made the Puritan covenant morally untenable was the Puritans' refusal to consider as covenant partners the many other people who also occupied the land. Native Americans and African slaves had no willing part in the formation of the covenant, which was instead a relationship interpreted primarily for the benefit of European-American settlers.[5] But Blacks and Native Americans were never afforded even the limited protection of sojourners in the land, as was available in the biblical covenant.[6] The American covenant reflected the needs of the new society that required Native American land (but not Native Americans) and African slave labor (but not for the benefit of Africans).

Yet Puritan theology was sufficiently developed to be concerned with the problem of being a "new Israel," in a "new Canaan" with "new Canaanites." Part of the rationale for the conquest of the land was to convert the "savages," and part of the justification for slavery was to convert the slaves.[7] The conquest of America and the establishment of the new covenant meant that certain occupants of the land had to be eliminated, and certain others had to be subjugated and kept subjugated. Whereas the biblical covenant did not have expendable people, the American one did.

European-American male settlers who were over twenty-one years of age, who owned real property in freehold could vote, and, accordingly, were considered full-fledged citizens of the "new Israel." After the Revolutionary War, this select group also became full-fledged citizens of a new nation legitimated by a Constitution and a Bill of Rights that settled for them, finally, all the major issues concerning their civil and political rights. At the same time, however, the Bill of Rights and subsequent Constitutional law made it clear that the United States of America was to be not a theocracy but a democratic republic—at least for the fortunate few. This was indeed fortunate for the few, as early colonial history was replete with capital punishment for Quakers and other religious groups beyond the pale of acceptable practice. The theocratic flavor of the Biblical covenant can be seen most clearly in its

American version in the Salem witch hunts and, especially, in the persecution and execution of Quakers such as Mary Dyer.[8]

It is with Dyer that the link between covenant and capital punishment is so clearly revealed. Dyer represented a challenge to the old status quo and a perfect scapegoat to relieve societal friction in the settling of a "New World." Her religious persecution was possible only in a theocratic society that did not fully recognize religious tolerance by custom or by law. Such persecution sought to insure the uniformity of Puritan Christianity. Mary Dyer and others were executed as part of the process of attempting to keep the Puritan understanding of covenant intact. Yet this approach was never very successful and lost out in the progressive development of political and religious freedoms. Thus, the original American notion of Christian covenant became subject to the Constitution and the Bill of Rights. These were positive laws, but they were presumed to be more than simply the action of a secular state. European American colonists believed that they were a nation set apart by God and that they had received from God "inalienable rights." These rights were not automatically extended, however, to the oppressed, to the silent covenant partners, who were, instead, constrained by force to carry out their roles in subservient acquiescence to the oppressive majority. Thus the new Israelites forgot even their foundational moral obligations to avoid oppressing the foreigner or sojourner in the land. Accordingly, the old notion of covenant was broken in the new world, and the judgment of God was visited upon our ancestors in the form of a bloody civil war.[9]

The Civil War established the possibility of recognizing some of the oppressed as full-fledged covenant partners.[10] Yet the ending of Reconstruction aborted the tentative and preliminary recognition of African Americans as participating covenant partners and instituted a reign of terror in the South—lynchings, violence, and the reintroduction of peonage to landless peasants who continued to survive by sharecropping. Social relations throughout the country were maintained by force and nowhere were African Americans recognized as full-fledged citizens.[11] The threat of deadly force, even when held in check, was always present to intimidate some and to reassure others.

One means by which African Americans tried repeatedly to demonstrate their humanity was to take on the causes of this country in fighting its wars. To prove their full humanity required them to be complete citizens, and this goal required that they risk their lives. African Americans believed that the willing loss of their lives in defense of

America was a clear proof of their absolute loyalty to America and of their competence to be citizens. Thus African Americans have fought in every American war and police action. Yet African-American lives have never been considered equivalent in value, no matter how many have been lost in fighting campaigns from the American Revolutionary War to the Second World War. All of those wars were fought in separate and segregated units, generally speaking. Thus the sacrifice of African-American lives never yielded one of the sought after goals, namely the acknowledgement of equality between races. This depressing fact is still true after the integration of the Armed forces, schools, colleges, public transportation and even the problematic extension of "affirmative action."[12]

What is now clear is that there are several notions of community, in contrast to covenant, and that the extent to which America can still be understood as a covenanted community is very much in doubt. Previously "silent" covenant partners—Blacks, Native Americans, Hispanics, and Asian-Americans—are no longer silent. The continuance of covenant is also doubtful because of the continued characteristics of "broken covenant" manifested in America in watershed events like the Los Angeles riots following the Rodney King incidents, and in ongoing signs of social hatred such as white flight. Equally problematic is the continued exploitation of urban areas and populations and the overall abdication of moral obligations by most Americans.[13]

Advances achieved by the Civil Rights movement have not solved the widespread and chronic disparities in income and in wealth between blacks and whites, or removed from current racial relations other vestiges of oppression that hearken back to the white supremacist origins of this country. Indeed, Robert Bellah, whose notion of "broken covenant" informs this essay, has maintained that certain watershed events, such as the Civil War and the Civil Rights movement, have been merely partial attempts to correct skewed notions of covenant as well as movements to fulfill the hidden potential residing in biblical notions of covenant.

The issue of capital punishment, particularly in relation to minority communities, can now be addressed as the most troubling dialectical interaction of law, morality, and covenant. This issue demonstrates clearly that we Americans still live within a broken covenant.

The Law's Formation and the Maintenance of "Brokenness"

Racial injustice persists in America, particularly in our criminal justice process. This injustice is most clearly seen in the peculiarities of capital punishment. Numerous studies have demonstrated that capital punishment is used primarily, though not exclusively, as a tool of vengeance to punish minorities for crimes against white victims. Rarely are white perpetrators executed for the murder of Blacks.[14] Along these lines, Richard C. Dieter writes:

> There is certainly considerable evidence that the death penalty is discriminatory. For example, the United States General Accounting Office in 1990 found "a pattern of evidence indicating racial disparities in the charging, sentencing, and imposition of the death penalty after the Furman decision. Presently, about half the people on death row are from minority groups that represent only about twenty percent of the country's population. About forty percent of those who have been executed since the death penalty was allowed to resume in 1976 have been African-Americans, even though they constitute only twelve percent of the population.[15]

The history of capital punishment in this country reveals the ongoing process of subjugation of African Americans that has never been effectively impeded by the immunities ostensibly afforded by Civil Rights Amendments. The odious practice of lynching has now given way (by high tech or low, to paraphrase Justice Clarence Thomas) to the practice of capital punishment. Capital punishment reveals, as few other practices do, the ongoing devaluation of African Americans. Manning Marable, a noted social critic, has compiled a statistical history of the use of capital punishment that shows how punishment in America is much harsher for African Americans than for European Americans.[16] Additionally, his findings suggest, that the murder of African-American victims seldom invokes the severity of punishment that attends the dispatch of European-American victims.[17] These statistics also suggest that when lethal conflicts occur between blacks and whites, our system of law maximizes the severity of the punishment when the victim is white and the perpetrator is black and conversely minimizes punishment when the victim is black and the perpetrator is white. These practices suggest that the recent attempts of the Congressional Black Caucus to amend the recent crime bill are of special interest and importance. The Racial Justice Act was a piece of special legislation designed to allow for the possibility of escape for some African-American murderers from the ultimate sanction of capital punishment. Among others, the Congressional Black Caucus has sought to minimize the harm of racial injustice not by directly eliminating the racial bias and discrimination found throughout the American judicial process but by means of legislation. This is, of course, a dubious proposition at best. The majority of members of Congress found little enticement for passing a bill that would have been politically risky for them to support. When the 1994 crime bill was passed, the Racial Justice Act was severed from the legislative package and abandoned.

The Racial Justice Act: Justice or Just Us?

Despite the setback of the Racial Justice Act, the odious, arbitrary, and discriminatory process of capital punishment in this country so offends so many consciences that the desire to change things was not limited to minorities and their representatives. Senators Kennedy and Biden, among others, have been consistent supporters of the Racial Justice Act. This act would have created the possibility that Blacks and other oppressed minorities, individually, and after their convictions on capital murder offenses, might mitigate their racially disproportionate sentences by means of an evidentiary showing that their sentencing jurisdiction was one that disproportionately meted out death to minorities.[18] The legislation would have compensated for the inability to stamp out white supremacy in the American criminal justice system by mitigating its effect in terms of actual life and death sentences case-by case. Successful applicants would not be considered supplicants for mercy but would be viewed as potential victims of discrimination who also had committed heinous crimes; they would not go unpunished. They would, of course, remain convicted of murder or other capital offenses. At best they could hope only to commute their death sentences into life sentences. Furthermore, the Act did not guarantee the success of any particular applicant. In theory, minorities would be more successful in jurisdictions that had proven to be the most discriminatory. In other words, most of the appeals initially would have more plausibility where there had been huge gaps in disparity in sentencing; however, as applicants in a jurisdiction became more successful and began to serve mediated life sentences, subsequent minority applicants would not, presumably, find this approach nearly as successful. Though the juries and judges in the jurisdiction could remain as racist as ever, the *statistics* would change. At some point, some member of an ethnic minority who had been convicted of murder would have a poor evidentiary case; the success of murderous minority predecessors in having their capital punishment commuted would make this latter appeal untenable. At this point an equilibrium could be said to have been reached. African Americans, Hispanics, and others would then be executed at rates comparable to and corresponding to the percentage of European-American murderers executed in the district in question. Though still depressing, this scenario is, nevertheless, extremely interesting. Capital punishment was never intended to eliminated by the Racial Justice Act, and in no way would minorities have been executed at a rate lower than that for whites. Indeed, most appeals by this route would begin to fail (assuming they were ever successful) as soon as minority execution rates got within striking distance of those of whites. As a controversial addendum to the hotly contested Crime Bill, the act had the potential to address at long last the problem of disparities in sentencing. Such action also would have effectively mitigated the thirty additional crimes in the new federal bill that became *new* capital offenses.[19] The failure to keep the Racial Justice Act in the enacted Crime Bill demonstrates a settled American disposition for several issues.

The Moral Meaning of Rejection

Several things can be said of the rejection of the Racial Justice Act. First, that act and the Crime Bill of which it was intended to be a part were not designed to outlaw capital punishment. Indeed, it is unclear whether the Racial Justice Act would have aided or frustrated capital punishment abolitionists. Second, the unsuccessful push for the Racial Justice Act shows that it was a concern of a minority of American citizens. Its supporters, primarily liberal Democrats and African-American members of Congress, were isolated in their desire for a change in the criminal justice system. Any reasonable critical analysis of this lack of enthusiasm for change must conclude that most Americans do not feel any need to rectify any social injustices of the past or to make radical changes with regard to discriminatory capital punishment in the present. Thus the history of lynching is either denied as an historical reality or merely regretted as an immutable horror of the past, with no current effect on criminal justice. The statistically disproportionate use of capital punishment against African Americans is not understood by most European Americans as a continuation of an historical policy of both the subjugation and denigration of African Americans, though that is precisely what it is. In other words every time a European American is given a lenient sentence for killing an African American, the past history of lynching is re-affirmed. Similarly, every execution of an African American who has killed a European American, particularly in a jurisdiction that does not severely punish African Americans for killing each other exponentially, re-affirms that message: White lives matter, Black lives do not.[20]

Third, the inadequacy of the arguments in opposition to the Racial Justice Act demonstrates a lack of moral insight on the part of opposing legislators and a lack of moral discernment upon the part of their constituencies. This assertion cannot be fully developed now but will be examined shortly. Fourth, the rejection of the Racial Justice Act reaffirms a primary American social value, namely, the preservation of the right to exact vengeance against minority criminals who have violated the holiest of holies: who have murdered European Americans. Finally, the rejection of the Racial Justice Act reaffirmed yet another primary American social value, namely, the refusal to protect the lives of African Americans adequately, giving the distinct impression that Black victims are of little worth and the African-American community is of little value.

Thus, the most disturbing aspect of the failure of the bill was that it brought to full and obvious scrutiny the reality of racism in American criminal processes. This failure then aggravated the insult into injury by reminding European Americans that minorities in America, who come into conflict with European Americans, will always be punished to the fullest extent under the law. Already tense social relations were thereby exacerbated by this exercise of rubbing all American noses into the confusing mess that capital punishment has been. The only saving grace in this affair is of a dubious nature; with so few Americans aware of the rejection of the Racial Justice Act and the discriminatory application of capital punishment against minorities, psychological damage has been limited because of the obscurity of the harms done. Thus the triumph of racism over reason, especially galling to concerned citizens, is not even recognized by most Americans, biased or innocent. In other words, most average Americans are, justifiably or not, blissfully ignorant of American criminal justice atrocities. Our disgrace looks even more primitive in comparison with the recent changes in South Africa, where the new, nonwhite government has reversed the course of its predecessors by refusing to seek the death penalty for the clearly racially motivated murder of a European American scholar/activist, who was, ironically, working with Black South Africans in a voter registration drive to secure their freedom at the time of her demise.

Lastly, the failure of the Racial Justice Act could not have come at a more inopportune time with the notorious spectacle of a quintessential and stereotypical "race" murder trial, namely, the O.J. Simpson case. That the prosecutors refused to seek the death penalty for O.J. simply confuses the whole issue, since, aside from his celebrity-status and wealth, he would (provided he is convicted), in all probability, have been a classic example of discrimination in sentencing, namely an African-American male who had brutally slashed and killed an attractive, young White woman, his ex-wife. Assuming for the sake of argument that O.J. is found guilty, his life sentence will confirm the erroneous assumption that there is rough equality of justice between Blacks and Whites in America. His high profile and likely acquittal are anomalies that mask the problem that the Racial Justice Act was designed to address. In the future, other African-American celebrities, or those wealthy enough to hire a "dream team" of high priced attorneys, will similarly provide aberrant, anecdotal examples that further obfuscate the seriousness of this problem. Obviously there is also a class issue that figures into the capital punishment equation that cannot now be addressed.

Thus Robert Bellah appears to be correct in his assessment that America envisions itself as an "Anglo-Saxon" nation and thus its criminal justice system resolves violent crimes involving parties of different ethnic backgrounds in ways that invariably valorize Anglo-Saxon security over the security of all other ethnic groups.

In addition, this system remains emotionally and spiritually untouched by any resulting injustices that are the result of this valuing process. Indeed the use of capital punishment as a tool of social control and genocide of ethnic minorities is either categorically denied by most Americans as an actual state of affairs, or, alternatively, is understood as being a morally justifiable account of justice as it relates to the police protection that the state is charged with providing for its citizens: that is its first class citizens.[21]

That the opposition to the Racial Justice Act was absolutely insensitive to the tortuous functioning of capital punishment is clear from the arguments against it. There were two primary arguments. First, it was alleged that if the Racial Justice Act were passed it would act in effect as an abolition of the death penalty.[22] The speciousness of this argument is revealing. It implies that only racial minorities are executed in this country, since only racial minorities could invoke and utilize the act. This implication is, of course, factually false since (to our disgrace) a sizable number of European Americans are executed annually. But if it were true of American capital punishment, it would be even more problematic if *only* minorities were executed; because if only minorities were executed, what other argument could be more forceful that the Racial Justice Act is necessary? The further implication of this argument is revealed in the weighing of evil outcomes. The argument in favor of the "lesser of two evils" assumes that the continuance of capital punishment, no matter how unfairly it is administered, no matter how, presumably evil it is, is still a more crucial value and constitutes a lesser evil than the abolition of the death penalty. In essence this argument cries, "Damn the torpedoes, full speed ahead!"

The second primary argument in opposition was that the Racial Justice Act should not be enacted because it would create quotas vis-a-vis the death penalty. This argument would be amusing if it were not so ironically cruel. In the absence of the Racial Justice Act, the forty percent of the people executed for capital punishment in America that are minorities, already constitute a quota and have done so for decades![23] Supporters of the bill were trying to *diminish* the size of the quota by the *passage* of the bill. Thus opponents to this measure who were against it in principle because it would create a quota unwittingly became the *greatest* supporters of a racial minority quota system. The disturbing underlying implication of this argument is that for whatever reason, deterrence, vengeance, etc., that constitutes the need for capital punishment, no lessening in the numbers of victims is tolerable: if racism should skew the racial identity of those executed by the state then all for the better.

Ethical Responsibility in Relation to Capital Punishment

The mendacious and capricious spirit behind these arguments behooves the morally responsible self in America to reject the history of oppression and the privilege of *lex talionis*. At the minimum, the brokenness of the covenant is evidenced by these practices. The devaluation of African-American lives summons responsible selves to create and maintain legal escape hatches for oppressed minorities to escape the wrath of a relentlessly racist society. In other words, morally responsible agents need to work to dismantle the system of racism that necessitates the use of capital punishment as a tool of repression; and they need to approve legal mechanisms, such as the Racial Justice Act. Or, perhaps the creators of a new covenant need to do both.

Healing the Hurt

While many are deeply upset at the loss of opportunity that the Racial Justice Act presented, other opportunities to exercise ethical responsibility are still available. The abolition of the death penalty would, of course, eliminate part of the problem. That is to say, without capital punishment the loss of White lives at the hands of homicidal Blacks (one possible terrible scenario) would no longer be so readily avenged by the state's spilling of Black blood. Whether or not Whites can let go of this racial bloodlust is questionable, since capital punishment is statistically popular even when inflicted on European Americans. Yet the message delivered by the abolition of capital punishment would not go unnoticed in the African-American community. Though the Racial Justice Act was more specifically racially oriented, the abolition of the death penalty would itself tell African Americans that *racial relations had changed.* And it is this message that is so crucial, as it is the one that transcends the issue of capital punishment. But to change the present it is necessary to acknowledge the impact of the past. This need to re-interpret the past is one that was well-understood by H. Richard Niebuhr. For him the creation of a new future required a re-interpretation of the past. He once wrote:

> Insofar as the reinterpretation of our past has led us to some new understanding and acceptance of the past actions of and upon our groups, our present encounters with each other as North and South, Negro and white, have been guided by somewhat new ideas. Every nation with similar social recollections of past animosities, with a similar inherited complex of emotional and personal attitudes of group to group, seeks, I believe, to move toward freedom, toward freshness and fittingness in present interaction by similar reconstructions of its past. [24]

To feel finally that one's community is not of lesser value, that in wars against crime one's people are not cannon fodder, would have a greater effect on African Americans than the prevention of the loss of the lives of the executed murderous minority. Frankly, many of the executed are not missed, and African Americans are very American in their appetites for violence and revenge. Yet the relinquishment of the eye for an eye would not signify merely that a more peaceful state had come into being. It also would signify that, however hateful European Americans are of capital offenders, a foregoing of vengeance would be the greatest acknowledgement that great wrong has been done to the previously silent covenant partners. A foregoing of blood would be seen as a request for forgiveness for the millions of African Americans killed in the slave trade and transport. The strange fruit of the American Southern lynching tradition would finally begin to bear fruit of healing rather than rage. Such an admission could then begin to put the tragic origins of this country in the past, rather than continue to remind oppressed people that the awful past is still present in strange and tragic ways. The brokenness of the American covenant would itself begin to break down. Forgiveness for the past wrongs of lynching and oppression and discriminatory prosecution could actually be recognized and received. Genuine repentance for the social sin of racism in America could finally be achieved. Finally a new covenant, no longer broken on the altar of White supremacy, could be established. And, this covenant could be kept without the sacrifice of a minority scapegoat. No longer viewed primarily as scapegoats, the greater valuation of black lives would also have the salutary effect of disinclining the spilling of Black blood by Black brothers and sisters. Social recognition of the value of the Black community would further more peaceful resolutions to problems and thus further more law, order and morality. And, in the final analysis, isn't this what every system of justice, law, and morality desires?

We are all witnesses to a variety of stonings, yet we are not called to be modern day Sauls, eagerly standing by, holding the coats of the executioners. Still we are not innocent; we are not modern day Stephens. Once again the memory and presence of Jesus appears to this adulterous generation and tells us to go in peace, and to sin no more.

Notes

[1] The Gospel of John, Chapter eight, verses five through seven, reads as follows:

"Now in the law Moses commanded us to stone such women. Now what do you say?" They said this to test him, so that they might have some charge to bring against him. Jesus bent down and wrote with his finger on the ground. When they kept on questioning him, he

straightened up and said to them, "Let anyone among you who is without sin be the first to throw a stone at her."
Holy Bible, New Revised Standard Version, Nashville: Thomas Nelson Publishers, 1990.

[2]Gardner's most pertinent essays are "Justice, Virtue, and Law" in *Journal of Law & Religion* ,Volume 2, 393-412, "Responsibility and Moral Direction in the Ethics of H. Richard Niebuhr" in *Encounter* Spring, 1979 Volume 40, no. 2, 143-168, and "The Role of Law and Moral Principles in Christian Ethics" in *Religion In Life* 236-247.

[3]Gardner acknowledges this regulatory aspect of law as a positive attribute, writing:

But surely there is some justice in the world, and simply to break down and overthrow existing structures of power and existing cultural and social patterns would bring injustice as well as invite chaos. Doubtless some structures are so evil that they should be overthrown radically, but in other cases the cause of justice would be best served by the transformation or conversion of the existing structures so that the good in them would be preserved while the evil is being purged away.

From "The Role of Law and Moral Principles in Christian Ethics" in *Religion In Life* at 239.

[4]Indeed, Gardner's work has been to show how concepts of covenant make for broader rather than narrower notions of community. He writes:

Understood in terms of covenant, pluralism is part of God's design for the ordering and enrichment of human history. Its inclusion in the political process is prerequisite for the achievement of justice. In a covenantal understanding of public life, accountability is the willingness to be held accountable by the community as a whole. Pluralism provides the broadest possible resources not only for a fuller insight into the meaning of justice but also for the practical implementation of the latter with the limits of history.

"Justice, Virtue, and Law" in *Journal of Law and Religion* 2, 409-410.

[5]It would be incorrect to say that Native Americans had no part to play in the formation of the new covenant. Native Americans were consigned unwillingly into playing the role of the "New Canaanites" in a "New Israel" in which they served as convenient "heathens" to be converted and/or divested from their traditional holdings in land. African slaves, through a tortured but useful interpretation of the curse of Ham, proved to be very profitable slaves in which they were consigned to be hewers of wood and drawers of water. With reference to the curse of Ham (Gen. 9:18-27) one New Testament scholar, Cain Felder writes, "The idea that the blackness of Africans was due to a curse, and thus reinforced and sanctioned enslaving Blacks, persisted into the seventeenth century." *Troubling Biblical Waters: Race, Class, and Family* (Maryknoll, N.Y.: Orbis Press, 1989), 40.

[6]Deuteronomy 10:17-19 reads as follows:
For the Lord your God is God of gods and Lord of lords, the great, the mighty, and the terrible God, who is not partial and takes no bribe. He executes justice for the fatherless and the widow, and loves the sojourner, giving him food and clothing. Love the sojourner therefore; for you were sojourners in the land of Egypt.
It is this very loss of the sense of being a redeemed covenanted community that goes so wrong in Israel and America.

[7]Albert Raboteau, *Slave Religion* (Princeton: Princeton University Press), at 100.

[8]D. Elton Trueblood writes of this period:
The persecution on the part of the old religious establishment in England might have been expected, but the paradox is that the most severe persecution arose in the New World, in the establishment of Massachusetts. A law was made which provides later generations with an unintentional yet unmistakable evidence of the vitality of the infant Quaker Movement. The law, which was to the effect that Quakers who were banished and who returned, would be put to death, showed how deep and almost frantic the fear of the Quakers was. . . .
Four were actually hanged, William Leddra, Marmaduke Stephenson, Mary Dyer, and William Robinson.
The People Called Quakers (New York: Harper & Row, 1966), 13,14. See also "The Quaker Executions as Myth and History," *The Journal of American History* (September 1993), 441-469.

[9]The Civil War as a punishment for slavery is given its clearest enunciation by President Abraham Lincoln.

[10]The Civil War did nothing, of course, to stop the ongoing genocide against Native Americans. Indeed, Buffalo soldiers, newly freed African Americans, also participated in pogroms against Native Americans.

[11]The status of African Americans in this country has always been tenuous and tempestuous. It has been similar to the experience of European Jewry. During times of prosperity and peace, Jews in Europe and African Americans in the United States could move about with some semblance of acceptance. Such acceptance was, however, always maintained with the understanding that such people were inferior, and if conflicts arose legal and nonlegal force could be used to "put people in their places." For African Americans this usually meant lynching, for Jews periodic pogroms would arise. I have previously commented upon this unpredictable status elsewhere, writing:
In contrast, [to infantilization] the latter membership problem, or experience of oppression, consists of a kind of sustainable marginality. It is the experience faced by people such as this writer, people who are not necessarily poor or economically deprived, who are often successful in their careers, but are oppressed, nevertheless, because their belonging to a hated or traditionally subjugated ethnic or religious group subjects them to sudden, drastic, destabilizing acts of oppression. Such 'members' of society feel reasonably secure until an incident of police

brutality or a lynching occurs to remind us that we skate in the thin ice of a hostile society and are subject to sudden, fatal plunges into unseen, unanticipated fissures in the frozen depths of white supremacy. *Voices of the Silenced: The Responsible Self in a Marginalized Community* (Cleveland, Ohio: Pilgrim Press, 1993), xvi.

[12]Some African-American conservatives, such as Shelby Steele, are deeply disturbed by the very self-imaging of Blacks as victims. While taking on solely the role of victim does seem to be self-defeating, refusing to recognize ongoing oppression seems to an equally clear case of denial and wishful thinking. See Steele's famous piece, *The Content of Our Character: A New Vision of Race in America* (New York: St. Martin's Press, 1990).

[13]My notion of broken covenant is liberally borrowed from Robert Bellah's influential text, *The Broken Covenant* (New York: The Seabury Press), 1975.

[14]The case of Donald Gaskins clearly illustrates this issue. Mr. Gaskins was executed on September 8, 1991. He was only the second white in American history to be executed for killing a black and the first in over forty years. See "Rarity for U.S. Executions: White Dies For Killing Black, First Time in Decades" *New York Times* (7 September 1991), 1.   .

[15]Richard C. Dieter, "Secondary Smoke Surrounds the Capital Punishment Debate", *Criminal Justice Ethics*, volume 13, number 1, Winter/ Spring 1994, at 2.

[16]Manning Marable, *How Capitalism Underdeveloped Black America: Problems in Race, Political Economy, and Society* (Boston, MA: South End Press, 1983), chapter 6. See also more recent statistics in Michael Tonry's article, "Racial Disproportion on US Prisons" *British Journal of Criminology*, 34 (Special Issue 1994), 97.

[17]Manning Marable, *How Capitalism Underdeveloped Black America* (Boston, Mass.: South End Press, 1984), Chapter 6.
   The act reads as follows:
(a) In General.-No person shall be put to death under color of State or Federal law in the execution of a sentence that was imposed based on race. "(b) Inference of Race as the Basis of Death Sentence.-An inference of race was the basis of a death sentence is established if valid evidence is presented demonstrating that, at the time the death sentence was imposed, race was a statistically significant factor in decisions to seek or to impose the sentence of death in the jurisdiction in question. "(c) Relevant Evidence.- Evidence relevant to establish an inference that race was the basis of a death sentence may include evidence that death sentences were, at the time pertinent under subsection (b), being imposed significantly more frequently in the jurisdiction in question- "(1) upon persons of one race than upon persons of another race; or "(2) as punishment for capital offenses against persons of one race than as punishment for capital offenses against persons of another race.

[18]The Honorable Cardiss Collins, of Illinois was clearly aware of the exacerbation of the problem of discrimination in sentencing. On the floor of the House of Congress she noted:

> While the deterrent effect of the death penalty has never been clearly shown, we have all witnessed the discriminatory way that it has been used. Time and again we have seen how African-American men and women are disproportionately sentenced to death--even when one accounts for the crime committed. Since 1988, 33 of the 37 Federal death penalty defendants have been African Americans. In the current Administration, which I look upon as being more enlightened regarding the unfairness of our judicial system, all of the defendants the Attorney General has approved for the death penalty have been African-American.

From the *Congressional Digest*, June-July 1994, at 181.

[19]Richard C. Dieter makes this point clearly, writing,

> The issue of race and the death penalty is compounded when one looks at the race of the victims in capital cases. Then it appears that not only is the death penalty targeted more often toward black defendants, it is used almost exclusively when the victim is white. Eighty-five percent of the victims in cases resulting in execution since 1976 have been white even though whites constitute only about fifty percent of murder victims overall. Thus, both the perception and the reality converge on the conclusion that if you kill a white person in this country, you're far more likely to receive the death penalty than if you kill a black person. To put it another way, the criminal justice system appears to place a higher premium on white lives than on black lives.

See "Secondary Smoke Surrounds the Capital Punishment Debate." At 81-82.

[20]This American lack of interest in the gross disparities ion the racial composition of death row inmates is noted by David Masci who finds it clearly evidenced in the McCleskey case. He writes:

> The Supreme Court seemed to agree when it ruled in 1987, in McCleskey v. Kemp, that statistics showing race-related disparities in sentencing were not enough to sustain a constitutional challenge to a death sentence and that courts could not accept such evidence. 'Apparent disparities in sentencing are an inevitable part of our criminal justice system,' Justice Lewis F. Powell Jr. wrote for the majority.

"Controversial Racial Justice Proposal. . . An Explosive Issue for Lawmakers" *Congressional Quarterly*, June 18, 1994, 1626.

[21]David Masci writes on this subject:

> To Rep Bill McCollum, R-Fla., the Racial Justice Act is anathema: Racial bias in sentencing may occur occasionally, he says, but the Edwards solution is not the answer. It could lead to racial quotas in death sentencing, or worse: 'This would mean the end of the death penalty in most jurisdictions where it currently exists,' McCollum said.

From "Controversial Racial Justice Proposal. . . An Explosive Issue for Lawmakers" *Congressional Quarterly*, June 18, 1994, 1626.

[22]By quota I do not mean that there is a conscious conspiracy to have a certain percentage of minorities make up a set percentage of executions. Rather I mean that American capital punishment continuously consigns a disproportionate number of minorities (in relation to their numbers in the total population) to the grave. Obviously some portion of the executed minorities make up a proportionate segment of capital punishment's victims.

[23]H. Richard Niebuhr, *The Responsible Self* (New York: Harper & Row, 1963), 1

Chapter 12

The Covenant with Distant Neighbors: A Theological and Ethical Argument for School-Mandated Community Service

Leslie F. Weber, Jr.

> In a speech unveiling key themes in his re-election campaign, President Clinton challenged all Americans on Friday to take direct personal action to help solve their communities social problems. Citing rising rates of out-of-wedlock births and violent crime by young people, Clinton said America is plagued by a "stunning break-down" of community life and insisted that the nation's shredding social fabric can be mended only if citizens take personal responsibility for doing it. Clinton challenged every high school in America to put community service into its curriculum.[1]

Should community service be mandated by schools as a high school graduation requirement? With or without the cajoling of an American president, this question is being asked in various forums throughout the nation. Answering it in the affirmative, a number of school systems have adopted community service requirements. It is estimated that over one million secondary students are engaged in school-based community service-learning.[2]

Many, however, disagree with school-mandated service. They believe that it places an unjust burden on certain racial or economic segments of the populace. They claim that it makes students do for free what it is difficult to hire people to do because of low funding for social programs. They say that it diverts teachers from the more important task of helping students to develop critical thinking and subject knowledge through academic course work, or that it invades students' privacy by denying freedom of choice and by imposing certain altruistic views.

The debate over school-mandated service underscores the broader issue of what responsibility citizens bear toward one another in a liberal democratic society. Should we meet the needs of others as well as our own? Should we concern ourselves with the common good as well as our individual goods? Or is our responsibility only to fulfill our own goods and needs, provided we do not harm others in the process? E. Clinton Gardner states that a liberal democracy forges a middle ground between the good of the individual and the good of the community:

> On the one hand [democracy] rejects the anarchic view that the individual is independent and sufficient unto himself; on the other hand, it rejects the collectivist view that the good of the individual is subordinate to a superpersonal state, or race, or class, membership in which alone bestows worth upon the individual.[3]

The debate over school-mandated service, however, illustrates that Americans are not clear about that middle ground.

I believe that the Christian theological tradition can shed light on this significant issue. What I will argue is that service for the well-being of the distant neighbor, a fundamental requirement of the biblical conception of covenant, can help us to focus more clearly on the middle ground noted above. On the one hand, serving the neighbor's needs prevents a lapse into self-interest. On the other hand, by concretizing the "public good," serving the neighbor's needs inhibits the absolutizing of a vague, impersonal collectivity.

This essay will first examine the strengths and weaknesses of two philosophical arguments by which advocates seek to justify mandatory community service: for the sake of the individual performing the service and for the sake of the public good. Departing from these common justifications, I will then develop a theological perspective that suggests that mandated service is, first and foremost, for the well-being of the neighbor, toward whom the creation is constrained by the force of God's will. As Gardner writes: "we are summoned to love the neighbor. . . . The will of God for us is related to the neighbor's needs in a particular, concrete situation."[4] I will also discuss the concept of vocation, because it helps to understand this constraint operating throughout a person's life and not merely in personally-chosen or socially-mandated ways.

After setting forth my arguments for neighbor-centered service, I will defend the justice of requiring only youth to perform community service. Finally, I will conclude by looking at arguments for and against the use of the school as the place to teach service.

The Current Debate

Arguments supporting school-mandated community service fall into several categories. These categories reflect more than attitudes toward school-based service; they also reflect attitudes toward civic responsibility in general. Two significant philosophical arguments for endorsing and for rejecting mandatory community service find their basis in two forms of individualism that stem from classical liberalism: utilitarian individualism and expressive individualism.

Utilitarian and Expressive Individualism. According to the utilitarian individualist, individuals are the "primary human reality," driven by passions of "fear of harm" and "desire for comfort."[5] Social relations are evaluated on an instrumental basis: do they foster the private ends of individual security and gain? According to the expressive individualist, "gain" is measured by enriched experience, enjoyment of all kinds of people, and the liberation or fulfillment of the individual.[6] Both proponents and opponents of mandatory community service draw on classical liberalism's two forms of individualism; however, proponents more often reason according to utilitarian individualism and opponents according to expressive individualism.

The utilitarian individualism of many proponents of mandatory community service is apparent in the claim that students will explore career possibilities, build self-confidence through risk-taking activities, and develop leadership, communication, critical-thinking, and problem-solving skills.[7] Service will make classroom learning relevant. Students will be more ready to learn,[8] and, thus, academic performance will improve.[9] Students will learn to work with people of different ethnic, racial, and socioeconomic groups, thereby helping to overcome stereotypes.[10] Virtues, such as justice and compassion, will be imparted or reinforced through service.[11] Many proponents stress the way that community service connects young people with adults, so that they learn mutual respect and trust.[12] In sum, "Students who serve others actually help themselves most."[13]

Expressive individualism is often invoked by opponents of mandatory community service. These opponents claim mandatory service infringes on various personal freedoms. They cite the possible violation of the Thirteenth Amendment to the Constitution, which bans involuntary servitude.[14] While courts have ruled that mandatory service does not constitute servitude,[15] critics of mandatory community service continue to say that it unfairly burdens working-class students who might already have jobs, as well as students whose participation in extracurricular activities, such as athletics, might enable them to attend college. Or, these critics say, mandatory service forces rural students to go to great lengths to find scarce volunteer opportunities. Opponents have also pointed to mandatory service as a possible violation of the First Amendment's guarantee of free speech, because they claim that a certain form of altruism is being imposed. One parent who objected to required service summarizes well the expressive individualist position:

> Don't get me wrong—I believe in community service, voluntary service. My whole family is involved in community service; we all volunteer. But this is getting into my private life. This is like Communism, and that's dead, isn't it?[16]

Although there may be some strengths to individualist arguments for and against required service, the weaknesses are greater. The problem with utilitarian individualism as an argument for mandatory service may be seen in the relationship between the servant and the one served. Contrary to the empathy and mutuality that usually exist in a caring relationship, utilitarian individualism objectifies people and controls circumstances.[17] The meeting of the servant's private ends and the fulfilling of the servant's desires mean that the one "serving" is "using" the one served. This utilitarian function runs contrary to the commonly accepted understanding of service, in which the well-being of the other is primary. Given the focus on service's utility to the individual servant, it is not surprising that service "lacks a vocabulary that draws attention to the public world that extends beyond personal lives and communities."[18] Instead, service is described using therapeutic language, relating educational goals to self-esteem, self-understanding, consciousness, and openness.[19] Utilitarian individualism is, therefore, not an adequate basis on which to support required service, even though utility is often used to sell such a requirement to the general public.

Expressive individualism, whether used to support service because it offers an enriching experience or, more often, to reject service because it interferes with one's freedom, is flawed as well. Against the arguments that service constitutes servitude and restricts free speech, I would contend that requiring forty or fifty community service hours over the four years of high school hardly seems burdensome, especially since students may choose from a wide variety of service options, including ones they might create themselves, to fulfill the service expectation. My fundamental objection to individualism in all its forms, however, is its tendency to center on the individual and away from the neighbor, a centering that I will show is theologically untenable.

Civic Republicanism and Democratic Education. A second major philosophical perspective that many proponents of mandated community service rely upon is "civic republicanism," which has precursors in the ancient world as well as in the "founding generation" of America. Civic republicanism asserts that one's self-fulfillment, personal identity, and orientation in the world are formed by involvement with others in community and by contributing to the public good.[20] These forms of engagement with the community make it possible to be human.[21] One is a "citizen" in a commonwealth or "community of mutual concern," linked with others through a "civic contract" or covenant.

Proponents of mandated community service who draw on the civic republican tradition suggest that it "knits" the community together,[22] "reconnects" the young with the institutions of the community,[23] or offers a way for students to "give something back to their schools and communities."[24] This engagement has traditionally been termed "civic education" or "democratic education" when it occurs through schools.

Democratic education consists in practicing democracy in the classroom by allowing students to participate in decision-making. It is believed that this participation will lead to empowerment and to students' confidence in their ability to make a difference in the world. At that point educational objectives emphasize "pro-social relationships" and the practice of "democratic values" such as respect, caring, trust, and cooperation.[25] One practical way of emphasizing these relationships and values, it is argued, is through community service. In short, students learn "citizenship."

Proponents of "voluntary" *vs.* mandated service criticize democratic education that does not honor its own belief in the decision-making capability of students by giving them complete freedom to choose whether to serve or not to serve. This apparent inherent contradiction, how-ever, is mitigated by the educational setting: In most aspects of school life, not only in service activities, students participate in but do not control the decision-making process.

Benjamin Barber has used the civic republican tradition to argue for a community service requirement at the collegiate level. He asserts that service is a "prerequisite of citizenship." Its principal end is not to improve the moral character of youth, nor to repay a debt owed to one's country, nor even to help the less fortunate. Service is not charity, which, in his opinion, has become an activity carried out in the private realm. Service is a duty that we "owe ourselves or that part of ourselves that is embedded in the civic community."[26]

Although the strength of the civic republican tradition is its emphasis on the communal over the individualistic, this tradition also falls short theologically because it lacks an eschatological point of reference. Civic republicanism is rightly concerned about those bonds that incorporate individuals into the whole, and in this respect the tradition shares in the biblical understanding of the oneness of humanity in creation and the inclusiveness of covenant love.[27] But since the civic republican tradition lacks an understanding of the Reign of God, the temporal, communal whole may become an end in itself. When this occurs, the self-centeredness of utilitarian or expressive individualism becomes the self-centeredness of the commonwealth. In respect to this, the state often has "pretensions to divinity."[28]

The New Testament describes the civil order as part of the old eon, which stands in tension with the new eon that Christ is bringing into the world. The new serves to judge the existing order and lure it to a higher level of covenantal relationship.[29] In the following two sections, I will describe the difference between the old and the new eons in terms of the difference between "worldly responsibilities" mandated by God's law and "vocations" made possible by faith in God's gospel.

The Theology of Neighbor Love

Service in general, and school-mandated service in particular, may be viewed theologically as two of the necessary means of God's ordering of creation through divine law. Our sense of the rightness about the teaching of service and the performing of service can be attributed to the fact that God's law is at work calling people to responsibility to others and to the creation. God's law is a *dynamis*, a force that "subdues the destructive forces of humanity" and "lays the foundation necessary for maintaining human fellowship, in the first place then, the foundation of justice."[30]

God's law leads people to "take care of their neighbors," whom they encounter as individuals and in the form of the community.[31] Unlike the notion of natural law, God's law is not a theoretical source of general norms about what is right or wrong, but it is a "force" working in the world through which God reveals God's will that people "shall live 'in love' to each other, and not in selfishness."[32]

On the basis of this understanding of God's law, I wish to argue that school-mandated community service and service in general are performed not for the sake of the one serving nor for the sake of the "civic republic" but for the sake of the neighbor or neighbors being served. God's law "demands the performance of good works" for the neighbor's good.[33] "Our neighbor, simply because he is our neighbor, puts us under obligation to him."[34] Unfortunately, the priority of the neighbor has been forgotten in a great deal of the discussion of community service.

In the on-going work of creation, God has placed all people in certain "covenantal structures of creation," such as family, work, nation, gender, race, and economy.[35] These structures are an expression of God's law in the creation. They are modes by which God expresses the divine will to unite individuals into covenant community. As such, these covenantal structures are "ethical agents" of God, and they perform a "pedagogical function" on behalf of God's law.[36] They are "a school in which all citizens are educated to care for each other, to do their duties even against their egoistic drives."[37] These structures hold people responsible for their neighbors. Whatever good is done for the neighbor is really the Creator's goodness extended through human instruments.[38]The good done for the neighbor is not necessarily freely chosen. Love or other altruistic feelings need not be, though they may be, the motive for meeting the neighbor's need. Owing to human sinfulness and to the power of evil in the world, which threatens the covenantal structures,[39] the law of God is a "coercive power." God's coercion, unlike other forms of coercion at work in the covenantal structures, takes the form of justice.[40]

Because sin diverts people from the neighbor's good, God's law must constrain people toward the neighbor's need. Wherever we are called to responsibility, God's law is at work; we are constrained not only by covenantal structures but also by conscience, social pressures, "habits of the heart," convention, previously chosen courses of action, and positive law.[41] These things eliminate the need constantly to decide what to do for the neighbor.[42]Social conventions and pressures are fallible approximations of God's law and, so, may be criticized. But they should not be totally replaced.[43]

That people are forced by God's law to respond to their neighbors' needs means that the intention of the law is not to make people inwardly good or righteous but to produce "civil righteousness." Inward, spiritual righteousness is the unique work of the gospel of forgiveness and salvation in Christ, which is distinct from God's work through the law. The work of God's law, unlike the gospel, is "nonredemptive." The law "makes the world a better place to live but does not complete or fulfill it."[44] Though created by God, the covenantal structures of creation are permeated by sin and death. God intends them to preserve life, but destructive forces are at work in them, too. We experience life within these structures as both blessing and curse—that is, ambiguously. These structures "must be examined as to whether they measure up to God's intention for them, whether in their current form they work for the common good in the service of justice, liberty, and community."[45]

Service as Vocation

Given that God's law permeates the creation and cajoles people to take responsibility for others and for the creation, it would appear that service is not simply one option for action among many. It is mandated by various covenantal structures, as well as by conscience, social conventions and pressures, virtues, and so forth. Through service in these structures, the creation is preserved and life is made possible. Because all people live under God's law in these covenantal structures, Christians, too, though also living under the gospel of Christ, live in the covenantal structures and, thus, are subject to the law's demands to be responsible for the neighbor. Faith in God's grace makes them members of God's reign and elevates "worldly responsibilities" to "vocations," God's callings for them.

Vocations are filled with constraint, according to Martin Luther.[46] That is, they are supplied with "trouble and toil," a "cross on which the old human nature is to be crucified."[47] Through these struggles, God helps people die to sin daily, so that they might rise daily and live with Christ in newness of life. Vocation is God's way of advancing a person to salvation and Glory. Where there is faith in God's forgiveness and providence, love is defined as the "inner willingness" to do what vocation requires.

The concept of vocation eliminates the need to seek extraordinary or heroic ways to serve one's neighbor, as the young Holden Caulfield in *The Catcher in the Rye* would like to do by "catching" rather than "meeting" a body "coming through the rye."[48] One's callings in life provide sufficient opportunity. Each calling has its own work, and in that work one person complements the work of others with different callings. God may, however, require a person to do the extraordinary through "the infinite and unpredictable variety of encounters."[49]

Living out one's vocation is never easy because every individual has overlapping vocations. As a member in a family, one might have the calling of son, daughter, or parent. Yet, as a student, this same person has a calling to study and learn; or as a citizen, the calling to fulfill the responsibilities of citizenship. The duties of one calling are not easily demarcated from the duties of another. If individuals take the responsibilities of their callings seriously, there will be no end to what they must do.[50] Realizing this, the individual lives with a dialectic of God's judgment and forgiveness, for the individual can never be fully responsible.[51] People who take their responsibilities seriously must also remember that the world will be transformed only at the eschaton. They need to be careful about overly optimistic and pietistic views of changing the world. Only the gospel, not vocation, is redemptive.

The concept of vocation illuminates the matter of mandated community service for students in a number of ways. To begin with, it must be granted that young people, along with adults, have more than one calling at a time. They are simultaneously family members, students, citizens, employees, and often members of religious institutions. Family life for today's young people involves a host of activities from child care to housework. Being a student means extracurricular activities in addition to classroom learning and homework. Many young people hold part-time jobs that require them to meet the expectations of the workplace. Membership in religious institutions often includes participation in youth organizations. There are, however, relatively few ways that nonvoting youth live out their citizenship, other than by obeying the law—though this is important!

Within each calling, an adolescent is mandated to serve. This is God's command to love through service to one's neighbor. Nor is there any covenantal structure in which such service is not mandated. Consequently, the service required in one calling is not superior in God's sight to the service commanded in another, though it may take on a different cast, be given higher status, in the eyes of society. Love is not more necessary, say, in baby-sitting a sibling than in driving soberly or wearing a seatbelt. Nor is love more involved in feeding the homeless than in studying Cicero for a Latin test. This may not be clear in terms of the responsibilities involved or the immediate effect of these activities. It becomes clear only in the long-term view of God's creating and preserving of life. From this standpoint, the life of the son or daughter is as vital as that of the student or the involved citizen. In each of these vocations, the young person participates in God's bringing of order and justice to the world.

While the service required in one calling is not superior to the service required in another, in the eyes of God, it is possible for one calling to consume so much time and attention that little remains for another calling. Gilbert Meilaender makes this point when discussing the so-called "apathetic citizen." The "apathetic citizen" is not necessarily selfish—he or she may be "an active participant in many personal relationships where the bond is love and affection," while being inactive in the impersonal relations called for by citizenship.[52] Sometimes these personal forms of community, such as in the family or among friends, may take moral priority over broader, civic relationships.[53] Meilaender concludes, however:

> We ought not forget . . . that no matter how highly we exalt the
> ties of personal love, they are capable of being greatly misused
> and distorted by those for whom Christian theology has reserved
> that old-fashioned but inclusive term "sinners." If all our bonds of
> affection are, as Niebuhr would put it, "tainted" by inordinate
> love, they offer many opportunities for ignoring or retreating from
> the needs of others under the guise of love for the near neighbor.
> And we may well imagine that it is the weak and powerless who
> are most likely to be ignored or, worse, misused.[54]

Thus, at the hands of "sinners," certain callings may "offer opportunities for ignoring or retreating" from other callings in which the needs of
distant neighbors are addressed. One such neglected calling for many
youth is that of citizen.

Justice and Community Service

Certainly youth are not the only "apathetic citizens" in our society.
So why should adolescence be the time selected to mandate community
service? Earlier we examined the reasons for selecting adolescence by
those who are interested in reforming youth. Charles Moskos, referring
to a national service program for older youth, cites several practical reasons for selecting this general period in a person's life to educate for
civic responsibility. In many ways, "young people are more flexible"
with "fewer family obligations." They also possess physical strength
and efficiency. Service has the potential to enhance their value as workers. Moreover, youth do not have the same work obligations as most
adults. Finally, youth is a good time to learn civic values that will be
important later in life.[55]

One suspects, however, that at least as important a reason as these is
that young people can be forced to perform service, especially when it is
part of their education. A teacher at an independent school in Atlanta
expressed his opinion on a service requirement at his high school by
saying, "We require them to be able to swim to graduate. I require
homework. Why not require service? It's certainly as important as
swimming!"

Adolescents are not responsible as a group for the current breakdown
in civic responsibility, though many adults might think that young
people need reforming. "Adolescence" is a relatively recent cultural
construction, a product of the modern era. It became identifiable as a
"life stage" through the advance of industrialization in the nineteenth
century, urbanization's effect upon the social habits of youth, the pro-
longing of education, and psychology's findings of youth as a time of
storm, stress, and developing identity.[56] Many of the same forces

behind the specifying of "adolescence" are responsible for the societal stresses that school-mandated service is intended to address.

Youth, as citizens, have a calling to serve. And evidence suggests that many adolescents heed this calling. A 1991 survey of adolescent charitable behavior showed that slightly more than 60 percent of twelve- to seventeen-year-olds "worked for a service organization or helped others without pay an average of 3.2 hours a week."[57] While 79 percent of these youth became involved in service through school, only 8 percent said their school required community service. Many adolescents are already involved in service voluntarily; but a sizable percentage is not.

In advocating mandated community service, we must take seriously the concerns of opponents over the fairness of community service as a high school graduation requirement to youth. Mandating community service should not be viewed as "reform" or correction for adolescents who are presumed to have created a crisis in civic responsibility by leading lives that are completely self-centered. Adolescents are the products of this crisis, but given their limited decision-making capacity, they are hardly its creators.

In addition, fairness requires that society acknowledge the forms of service that are already performed by adolescents. Wherever youth are constrained by the covenantal structures they are part of, they are mandated to serve. Seldom are they given credit for this service. But because this service may not involve them with "distant neighbors," mandated community service is still important, especially as age-appropriate training in civic responsibility for all citizens.

Finally, fairness requires that society insure that mentoring adults accompany adolescents in their mandated service. If community service is a way of learning what responsibility to others means, then community service involving youth and adults is an immediate expression of community, in which teaching responsibility is not merely a goal but a realized accomplishment. Future discussions of mandated community service should incorporate creative proposals for youth and adults to work side-by-side.

School as the Locus of Community Service

Should the school be charged with the responsibility of training youth in their responsibilities to others? To one degree or another, all covenantal structures in which youth are involved have this responsibility, including the family, the church, and the workplace. Why, then, should we single out the school as the locus for this training?

Some might argue against using the school for this purpose, offering a number of reasons. They might contend that if the school is the vehicle for service learning, a significant body of mentoring adults might be excluded from the process, namely, parents. Although some parents might be able to be involved in guiding young people during the school day, for the most part their involvement would take place during the evenings or weekends; in that case, however, teachers would no longer be on duty.

Furthermore, it might be argued, public schools may acknowledge, but may not encourage, reflection about service from a religious or theological perspective. Moreover, mandating service through the school presents simply another claim on already-limited school time, giving students less time to learn the skills that will be necessary in their future occupations. In response to these two objections, one must acknowledge first that the absence of theological or religious perspective in the schools, while a limitation, does not mean that reflection about service will be worthless without a religious component. Second, it seems that, in view of the amount of time most students spend in service to "distant neighbors," the use of school time for this function does not seem unreasonable.

Yet another possible reason to oppose the use of the schools for community service is that few teachers are trained to guide this type of learning. In the same way that not everyone is capable of teaching English or algebra, not everyone is capable of teaching service. This handicap, however, should change over time as schools develop service programs. A more powerful argument, perhaps, is that mandating service through schools does not insure its continuity with the rest of the student's life, either earlier in life or after graduation. Is it possible for service to become a "habit of the heart" if there is no continuity? Yet it must be pointed out that, while there is no guarantee that service will continue later in life, there is even less reason to expect it without some exposure to the concept and the practice.

Finally, one might question whether mandated community service is simply another educational fad. Is civic service being taken seriously in other quarters of society, outside the educational institutions? This is a legitimate concern, to which it can be said only that it is too early to tell how much staying power the idea of community service will have; on the other hand, its newness as a concept is not in itself a strong enough reason not to test its substantive and long-term value.

In favor of using the school as the locus for service learning, it must first be recognized that there is a long history of its use for training in character and civic responsibility.[58] Moreover, the school has the legitimacy of being the place where learning and training traditionally occur. School districts may develop curricula and legally require students to complete courses of study in order to receive a diploma. Unfortunately, but not surprisingly, many students will do only what they are required to do; once involved in these required curricula, however, they often find significant rewards in experiences they would not otherwise have had. Society might criticize the school's lack of effectiveness, but it does not dispute the school's role in learning and training.

The school also has an organizational capability that few other institutions in society have. The school employs people with varied training, has a daily and yearly schedule, and has the capacity to transport people. In addition, the school offers the potential for reflecting upon service as well as performing it. Students need guidance in sorting through all their responsibilities and deciding which take priority, and the school has teachers and counselors who have assisted students in this process in many other areas. And the school program offers the possibility for integrating service with other disciplines. It is preferable that service not simply be an "add on" to the existing curricula, but that it support instruction in other humanities-related subjects. Experiential education is an important way to learn, and service is an excellent form of experiential education.

Finally, by utilizing the school in this way, society would push the school into relationship with the broader community and away from self-interest or isolation. Other covenantal structures—the family, the church, and the workplace—have unique contributions to make in training youth to serve, but the school is the primary public vehicle for this purpose.

Conclusion

Public service is at a crossroads in American society. While many citizens volunteer on their own or through various groups and organizations, individualism entices all citizens to retreat into homogeneous enclaves and away from "distant neighbors." God mandates service through the various covenantal structures in which people live. This mandate is embraced as people understand their life within these covenantal structures as composed of "vocations." God mandates service primarily but not exclusively for the sake of the individual neighbor or neighbors in community.

School-mandated community service is a recognition of the relationship of responsibility implicit in these covenantal structures. Adolescents are at a point in their lives when such training in responsibility and service can be meaningful and more easily accomplished. Moreover, the school has the history, legitimacy, and capability of overseeing mandated community service. Clearly, if Americans are to discover anew that balance between individual pursuits and the common good so important to liberal democracy, school-mandated community service can provide an important step in that discovery.

Notes

[1] Robert A. Rankin and Steven Thomma, "Clinton, Dole share vision with Students," *The Atlanta Journal/The Atlanta Constitution* (11 May 1996): A3.

[2] Rob Teir and Suzanne Goldsmith, "Teaching Citizenship Is Not Slavery," *Education Week* (24 May 1995): 35.

[3] E. Clinton Gardner, *Biblical Faith and Social Ethics* (New York: Harper and Row, 1960), 322.

[4] Ibid., 335.

[5] William M. Sullivan, *Reconstructing Public Philosophy* (Berkeley: University of California Press, 1986), 19.

[6] Robert N. Bellah, et. al., *Habits of the Heart* (Berkeley: University of California Press, 1985), 34, 47.

[7] Scott Willis, "Learning Through Service," *ASCD Update* 35 (August 1993): 5.

[8] Ibid., 4.

[9] Cathryn Berger Kaye, "Essentials for Successful Community Service Programs," *The Educational Digest* (November 1989): 59.

[10] Ibid., 58.

[11] Maurice B. Howard, "Service Learning: Character Education Applied," *Educational Leadership* 51 (November 1993): 42.

[12] Alliance for Service Learning in Education Reform, "Standards of Quality for School-Based Service-Learning," *Equity & Excellence in Educa-tion* 26 (September 1993): 71.

[13] Willis, "Learning Through Service," 8.

[14] Teir and Goldsmith, "Teaching Citizenship," 35.

[15] Marie Bittner, "The Constitutionality of Public School Community Service Programs," *The Clearing House* (November/December 1994): 116-117.

[17] Sullivan, *Reconstructing Public Philosophy*, 62, 65.

[18] Harry C. Boyte, "Community Service and Civic Education," *Phi Delta Kappan* 72 (June 1991): 766.

[19] Loc. Cit.

[20] Bellah, et al., *Habits of the Heart*, 142.

[21] Sullivan, *Reconstructing Public Philosophy*, 158, 173.

[22] "Excerpts from Report by U.S. Commission on National and Community Service," *The Chronicle of Philanthropy* (January 1993): 10.

[23] Willis, "Learning Through Service," 5.

[24] Kayte, "Essentials," 58.

[25]Susan Seigel and Virginia Rockwood, "Democratic Education, Student Empowerment, and Community Service: Theory and Practice," *Equity & Excellence in Education* 26 (September 1993): 65.

[26]Benjamin R. Barber, "Service, Citizenship, and Democracy: Civic Duty as an Entailment of Civil Right," in *National Service Pro & Con*, ed. Williamson M. Evers (Stanford: Hoover Institution Press, 1990), 36.

[27]Gardner, *Biblical Faith and Social Ethics*, 327-328.

[28]Robert Benne, *The Paradoxical Vision* (Minneapolis: Fortress Press, 1995), 83.

[29]Ibid., 88.

[30]Gustaf Aulen, *Church, Law and Society* (New York: Charles Scribner's Sons, 1948), 62-63.

[31]Ibid., 66.

[32]Ibid., 65-66.

[33]Gustaf Wingren, *Creation and Law* (London: Oliver and Boyd, 1961), 153.

[34]Ibid., 160.

[35]Benne, *The Paradoxical Vision*, 88.

[36]Gustaf Wingren, *Luther on Vocation*, trans. Carl C. Rasmussen (Philadelphia: Muhlenberg Press, 1957), 6.

[37]Carl E. Braaten, "God in Public Life: Rehabilitating the 'Orders of Creation,'" *First Things* 8 (December 1990): 35.

[38]Ibid., 154.

[39]Benne, *Vision*, 82, 85.

[40]Braaten, "God in Public Life," 37.

[41]Benne, *Vision*, 82.

[42]Wingren, *Creation and Law*, 155.

[43]Ibid., 165.

[44]Benne, *Vision*, 85.

[45]Braaten, "God in Public Life," 35.

[46]Wingren, *Luther on Vocation*, 65.

[47]Ibid., 29.

[48]J. D. Salinger, *The Catcher in the Rye* (New York: New American Library, 1953), 156; quoted in Bruce C. Birch and Larry L. Rasmussen, *The Predicament of the Prosperous* (Philadelphia: The Westminster Press, 1978), 97.

[49]Paul Althaus, *The Ethics of Martin Luther*, trans. Robert C. Schultz (Philadelphia: Fortress Press, 1972), 41.

[50]Ibid., 39.

[51]Ibid., 40.

[52]Gilbert Meilaender, "Understanding the Apathetic Citizen," *Dialog* 17 (Autumn 1978): 303.

[53]Ibid., 307.

[54]Ibid.

[55]Charles C. Moskos, *A Call to Civic Service* (New York: The Free Press, 1988), 3.

[56]Steven Mintz, "Life Stages" in *Encyclopedia of American Social History* (New York: Scribners, 1993), Vol. III, 2013.

[57]Meg Sommerfeld, "60% of Adolescents Volunteered in '91, Survey Finds," *Education Week* (9 December 1992): 8.

[58]See Charles L. Glenn, "'Molding' Citizens," in *Democracy and the Renewal of Public Education*, ed. Richard John Neuhaus (Grand Rapids: Wm. B. Eerdmans, 1987); and Dan Conrad and Diane Hedin, "School-Based Community Service: What We Know from Research and Theory," *Phi Delta Kappan* 72 (June 1991): 744.

Chapter 13

Complex Responsibility in an Age of Technology[1]

Russell E. Willis

For those of us living at the dawn of the twenty-first century, technology pervades virtually all aspects of human life. Whether we like it or not, we live in an "age of technology." Technological innovation, and the social and cultural changes it fosters, has so influenced our daily lives that it has become second nature to us. Human potential is increasingly tied to scientific advancement and technological innovation; we dream new dreams or discover new ways to fulfill age-old dreams through science and technology. We anticipate technological "fixes" for our personal and social problems. At the same time, technology threatens to overwhelm us with information, sensory overload, unremitting change, unprecedented human capacities, and even sheer power. For both good and ill, we live in a time when technology—in its complexity, magnitude, dynamism, power, and pervasiveness—is definitive of human life.

The tremendous promise and threat of technology raise questions for the moral life. What does it mean to be morally responsible in this "age of technology"? Does technology in any way affect the capacity for responsibility? Is there anything about technology, or life in a technological society, that either promotes or restricts responsibility? Is there a way to understand technology that not only provides an accurate and insightful view of technology but also offers a vision for moral responsibility?

In this essay, I suggest answers to these important questions. First, I examine briefly the nature of moral responsibility. What does it mean to be responsible? What capacities must an individual possess in order to be responsible? What is the scope of responsibility? Under what circumstances and within what time-frame do we remain responsible for any particular act?

I then explore the relationship of technology to responsibility by examining those dimensions of technology that affect responsibility, especially in an age of technology. I contend that technology is not merely a set of tools, instruments, machines, and systems that humans manipulate for various purposes; it is a mode of human activity. This view of technology provides the basis for constructing a model of the responsible self grounded on the metaphor of "participation."

Next I focus on the ways technology orders human life today and demonstrate how this technological ordering affects our capacity for responsibility. Finally, I propose the concept of "complex responsibility" as a model for those seeking to be morally responsible in an age of technology.

What Does It Mean To Be Responsible?

To be morally responsible[2] is to be accountable for what one causes to happen (either through one's own agency, or through the exercise of one's authority) and to be obligated to act in relation to others in an appropriate manner. This obligation includes the duty to be reasonably diligent in one's efforts (negligence is a form of irresponsible behavior). To be morally responsible, one must have the capacity for self-determination (the ability to have some control over one's actions in pursuit of one's goals) and the capacity for reasonable foresight (the ability to determine accurately the nature and outcome of one's actions given the constraints of limited knowledge and perception). Responsibility also requires moral reasoning—reflection on the moral relevance of the agent's action. Finally, responsibility entails acting in ways that foster responsibility (in oneself and in others) and create and sustain an environment conducive to responsible behavior.

Human agency is fundamental to responsibility. Responsibility must, therefore, be understood in terms of the expansion or limitation of what is humanly possible. An agent is capable of a finite range of possibilities, which are limited by physical, biological, psycho-emotional, social, and cultural conditions. For example, my actions are limited by such things as the laws of physics, by my vulnerability to disease, by the legal requirements of my university contract, and by my education, religion, and politics. Changes to these conditions promote or restrict responsibility by broadening or limiting what one can cause to happen, what foresight into the nature and consequences of one's actions are possible, and how these changes affect the web of relationships that have moral significance. Technology is described below in terms of the expansion and enhancement of the humanly possible, as a means of mitigating or even overcoming limitation. This places technology at the heart of a model of moral responsibility, especially in an age of technology.

The issue of responsibility and limits must also be considered from a different angle. Although our actions are conditioned, over time conditions may change, sometimes as a result of technology. Nevertheless, at any particular time we are limited by some forces beyond our control. We also impose limits on ourselves. If we are in fact agents—persons with some capacity for self-determination—then self-limitation must be considered an option of responsible conduct.

This is particularly true in relation to modern ideologies based on the ideal of inevitable progress, and political ideologies that construe "freedom" (agency) as freedom from limitation. The idea that "if we can do it, we must do it," is often engendered by these ideologies. This position, ultimately, either is simply irresponsible or indicates a form of determinism that makes nonsense of the very notion of responsibility.

Relationship is also a crucial aspect of responsibility. Responsibility makes no sense without reference to an "other."[3] The very notions of obligation and accountability suggest relationship; we are obligated to others and held accountable by others. Even the language of responsibility reveals relationship, for we speak of having responsibility "to" or "for" someone or something. Therefore, we must view responsibility as functioning within a web of relationships. The web encompasses relationships of dependence and interdependence between the agent and other humans. This web also involves relationships between human beings and sociocultural and natural environments.

In the broadest sense, the various relationships of this web provide the basis for existence. This web is the context within which human life, including the moral life, is expressed. More specifically, this web embodies the causal relationships and patterns of obligation and accountability that form the basis of responsibility. In addition, the web of relationships must itself be considered an object of responsibility; we are responsible for fashioning patterns of relationship that foster responsible behavior, if possible. A central theme discussed below is how technology affects the web of relationships, and, thus, affects responsibility.

When considering contemporary technology, the issue of the scope of responsibility must also be addressed. Under what circumstances and within what time-frame do we remain responsible for any particular act? Traditional ethics generally is based on face-to-face or other limited encounters. Time is morally relevant only at the moment of decision and action. Responsibility is rarely considered beyond the life-times of those directly involved in the matter (or their immediate progeny). Traditional ethics also assumes that indirect and unintentional consequences will also be of a relatively limited nature.

As we shall see in what follows, however, modern technology has the potential to expand greatly the effects of human conduct in both space and time. The scope of responsibility fluctuates with the scope of technology. Today, technology engenders a wide range of indirect and unintended effects that are magnified by the far-reaching power of contemporary technology. Technology thus has the potential to reach far into the web of relationships, even far into the future.

The difficulty with assessing responsibility in an age of technology arises when the magnitude of a particular action is far-reaching in terms of the number of relationships involved and the extent in time and space of the consequences. For example, what is the appropriate scope of responsibility for storing nuclear waste that remains highly toxic for thousands of years, or for performing germ-line genetic manipulations that will be passed on to future generations? There is also a problem when an action introduces some unprecedented factor with no reasonable analogies to help predict the near- or long-term effects on the web of relationships.

These conditions certainly strain traditional notions of the scope of responsibility. How and where do we draw fitting lines of responsibility—lines that accurately trace accountability (in terms of both cause-and-effect and authority), that reasonably weigh the degree of diligence or negligence of the agents involved, and that are also practical? A universal answer to this question is impossible. Nevertheless, an adequate model of responsibility must have a broad view of cause-and-effect and authority within the web of relationships, the future, and the nature and scope of potential unintended consequences. The role of foresight (or its lack) becomes especially crucial to such an expanded view of responsibility.

This brief discussion is far from a full-blown theory of moral responsibility. Rather, it is meant to provide a framework for considering moral responsibility in relation to technology.

Technology Revealed

It is common for technology to be described in terms of tools, instruments, machines, and systems that humans use for a wide range of purposes. From this perspective, technology is "simply a means that humans are free to employ or not, as they see fit."[4] There is no intrinsic value or purpose to technology. Technology is used to achieve the ends or pursue the purposes of other types of activity, such as art, religion, or politics, for instance. According to this position, technology "merely opens a door, it does not compel one to enter."[5]

This is an accurate description, as far as it goes. Indeed, the concept of technology does encompass such things as plows, microscopes, computers, and space shuttles. The question is whether this *instrumental* view of technology reveals the essence of the phenomena we refer to as technology. If technology (in its essence) is simply a thing to be used, then technology has a very limited moral significance. In fact, the conclusion commonly drawn from this instrumental view is that technology is morally neutral. If this conclusion is correct, we should not concern ourselves about questions involving technology (as a general concept) and responsibility. After all, responsibility would make sense only in reference to the activities served by technology and not technology itself. In this view we should deal only with problems related to how specific technologies are used in good or bad ways, or how specific technologies are, or can be, used to promote or thwart the achievement of the "good."

There is another perspective, however, based on a phenomenological interpretation, that reveals something beyond the merely instrumental character of technology.[6] This broader, more nuanced view paints a very different picture of the moral significance of technology. According to this view, technology is essentially a mode of human activity, not simply a set of human artifacts. In addition, technology functions as a factor in the ordering of human life. In fact, in an age of technology, this technological ordering becomes a primary mechanism and form of order. Analysis of these two dimensions (technology as a mode of activity and technology as a form of order) reveals crucial ways that technology affects responsibility, and even signals the need for a reevaluation of the nature of responsibility. The remainder of this essay explores responsibility in light of these two dimensions of technology.

Robert McGinn argues that technology encompasses a specific activity—the "expansion of the realm of the humanly possible."[7] McGinn's definition of technology, however, is too broad. Ironically, it suffers because it lacks any reference to technology as a human artifact. Also, the notion of "expanding the humanly possible" is too vague. Embracing the spirit, if not the letter, of McGinn's definition, we can define technology as a mode of human activity, namely, *the extension or enhancement of human capacity or power by artificial means.*

In this definition, "human capacity" simply connotes the various mental and physical capabilities and potentialities that are native to or assumed by human beings. The phrase "by artificial means" implies that not all activities of extension or enhancement of human capacities and power are technological. For instance, mental techniques can be used to improve one's memory. Neither is the use of artifacts, nor the activity of making artifacts, sufficient for describing an activity as technological. For instance, though it is a human artifact, a decorative bowl made of clay and painted with natural dyes is art, but not technology. In order to be technology, a phenomenon must be associated with some mode of activity in which human capacity or power is extended or enhanced, and this extension or enhancement must be brought about directly by the use of some artifact. The use of a potter's wheel to produce the bowl, or even the use of the bowl to mix ingredients, would be technology.

What makes something "technological" is its relation to a distinctive mode of human conduct—the extension or enhancement of human capacity or power by artificial means. However, though it can be differentiated from other pursuits, technology is not generally pursued for its own sake. Rather, technology serves other purposes, such as producing food, winning battles, and communicating with others. In fact, technology potentially can be used to accomplish any human purpose. For instance, agriculture is the activity of producing crops or raising animals for various human uses. Agriculture is not intrinsically technological—one need not use artificial means to do this activity. Removing a seed from a piece of fruit and planting that seed in the ground is an agricultural, not technological, activity. However, agricultural activities can be enhanced or extended technologically. That is to say, certain human capacities and power (such as the ability to dig holes or otherwise manipulate rocky or dense soil) may be extended or enhanced by the use of artifacts (such as the hoe or plow). Thus we have agriculture and technology, coincidentally.

Technology can become so intertwined with another form of activity that the activity is practically conceived in its technologically-extended or -enhanced form. This is especially true for activities, like agriculture, that have been pursued technologically over long periods of time during which there have been numerous technological innovations that have come to represent the state-of-the-art of practice. This is also true of activities, like space flight, that were born and will always be practiced in a technological mode.[8]

When something is enhanced or extended, a change of some sort takes place. Therefore technology entails change. This is true whether the agent realizes or intends it or not. Yet, though the activities of extension or enhancement inherently involve dynamism and change, technology is not thereby necessarily associated only with practices characterized by innovation. After the original innovation (that may take place many different times in isolated incidents), the mode of activity (now constituting the original activity plus technology) may become a practice. In some ages and circumstances (most of human time, in fact) the state of technological innovation is best viewed in evolutionary, rather than revolutionary terms.

Take agriculture again as an example. At the point of the original innovation (e.g., when a hand-plow was first used to break up rocky soil), technology involved change, possibly dramatic change, in the primary practice (in this case, tilling). The culture, however, ultimately adapted to this technological practice (tilling with a hand-drawn plow), which then persisted for centuries before another technological innovation was introduced (the animal-drawn plow). To some degree, therefore, technology becomes a component of the practice at a particular stage of development—it becomes part of the *status quo*. Nevertheless, human capacities or power continue to be enhanced or extended, whether this is recognized or not. The activity remains technological even long after the innovation was first realized.

In an age of technology, technology is a primary mechanism of change, a source of sociocultural dynamism that shifts the boundaries of both possibility and limit. The degree of dynamism engendered by technology depends on the conditions within which the technology is employed, the amount of power utilized, the degree of innovation, and the length of time between the innovation and the sociocultural adaptation to it. In an age of technology, the evolutionary development of technology continues, but the revolutionary character of technological innovation and its effects on society and culture become the norm.

Homo Technicus as the Responsible Self

The interpretation of technology as a mode of human activity suggests an anthropological ideal-type: *Homo technicus*—the being who has the capacity and propensity to extend and enhance its capacities, and subsequently its power, by artificial means in the service of human purposes. *Homo technicus* is that aspect of human being that intervenes purposively into its various natural and sociocultural environments, inventing, perpetuating, and enhancing new modes of, and environments for, human conduct and being. *Homo technicus* constitutes an aspect of human agency and, therefore, is a locus of responsibility.

Though the presence of *homo technicus* distinguishes the present age of technology, it is not an offspring of this age. Rather, *homo technicus* is as old as *homo sapiens*.[9] As Langdon Winner suggests,

> No evidence exists of any culture that has gotten away without some attempt to understand, alter, and explain nature. No evidence can be found of any human society that has not employed tools and techniques to expand or enhance the capacity to alter nature.[10]

Thus, the technological impulse constitutes an essential characteristic of human being. In an age of technology, however, *homo technicus* has become a definitive feature of human being and a primary facet of the responsible self.

Clinton Gardner's mentor, H. Richard Niebuhr, clarified the notion of the moral self by proposing three models of moral responsibility.[11] The first, the human-as-maker, is the quintessential teleologist or consequentialist. Human making leads to consequences that are good or bad. As Gardner describes it, the human-as-maker "is like an artisan, or craftsman, who shapes or constructs things in accordance with some idea of the good and for the sake of some end."[12] This symbol "accents the purposive nature of moral action; it also implies an understanding of human freedom as self-determination by final causes."[13] This rendering of moral responsibility clearly resonates with an instrumental conception of technology. Technology allows humans to make things that produce good or bad consequences. Moral responsibility simply involves making and using technology to produce good consequences.

The second model of the moral self, the human-as-citizen, was the quintessential deontologist or formalist. It is the nature of the act itself, not the consequences of the act, that has moral significance. From this perspective, responsibility consists of obeying the law. In this sense, law consists of the moral law and cultural norms (including the legal system) that are explicitly or implicitly sanctioned by the moral law. The model of the human-as-citizen also resonates with the instrumental paradigm. Technology is neither good nor bad, it is only rightly or wrongly used. That is to say, the only issue regarding responsibility is whether technology is used in ways that follow or subvert the law.

Niebuhr suggested that both of these models accurately depicted an aspect of the moral life. Each was true to a point. The same can be said of the instrumental paradigm of technology. Therefore, in a limited way, each of these models of the moral self resonates with this limited view of technological being.

Niebuhr's choice for the responsible self was a third paradigm—the human-as-answerer. This model, he believed, was a fuller representation of moral existence. In this model, dialogue was the chief analogy to responsibility. Here the agent is understood "predominately in terms of interaction, in terms of challenges in [humanity's] natural and social environments."14 Human being is defined in terms of human

> relationships to that upon which they and all their actions are contingent—in terms of the possibilities and limits which are given, not primarily in terms of human autonomy. Here the primary question is "What is going on?"; and the action of the agent is understood as a response to that prior action.15

While the human-as-maker seeks to do the good and the human-as-citizen seeks to do the right, the human-as-answerer seeks to do the fitting. The fitting is "a response of the self to the needs, capacities, and potentialities of other selves to which it is related."16

I agree with Niebuhr's reaction to the traditional models of teleology and deontology. They both fall short of an adequate view of responsibility, especially in relation to technology. The model of the human-as-answerer more fully reflects the general nature of moral responsibility and resonates with crucial aspects of technological being. Most importantly, it comprehends agency and responsibility in terms of response to possibilities and limitations within the web of relationships. The model of moral responsibility that I am suggesting follows Niebuhr's lead, but pushes the metaphor beyond answering.

Homo technicus does not just answer, but participates.17 *Homo technicus* is not just caught in a web of dependence and interdependence. Through activities of enhancement and expansion, *homo technicus* modifies this web. *Homo technicus* relates to "others" in new ways. *Homo technicus* expands the web of interrelatedness to greater wholes, to larger communities, to future generations, and so on. *Homo technicus* is a finite creature but acts at the intersection of possibility and limit to change the conditions of human finitude. At this intersection, *homo technicus* expands the humanly possible, intervening in sociocultural and natural systems, molding the world in its own image. Advances in science and technology provide unprecedented insight into and control of human and nonhuman systems, curtailing uncertainty and risk, and altering limits to expand possibilities. At the same time, the fitting response is one that accepts the fact that contingency can be modified but not ultimately escaped. *Homo technicus* must bear the costs and risks involved with overcoming some aspects of finitude.

The human participant seeks to do the fitting, but does so realizing that responsibility includes fashioning the mold into which the participant must fit. Yet *homo technicus* is not simply the human-as-maker, because the responsible self is, to some degree, the product as well as the producer of its conduct, including technology. In addition to asking "What is going on?", the responsible self must also ask "What am I doing that affects what is going on?" Only in answering this question can a fitting response be made. The fitting in this case is a response of *homo technicus* to the needs, capacities, and potentialities of other selves to which it is related through technological activity. The fitting now incorporates response to a condition caused, to some degree, by the agent itself. The fitting is a participation by oneself in the life of the other, not merely a response to the other.

Technological Determinism and Responsibility

Homo technicus does not function in a vacuum. Rather, *homo technicus* functions within, and is inexorably bound to, the complex web of relationships that makes up the world of human existence. This implies the need to develop an ecological frame of reference when considering the scope of responsibility vis-a-vis technology.

Ecology is the relationship between organisms and their environments. The ecological dimension of technology encompasses the various ways technology relates to the human condition and to the various environments within which human beings exist. The ecological dimension of technology is the evolution of a "second nature," one inexorably bound to the first (what we refer to as Nature). One way to describe this relationship is with the concept of order. From this perspective we can describe the ecological dimension of technology as the various ways technology fashions an order of being—a form of life—that alters the capacity for human agency, and thus responsibility, often in very deterministic ways.

Melvin Kranzberg, an historian of technology, has identified a crucial characteristic of the technological order. In what he (no doubt humbly!) refers to as "Kranzberg's First Law of Technology," Kranzberg states, "Technology is neither good nor bad—nor is it neutral."[18] By this statement he rejects three basic views of technological determinism. First, although technology has produced much good, he argues that technological progress, and the ultimate creation of a technological utopia, are not inevitable. Second, he argues that the specter of "autonomous" technology, where technology becomes the master and humanity the slave, is an illusion that misinterprets the nature of technological determinism and undervalues the role of human agency. He also rejects, however, the notion that technology is "simply a means that humans are free to employ or not, as they see fit."[19]

Kranzberg claims that technology does indeed have a deterministic character. Technology orders life, often at the expense of human control. Technology, he claims, is not simply ambiguous, i.e., equivocal, uncertain, or susceptible to multiple interpretations, though it is certainly all of these things. Rather, technology is ambivalent. It involves conflicting (dialectical) factors and embodies various and competing values. Some of these factors are healthy, productive, and life-affirming, while others are debilitating, destructive, and life-destroying. These factors and values create an ordering of human life and the world within which humanity exists. This ordering affects, but does not necessarily overwhelm, human agency and responsibility. This deterministic quality is what I call "ambivalent technological determinism."

One form of ambivalent technological determinism is what Langdon Winner refers to as "technological drift."[20] In an age of technology, our society "drifts" on currents produced by the "directionless imposition of [technologically influenced] structures, interactions, and values without meaningful [human] participation."[21] Though technological drift is unintentional, it is not necessarily bad and, in fact, is a predictable consequence of contemporary technology. As Winner states,

> *technology is most productive when its ultimate range of results is neither foreseen nor controlled.* To put it differently, technology always does more than we intend; we know this so well that it has actually become part of our intentions. Positive side effects are in fact a latent expectation or desire implicit in any plan of innovation. Negative side effects, similarly, are experienced as necessary evils that we are obligated to endure. Each [technological] intention, therefore, contains a concealed "unintention," which is just as much a part of our calculations as the immediate end in view.[22]

This raises the issue of how the inevitability of technological drift can be responsibly anticipated.

A second form of ambivalent technological determinism is linked to a strong innovative and deterministic force generated by technology itself. This property of technology is captured in Kranzberg's second law. Standing traditional wisdom on its head, Kranzberg claims, "Invention is the mother of necessity." Stated simply, this means that "every technical innovation seems to require additional technical advances to make it fully effective."[23]

This property of technology is seen vividly when viewed at the level of large technological systems. Here it is clear that as systems develop within specific social contexts, new properties of the system emerge and are discovered, new applications of the various technologies are recognized, and new problems (technical, social, and moral) are potentially revealed. Each of these aspects of technological development and application spawns potential change.

As Kranzberg indicates, the automobile is the prime example of this phenomenon:

> [The development of the automobile] brought whole new industries into being and turned existing industries in new directions by its need for rubber tires, petroleum products, and new tools and materials. Furthermore, large scale use of the automobile demanded a host of auxiliary technological activities—roads and highways, garages and parking lots, traffic signals, and parking meters.
>
> While it may be said that each of these other developments occurred in response to a specific need, I claim that it was the original invention [but not its purpose] that mothered that necessity.[24]

In this case, the intent to expand human mobility has resulted in the need to develop technologies (such as oil-spill clean-up technologies) far removed from the original intent. Without the development of these other technologies, however, the automobile-based transportation system as we know it would be simply impossible.

This property of technology goes by several names. Kranzberg calls it "technological imbalance," apparently wishing to stress the potential for the introduction of disequilibrium into the various technological and social systems involved. Langdon Winner stresses the ineluctable character of technology by referring to this phenomenon as the "technological imperative"—"the system's need to control supply, distribution, and the full range of circumstances affecting its operations."[25]

The technological imperative has become critical to the ordering of human life in a technological society. Such societies are characterized by large-scale systems, such as the information super-highway. The superstructure of contemporary society includes a vast array of technological and nontechnological structures, the primary purpose of which is the maintenance of technology. This superstructure creates demands on the society that must be met if the society is to function and prosper in its current form (i.e., as a technologically extended and enhanced society).[26]

For Winner (and other critics of technological society, such as Daniel Bell, Herbert Marcuse, Jacques Ellul, and Neil Postman) the ultimate issue related to the technological imperative is human control—or, more precisely, the lack of control—over megatechnological systems. These critics argue that modern technology tends to co-opt political control from human beings.[27] According to Winner, technology has the "capacity to transform, order, and adapt animate and inanimate objects to accord with the purely technical structures and process."[28]

Winner's point can be applied to the general context of human agency and, more specifically, moral responsibility. Kranzberg's Law also applies. Technological phenomena are neither good nor bad in and of themselves. But technology does tend to engender a technological ordering of life that becomes, in an age of technology, a primary context of moral responsibility. The implication of this for Winner is that technology should be viewed not as neutral but as a "political phenomenon." In a sense, the various technological systems "legislate" social policy in modern societies. As Winner suggests, "New technologies are institutional structures within an evolving constitution that gives shape to a new polity, the technopolis."[29] The question then becomes, what mechanisms for control of this situation are possible and necessary for the maintenance of responsible human agency?

One consequence of ambivalent technology is that technological ordering can spawn unavoidable choices, what Roger Shinn refers to as "forced options." According to Shinn,

> The forced option is a simple point of logic. Some options are avoidable and some are forced. That is, some decisions can be put off indefinitely or evaded forever; other cannot. To recognize a forced option is not to say that any single course of action is forced. . . . What is forced is the decision.[30]

Forced options are situations in which certain consequences of significant risk become unavoidable unless effective action is taken virtually immediately. For example, because of my eating habits, my sedentary occupation, lack of exercise for several years, and stress, I face a forced option. I must either take blood pressure medication, radically alter my lifestyle, or risk a stroke or heart or kidney failure. In other words, I must do something or suffer potentially dire consequences.

The forced option is similar to what Jacques Ellul refers to as a "threshold."[31] Thresholds are points that, when reached or exceeded, cause a contrary or negative reaction to a previously normal or benign activity. The unwillingness or inability (often because of ignorance) to react to forced options or thresholds forces the issue.

Forced options are not solely the product of modern technology. Persons and societies of other times and conditions have faced forced options. But as an aspect of contemporary technology,

> human beings have acquired technological powers that increase the pace of events and the scope of actions, so that decisions come faster and more hangs on these decisions than in past ages. Weapons, inventions that liberate us from drudgery and open new possibilities for human achievement, techniques that chew up irreplaceable resources—these are transforming the conditions for life for us and generations to come.[32]

The structure of contemporary technology is, therefore, part of the problem. But ignorance and denial of the real situation are also too often involved.

A particularly problematic example of a forced option is the dilemma posed by the disposal of nuclear waste. As a result of particular technical, economic, and political decisions (and partially as a consequence of drift) nuclear technology has been increasingly used over the past five decades without the benefit of a reasonably practical and safe program of long-term waste disposal. Highly toxic and long-lasting waste (some of which will be lethally radioactive for more than 10,000 years) is being produced and temporarily stored daily. We cannot choose for this not to be the case. We, the present human community and those who come after us, are forced to deal with this waste for an indefinite future. We do not have the option of living in a nuclear waste-free environment. We must deal with this issue or suffer the potentially dire consequences of catastrophic contamination of human and nonhuman environments.

The notion of the forced option clearly contradicts the idea that technology is neutral. While it is true that decisions leading to a forced option could be made differently, at the stage of development at which the forced option comes into play, the state of technology (in its ecological dimension) determines a context that affects human life in certain (potentially catastrophic) ways, and allows only certain courses of human response (if catastrophe is to be avoided).

Ambivalent technological determinism also functions at the level of ideas and values. An "ideological dimension" of technology exists that involves the association of certain ideas, values, norms, and aspirations with technological existence. Technology in and of itself does not intrinsically determine an ideology. Rather, as Kranzberg suggests, "values become attached to particular technologies and hence serve to determine the lines of future political, social, and, yes, technological action itself."[33]

The ideological force of technology issues from the (individual and corporate) intellectual, moral, religious, and aesthetic consciousness of, and response to, technology in any particular sociocultural milieu. The particular state of technology comes to embody these ideological factors, and therefore must be considered in light of them. In this context certain values are routinely associated with contemporary technology, particularly the values of progress and efficiency.

Of particular concern is the notion of limit. The modern technological ethos is an ethos of limitlessness, implying that overcoming finitude is both good and necessary. Whatever can be done should be done, especially if it has something to do with technology. Langdon Winner captures the heart of the ethical problem engendered by the ideological dimension of technology when he suggests:

> Rather than storm the metaphysical foundations of civilized existence hounding an illusory "new ethic," it may be more to the point to reexamine a number of the traits most closely linked to the development of Western technology . . . and then ask *when and how such impulses get out of hand.* . . . The interesting question is why the modern West has proceeded along these paths *with virtually no sense of limit.*[34]

Responsibility requires moral reflection on the ideological dimension of technology. This is especially true of the ethos of limitlessness and the role technology plays in kindling this ethos.

Consideration of limit in relationship to responsibility must begin with the fact that technology, by definition, is a means for overcoming limits. After all, technology is the extension and enhancement of human capacities and power. Technology expands the boundaries of possibility in part by altering the boundaries of limit. Human finitude is not conquered, but it is mitigated; however, technological drift, technological imperatives, forced options, and other aspects of technological determinism are critical factors in limiting human being and conduct.

Donald Shriver, Jr., is correct, therefore, when he describes technology as "the intersection of limit and possibility."[35] The notion of intersection implies a dialectical relationship. Technology creates new possibilities by overcoming various limitations, intervening in sociocultural and natural systems, and expanding the boundaries of possibility. At the same time, technological determinism alters the boundaries of possibility by imposing new limits to human agency. These limits involve the need to use valuable, scarce resources to maintain technology, instead of using them for some other purpose. At the same time, sociocultural and natural systems react to technological intervention, establishing a new boundary of limit. And so on.

Homo technicus, struggling to be a responsible agent, is caught squarely in this intersection of possibility and limit. In the context of ambivalent determinism—at the intersection of possibility and limit—responsibility compels *homo technicus* to consider both possibility and limit—limit in terms of not only limitations imposed on the agent but also self-limitation as a responsible alternative.

Under the influence of technological ethos, do we adequately consider the possibility of self-limit? Can we break the grip of compelling technology to insist on our true humanity? Only if this were a possibility would we really have an "intersection" at all. Otherwise we might have twists and turns, even forks in the road (choices among technological alternatives, but all choices that would go in the same direction). Is there a place to turn off our path, to choose a different kind of road, a fundamentally different direction, or even a new form of transportation to move us along this path.[36]

In light of the ethos of limitlessness that grips our contemporary age, the model of *homo technicus* as the human participant should draw special attention to *self-limitation* as a means of participation. The answer to the question "What am I doing that affects what is going on?" might be answered fittingly by seeking nontechnological solutions or by intentionally slowing the implementation of technology, for instance. This would especially be true when it can be determined that one is approaching, or has already reached, a forced option or threshold.

Winner places the issue of ambivalent technological determinism into the broader context of the experience of life in relation to contemporary technology, terming the technical order a "way of life": technological ordering functions as a way or form of life and thus is, as Winner suggests, hardly a notion that implies neutrality.[37] Simply stated, the idea of technology as a form of life implies that technological order becomes an aspect of human social order. This is not meant to imply that technological ordering is discontinuous with other, pre- or nontechnological patterns of ordering. For as Winner points out,

> Most changes in the content of everyday life brought on by technology can be recognized as versions of earlier patterns. Parents have always had to entertain and instruct children and to find ways of keeping the little ones out of their hair. Having youngsters watch several hours of television cartoons is, in one way of looking at the matter, merely a new method for handling this age-old task.[38]

That technology functions in relation to a traditional or natural human task does not imply that it does so with the same effects. For in other ways, being entertained and educated by television is different from directly interacting with other persons or with books. In an age of technology, technological ordering of human life should not be thought of merely as a "side effect" or "impact," but as the very stuff of human life.[39]

Technology-as-a-form-of-life embodies ambivalent determinism. It leads to the creation of dynamic patterns of interdependence, not only affecting the environments of human life but also creating new modes of human endeavor. As such it embodies various potentialities and determinisms that may or may not reflect the intended, direct purposes of the technologies employed in the particular sociocultural context. Different values are pursued, some with human direction, others without.

There are several ways ambivalent technological determinism is problematic for responsibility. First, the unintended consequences and by-products of technology generally emerge over time and have to be discovered after the technology has been designed and implemented, sometimes long after. Thus, unintended consequences generally are not accounted for in any evaluation of moral responsibility at the inception of technological development or implementation.

Second, the ecological dimension of technology tends to introduce uncertainty and loss of control (or at least the appearance of loss of control). Responsibility must comprehend such uncertainty, ascertain the actual condition of human control, and propose remedial action to reestablish responsible agency.

Third, someone (corporately or individually) must assume, or be assigned, responsibility for the costs associated with ambivalent technological determinism, regardless of whether the consequences are positive or negative. This situation is problematic for no other reason than that technological determinism depletes scarce social, cultural, economic, and political resources. But it is especially problematic if the society has not decided who is responsible (morally, economically, and politically) for bearing these costs. Should it be the designer of the technology, the owner of the technology, the user of the technology, those who otherwise benefit from the use of the technology, those directly affected by the costly consequences, some privately held insurance, or the government?[40]

Fourth, technological determinism introduces complexity and potential risk into what can already be a very complex and risk-filled situation. This is particularly problematic when one considers the magnitude and power of contemporary technology. Who should be responsible for making sense of this complexity and determining the risks? How should the risks of modern technology be shared, locally, nationally, regionally, and globally? What is an acceptable risk for society, and who should make this decision?

Fifth, some aspects of ambivalent technological determinism are so indirect, far-removed, or otherwise dissociated from their source, that it is sometimes difficult or impossible accurately to trace responsibility for them. Often in such cases, once the relationship is established between the effects of technological determinism and its source, a great deal of damage has already occurred and alternatives for solving the problem easily have long passed.

Complex Responsibility

Homo technicus, the human participant, faces a daunting task in the attempt to be a responsible self. The dynamism, expansion of scale, complexity and interdependence of contemporary technology, introduce uncertainty and risk, straining the ability of *homo technicus* to comprehend and control adequately the nature and consequences of human conduct. In addition, ambivalent technological determinism (technological drift, the technological imperative, the forced option, and the ideological dimension of technology) further confounds the foresight and control of *homo technicus*, generating additional uncertainty and risk.

Homo technicus stands at a true intersection, with many options representing a widening range of potential benefits and costs. While the potential benefits stagger the imagination and fuel the technological impulse, the costs could be catastrophes of unprecedented scale, including the annihilation of the human species, if not all life on Earth. The moral vision that guides *homo technicus* must include a vision of responsibility that encompasses and embraces the character of technology in the contemporary age. The basis of this vision is "complex responsibility."

Complex responsibility is meant to incorporate the intrinsic dynamism of technology (defined as the expansion or enhancement of human capacity or power by artificial means) as well as the various aspects of ambivalent technological determinism. The idea of complex responsibility also implies an awareness of the complications involved in the ethical task by this expanded moral vision. The notion of complex responsibility presents tremendous challenges, not simply for ethical analysis but for the attempt to bring such analysis into the realm of social-policy formation as well.

Complex responsibility includes the following requirements. First, technology is inherently dynamic, though in some settings the dynamism has an evolutionary rather than revolutionary character.

Therefore, complex responsibility must focus on the nature and consequences of technological innovation. In an age of technology, complex responsibility should have an iterative character. That is to say, we should anticipate change and routinely reconsider responsibility in light of these changes.

Second, there must be consideration of the expanded scope and multiplicity of purpose of human technological activity. This should include attention to larger wholes, including expanded constituencies and future generations. This expansion of the scope of responsibility should reasonably match the expansion of the scope of technological activity and its consequences.

Third, complex responsibility entails responsibility to, and for, changes in the sociocultural and natural systems affected by technology, including the future condition of these systems. This should include the responsibility to react to the factors of ambivalent technological determinism in ways that foster responsible agency (i.e., that foster human control of technology and the form of life it engenders).

Fourth, complex responsibility should anticipate that technology spawns unintended consequences as a matter of course, especially as a result of technological drift. This should lead to a heightened awareness of the introduction of uncertainty and risk. At a minimum, there needs to be an accounting of risk that, as far as is reasonably possible, anticipates the consequences of ambivalent determinism and assigns responsibility within society for making risk assessments. Since perfect foresight is impossible, and expanded complexity is a virtual certainty, social responsibility for bearing the costs and reaping the benefits of technological determinism must be assigned, at least tentatively.

Fifth, complex responsibility should also include the responsibility to foster technical and scientific literacy and to engage expert knowledge in the ethical task.

Sixth, in light of the ideology of limitlessness that seems to have grasped our technological age, complex responsibility must foster a model of self-limiting participation. This model would not simply say "no" in the face of any risk. Rather, it would foster a sense that ambivalent technological determinism is a product of the desire of humans to enhance and expand their capacity and power, and provide a moment of reflection in the midst of technologically-driven dynamism and the uncertainty it engenders.

In itself, the notion of complex responsibility does not suggest what one ought to think about each of these elements, only that one ought to consider them as morally relevant aspects of human conduct in the life of a technological society in an age of technology.

Notes

[1] I cannot remember which particular insights or conceptual frameworks Clinton Garner shared with me that can be traced directly to this essay. I am absolutely sure, however, that it was his nearly infinite patience, his insight into the human condition, his linking of ethics and social science, and his breadth of knowledge and experience in the field of theological ethics that nurtured my thinking about moral responsibility and life in an age of technology. And it is his personal example of self-restraint (embodied in his slow, cool, Southern drawl) that constantly reminds me that self-limitation can be a virtue and a means of grace—maybe a saving grace—for persons trying to live responsibly in an age of technology.

[2] In what follows I will use the term "responsibility" to refer to moral responsibility.

[3] A full-blown ethics would delineate which "others" (including God) have moral significance. For our purposes we need only note that consideration of the "other" is essential to the construal of moral responsibility.

[4] Melvin Kranzberg, "Technology and History: 'Kranzberg's Laws,'" *Technology and Culture* 27/3 (July 1986): 545.

[5] From Lynn White, Jr., *Medieval Technology and Social Change* (Oxford, 1962), 28, as quoted in Melvin Kranzberg, "'Kranzberg's Laws,'" 545. Kranzberg uses White to exemplify the "neutral" attitude toward technology, although White's position is much more nuanced than the "myth" of neutrality I am using White's language to characterize.

[6] For discussions of broad-based definitions of technology see: Carl Mitcham, "Types of Technology," *Research in Philosophy and Technology* 1 (1978), 229-294; Friedrich Rapp, "Philosophy of technology, " in *Contemporary Philosophy: A New Survey*, volume 2, ed. G. Floistad (Boston: Martinus Nijhoff Publishers, 1982), 361-412; and Nicholas Berdyaev, "Man and Machine," in *Philosophy and Technology: Readings in the Philosophical Problems of Technology*, ed. Carl Mitcham and Robert Mackey (New York: The Free Press, 1983 (1934)), 203-213. For a discussion of alternative approaches to a philosophy of technology as well as a more detailed account of this particular phenomenological approach, see chapters 1-3 of Russell E. Willis, "Toward a Theological Ethics of Technology: An Analysis in Dialogue with Jacques Ellul, James Gustafson, and Philosophy of Technology," an unpublished dissertation, Emory University, Atlanta, Georgia, 1990.

This phenomenological approach also identifies a third dimension of technology—technology as the material products of the technological mode of activity. This is the aspect of technology that represents the common instrumental view of technology (technology understood as tools, instruments, etc.). This dimension, and its ethical significance, are discussed elsewhere (Willis, 35-48).

[7] Robert E. McGinn, "What is Technology?" *Research in Philosophy and Technology* 1 (1978): 183.

[8]Space flight is impossible without some extension or enhancement of human capacity and power by artificial means. Therefore, it is necessarily technological.

[9]In fact, earlier species of *homo* apparently made and used tools.

[10]Langdon Winner, *Autonomous Technology: Technics-Out-of-Control as a Theme in Political Thought* (Cambridge: MIT Press, 1977), 133-134. See also, Don Ihde, "The Historical-Ontological Priority of Technology Over Science," in *Philosophy, Technology and Human Values*, ed. Larry Hickman (College Station, Texas: Ibis Press, 1985), 196-210.

[11]See H. Richard Niebuhr, *The Responsible Self* (New York: Harper and Row, 1963).

[12]E. Clinton Gardner, *Christocentrism in Christian Social Ethics: A Depth Study of Eight Modern Protestants* (Washington, D.C.: University Press of America, 1983), 119.

[13]Loc. cit.

[14]Ibid., 121.

[15]Loc. cit.

[16]Ibid., 77

[17]My choice of the paradigm of "participant" owes much to James Gustafson's portrayal of the human vocation in terms of participation. He develops this theme in both volumes of *Ethics From a Theocentric Perspective* (Chicago: University of Chicago Press, 1981, 1984).

[18]"Kranzberg's Law" is introduced in Melvin Kranzberg, "Introduction: Trends in the History and Philosophy of Technology," in *The History and Philosophy of Technology*, ed. George Bugliarello and Dean B. Doner (Urbana: University of Illinois Press, 1979), xxiv. Kranzberg further develops these ideas in "Kranzberg's Laws," 544-560. Kranzberg's analysis is phenomenological and historical, based on his reaction to the antitechnology movements of the 1960s and 1970s. See Robert C. Post, "Missionary: An Interview with Melvin Kranzberg," *American Heritage of Invention and Technology* 4/3 (Winter 1989), 34-39.

[19]Kranzberg, "Kranzberg's Laws," 545.

[20]Winner, *Autonomous Technology*, 88-100.

[21]Robert L. Stivers, *Hunger, Technology and Limits to Growth: Christian Responsibility for Three Ethical Issues* (Minneapolis: Augsburg Press, 1984), 53.

[22]Winner, *Autonomous Technology*, 98.

[23]Kranzberg, "Kranzberg's Laws," 548.

[24]Ibid., 549.

[25]Winner, *Autonomous* Technology, 251.

[26]Loc. cit.

[27]Here, "political" is not conceived solely in terms of the institutions of government or political parties. Rather, politics is viewed as the processes

and structures related to social power and authority, and to social policy formation and implementation. This raises fundamental questions regarding freedom in determining corporate and individual destiny and responsibility within the structures of the technological society. See, for example, Winner, *Autonomous Technology*, 257; and Herbert Marcuse, *One Dimensional Man* (Boston: Beacon Press, 1964), 250.

[28]Winner, *Autonomous Technology*, 237.

[29]Ibid., 323.

[30]Roger L. Shinn, *Forced Options: Social Decisions for the 21st Century*, 2nd. ed. (New York: Pilgrim Press, 1985), 3.

[31]See Jacques Ellul, "A Theological Reflection on Nuclear Developments: The Limits of Science, Technology, and Power," in *Waging Peace: A Handbook for the Struggle to Abolish Nuclear Weapons*, ed. Jim Wallis (San Francisco: Harper and Row, 1982), 114.

[32]Shinn, *Forced Options*, 4.

[33]Kranzberg, "Trends," xxiv.

[34]Winner, *Autonomous Technology*, 133-134 (emphasis added).

[35]Donald W. Shriver, Jr., "Invisible Doorway: Hope as a Theological Virtue," *Zygon* 8/1 (March 1973): 4.

[36]Here I find myself reflecting the roadway imagery of Stivers' "Forks in the Road," in *Hunger, Technology, and Limits to Growth*.

[37]Winner, *Autonomous Technology*, 201. Winner expands on this idea in "Technologies as Forms of Life," in Langdon Winner, *The Whale and The Reactor: A Search for Limits in an Age of High Technology* (Chicago: University of Chicago Press, 1986), 3-18. For a similar argument, see Stanley Carpenter, "Technology—Tool or Form of Life," *Journal for the Humanities and Technology* 6 (1984-1985): 13-18. The term "form of life" is borrowed by Winner and Carpenter from Ludwig Wittgenstein's *Philosophical Investigations*.

[38]Winner, "Technologies as Forms of Life," 12-13.

[39]Ibid., 10.

[40]A model for this is the U.S. Government's support of the Human Genome Project. Under current law, three percent of all government grants must go to social and ethical analysis of the project and its potential social consequences.

About the Contributors

Peter R. Gathje is Assistant Professor in the Department of Religion and Philosophy at Christian Brothers University, in Memphis, Tennessee. He has also taught at Kalamazoo College. His publications include *Christ Comes in the Stranger's Guise: A History of the Open Door Community* (Atlanta: Open Door, 1991), and "The Works of Mercy: New Perspectives on Ministry," in *Proceedings of the Theology Institute of Villanova University*, ed. Francis A. Eigo, O.S.A. (Philadelphia: Villanova University Press, 1992).

Frederick E. Glennon is Associate Professor of Ethics in the Department of Religious Studies at Le Moyne College in Syracuse, New York. He serves as a member of the Steering Committee of the Ethics Section of the American Academy of Religion. His published articles have appeared in *Currents in Theology and Mission*, *CSSR Bulletin*, and *The Annual of the Society of Christian Ethics*. He has recently coauthored, with Jennifer Glancy, Mary MacDonald, Kathleen Nash, and Nancy Ring, *Thinking About Religion: An Introduction to the Religious Experience* (Orbis Books, 1997).

Gary S. Hauk is Secretary of the University at Emory University, a position that engages him in all aspects of university life and the ethical dimensions of higher education. He has taught as an adjunct professor in the Candler School of Theology and regularly teaches a course in narrative and ethics in Emory's Alumni University. His essays and poems have appeared in *Christianity and Literature* and other journals.

Janet R. Jakobsen is Assistant Professor of Women's Studies and Religious Studies at the University of Arizona, in Tucson. During 1996-97 she is a Senior Research Fellow in the Center for Humanities at Wesleyan University, in Middletown, Connecticut. Her published essays have appeared in *The Journal of Religious Ethics* and *Hypatia*. She has recently authored *Working Alliances: Diversity and Complexity in Feminist Ethics* (Indianapolis: Indiana University Press, 1995).

Christine D. Pohl is Associate Professor of Social Ethics in the Department of Church and Society at Asbury Theological Seminary, in Wilmore, Kentucky. She is a recipient, from the Lily Endowment, of a 1996-97 Christian Faith and Life Sabbatical Grant for her work in hospitality to strangers. This study will be forthcoming in book form.

Adele Stiles Resmer is Assistant Professor of Practical Theology at the Lutheran Theological Seminary at Philadelphia, Pennsylvania, and is a pastor in the Evangelical Lutheran Church in America. She was formerly the Director of the Center for Ethics and Social Ministry, in the Division of Church in Society of the ELCA, in Lake Elsinore, California. Her most recent published essay is "Physician-Assisted Suicide: What is the Pastoral Task?" (*Word & World*, Winter 1996).

Rosetta E. Ross is Visiting Assistant Professor of Social Ethics and Acting Director of the Black Church Studies Program at the Candler School of Theology, Emory University. She also has taught at the Interdenominational Theological Center, in Atlanta, where she was assistant professor of ethics. She was a research fellow at the Coolidge Colloquium of the Association for Religion and Intellectual Life and a Hewlett Graduate Fellow in Religion and Health at Emory's Carter Center.

Louis A. Ruprecht, Jr. is Visiting Professor at Barnard College. He was formerly Visiting Professor of Religion and Classics at Emory University. His numerous published essays have appeared in *Diaspora*, *Religion and Literature*, and other journals. He is the author of *Tragic Posture and Tragic Vision: Against the Modern Failure of Nerve* (New York: Continuum Press, 1994), and *Afterwords: Hellenism, Modernism, and the Myth of Decadence* (Albany: SUNY Press, 1995).

James R. Thobaben is Associate Professor of Social Ethics and Medical Ethics in the Department of Church and Society at Asbury Theological Seminary in Wilmore, Kentucky, and is a United Methodist minister. He worked as the Vice President in Research and Ethics at the Mississippi Methodist Rehabilitation Center and is still a fellow there.

William A. Thurston is Associate Professor and Chair in the Department of Religion and Philosophy at Shaw University in Raleigh, North Carolina. He has also taught at Columbia Theological Seminary, in Decatur, Georgia, and Clark Atlanta University. He is currently researching and writing on the sociology and ethics of shared democracy.

Darryl M. Trimiew is Associate Professor and Chair of the Department of Church and Society at the Brite Divinity School at Texas Christian University, in Forth Worth, Texas. He serves on the Board of Directors of the Society of Christian Ethics and is a member of the Steering Committee of the Ethics Section of the American Academy of Religion. His publications include, *Voices of the Silenced: The Responsible Self* *in a Marginalized Community* (Pilgrim Press, 1993), and *God Bless the Child That's Got Its Own* (Scholars Press, 1996).

Leslie F. Weber, Jr., is Associate Executive Director of the Division for Church in Society of the Evangelical Lutheran Church in America in Chicago, Illinois, and is an ELCA pastor. He formerly taught ethics and served as chaplain at the Lovett School, in Atlanta.

Theodore R. Weber, Professor of Social Ethics at Emory University's Candler School of Theology, has published numerous essays, reviews, and journal articles. His books include *Biblical Faith and Ethical Revolution* (Nashville, 1964), *Modern War and the Pursuit of Peace* (New York, 1968), and *Foreign Policy Is Your Business* (Richmond, Virginia, 1972). He is a former president of the Society of Christian Ethics and is a United Methodist minister.

Russell E. Willis is Visiting Assistant Professor of Sociology and Religion at McMurry University in Abilene, Texas. He has also taught at Iowa Wesleyan College, Iowa State University, and Arizona State University. His most recent publication, coauthored with George L. Murphy and LaVonne Althouse, is *Cosmic Witness: Commentaries on Science/Technology Themes Based on the Three-Year Lectionary* (CSI, 1996).

Index